Glam Italia!

101 FABULOUS THINGS TO DO
IN ROME

BEYOND THE COLOSSEUM, THE VATICAN,
THE TREVI FOUNTAIN, AND THE SPANISH STEPS

Email corinna@corinnabsworld.com

ISBN: 978-1-7323799-3-0 (print)
ISBN: 978-1-7323799-2-3 (eBook)

DISCLAIMER

The author is not a travel agent. All opinions and views expressed are those of the author based on personal travel experiences. Businesses, websites and apps recommended by this author may change ownership, rebrand or close, through no fault of the author. The author has not received compensation or sponsorship from any recommended businesses.

Cover art and all images by Marta Halama www.martahalama.com © Corinna Cooke
Maps by Steve Doubles © Corinna Cooke
Photography by Tracy Battaglia Fully Alive Photography
Formatting by Polgarus Studio

Contents

Introduction

Roma Non Basta Una Vita
One Lifetime is Not Enough in Rome

So let's talk about Rome.

I love Rome.

I absolutely *love* Rome. In my opinion Rome is one of the greatest cities on Earth. It is the birthplace of civilization as we know it, the foundation of our political and legal systems. Sometimes called the *Eternal City*, it is a place of viewable, tangible, *touchable* ancient history. From the ruins to the statues to the endless art, you can visually trace history — a history accessible to us all.

Rome is beautiful. There are so many wonderful neighborhoods to wander, full of eateries and picturesque spots to stop for a glass of wine or a cup of coffee (or one of my favorites on a hot day – a Schweppes Limon), all with an incredible view. Maybe a view of a cobblestoned piazza, surrounded by centuries old ochre-hued palazzi, with flowers in the window boxes, ivy crawling up the walls and a Vespa or two parked in the corner. Or maybe a view across the hills of Rome, or ancient ruins that have been in situ for millennia.

Romans are a gregarious, fun-loving bunch. Even if you are by yourself, you will be welcomed, chatted to, included, and will have a wonderful experience. They have their own cuisine and if you know where to go, or more importantly *where not to go*, eating out is incredibly affordable.

1

Because I love Rome, it is really important to me that you love Rome. Not that you like it, not that you just enjoy it; I want you to completely fall in love with Rome so that your heart aches a little when you leave. Like mine does.

I often hear people say they didn't care much for Rome, or didn't like it. I hear people say it's dirty and crowded and expensive. (That's like telling me my baby's ugly!) When I start probing to find out more about their experience they all tend to tell me a version of the same story: they went to the Colosseum and there were thousands of people, it was really hot and even with a pre-purchased ticket they waited in line for hours. Or they have a similar story about the Vatican: insane crowds, feeling hustled, waiting for hours. Or the Trevi Fountain: being caught in a crush of tourists and pickpockets. The same with the Spanish Steps. And at some point they stopped to eat at a tourist restaurant near one of these tourist attractions and had a below average meal that cost the earth.

And so they don't like Rome.

I ask if they went to the Trastevere, or ate artichokes in the Jewish Ghetto, if they walked along the Tiber to Michelangelo's Unfinished Bridge or ducked up to Piazza Farnese, Campo di Fiori and Piazza Navona, if they went underground at the Palazzo Valentini, or if they ate in the Testaccio. I am met with blank stares. *Michelangelo made a bridge? Palazzo what?*

Everyone has heard of the Vatican, the Colosseum, the Forum, the Trevi Fountain and the Spanish Steps, but there is more to Rome than these. So much more. Most haven't heard of all the other amazing places I am going to tell you about. And for those who have, the effort of figuring out where they are and how to get there can be a bit overwhelming.

This is where I can help.

I am going to tell you all about 101 different, really cool things to see and do in Rome. I will show you where and how to find them, and which things can be grouped together so that you can maximize your time. The bulk of these places are within the heart of Rome which, although it may look like a huge area on the map, is actually quite small and very walkable. You will be amazed at how many incredible places there are to see within a one or two mile radius of Largo Argentina, my central point from which everything fans out.

I'm not going to say much about the biggest tourist attractions, because you already know about those. I'm going to focus on the lesser-known exquisite side of Rome. For example, if you have only five hours in Rome because you are on a day trip from a cruise I recommend you don't burn three of those hours on a tour of the Colosseum or the Vatican museums, but instead have a gorgeous walk through Rome, see some of the things mentioned in this book, eat some amazing food at reasonable prices, and leave at least a little enamored of this extraordinary city. If you have two or three days in Rome, by all means visit some of the big sites, but balance those with some lesser-known treasures.

Many of the places I am going to tell you about I found by accident. Or heard about from a local. Generally I see are very few tourists there (sometimes it's just me and my little group), yet just a hop, skip and a jump up the road at a big tourist attraction, there are literally thousands of people carted in by the bus load, all waiting to cram themselves inside like sardines.

GLAM ITALIA

Every year I bring small groups of women on Glam Italia Tours for a boutique experience that mixes a few big attractions with a lot of off-the-beaten-path places. I never intended to create a business taking people on private tours of Italy. My passion for the place is undeniable. Friends and then friends-of-friends, and then friends-of-friends-of-friends, asked me to show them the side of Italy they had seen in my Facebook and Instagram photos. So I began designing boutique private tours for women who wanted to experience another side of Italy, the one the tour buses can't show you. And they wanted to do it on a budget.

When I first started the Glam Italia Tours I would sit up at night studying dates and facts and figures about the places I was taking my travelers to the next day, then get up early each morning to review them. I was so prepped! However, I came to realize that my travelers didn't want that much information. They wanted a simple intro to whatever we were looking at and if they wanted more they would ask.

HOW TO USE THIS BOOK

My goal with this book was to let you in on some of the truly amazing things you can see and do in Rome, most of which are within a couple of minutes from the main tourist attractions.

I have always thought the big attractions are wonderful, and they are, but the experiences that turn a good trip into a completely fantastic trip are typically the ones where you stumble upon some mind blowing piece of history, just around the corner from a big monument, and have it all to yourself.

Don't try to see all 101 things in this book. Even if you were staying in Rome for a month it would still be too much to take in. Instead, read through the different chapters, identify the bits and pieces that are interesting to you, and add them into your Rome itinerary.

Chances are you won't want to visit all ten churches I talk about or all ten underground places, but you may want to add a couple of each, perhaps see a great market, a place to watch the sunset, and some Caravaggios. Pick and choose a few things, eat some great Roman food, and enjoy being here!

If you bought this book in paperback, consider adding the eBook version too. You can get it via the Kindle App and have it on your phone, which is easier to refer to when you're on the move than carrying a book all over Rome with you. (If you do carry the paperback around Rome, please take photos of it with you and share them with me!)

THE MAGIC OF ROME

Rome is like a living museum. Everywhere you turn there is something magnificent to see. As much as I always enjoyed the various sites and buildings, they took on a whole new excitement once I started learning the stories behind them. The madness, the hilarity, the pettiness and the decadence of those that were instrumental in their creation. The reason why something was built — be it to self-aggrandize, to appease a wife, or distract the people from crimes an emperor was committing — always makes it more interesting.

I found that my Glam Italia travelers would remember a building by the crazy story that went with it rather than by its name. (Trust me — there are some pretty crazy stories!) In this book I share some of these stories with you. You will learn about lunatic emperors and astoundingly accomplished ones. I introduce you to my two favorite villainesses as well as a wayward pope with a porn star name. We meet some brilliant artists who not only changed art, but also changed the face of Rome entirely, all the while enmeshed in drama, petty one-upmanship and rivalries that read like a Baroque soap opera. I find it fascinating how the history of this incredible city weaves back on itself, the stories intertwine, and how many brilliant tales all find their way back to one lovely piazza.

On my tours I hire experts – licensed guides with a wealth of knowledge. I am not an art historian or a Roman historian or any other kind of historian, and I don't pretend to be. I am just a girl who travels to Rome several times per year.

I keep a running list of things to do in Rome on my phone, adding to it every time I hear about somewhere that sounds interesting. I check items off each time I visit Rome but the list never gets smaller. There is a saying that one lifetime is not enough in Rome, and it is true. If I live to be a hundred and spend every day for the rest of my life exploring Rome I still will never see it all.

So I hope you will use this book to discover some fascinating places to add to your Rome itinerary.

This book is designed to introduce you to some sensational things to do in Rome beyond the Vatican, the Colosseum, the Trevi Fountain and the Spanish Steps — I'm not saying don't visit these big attractions, especially if you have plenty of time, but there is *so much more* to see than just these.

Don't plan on seeing all 101 fabulous things in one visit. (And yes, I know there are more than 101 fabulous things to do in this book. I just liked the sound of 101…) Skim through, flag what interests you, and then choose a handful (or more) for your must-see list.

Lastly, if you can — walk. The best way to experience Rome and to understand her is on foot.

More than anything, I hope you will truly fall head over heels in love with Rome.

Andiamo!

Maps

Ancient Rome

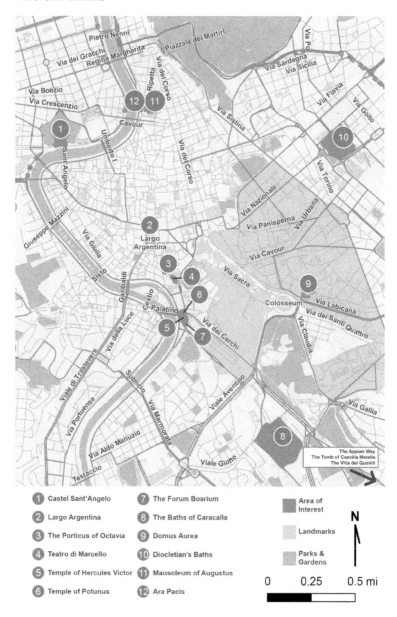

1. Castel Sant'Angelo
2. Largo Argentina
3. The Porticus of Octavia
4. Teatro di Marcello
5. Temple of Hercules Victor
6. Temple of Potunus
7. The Forum Boarium
8. The Baths of Caracalla
9. Domus Aurea
10. Diocletian's Baths
11. Mausoleum of Augustus
12. Ara Pacis

Area of Interest
Landmarks
Parks & Gardens

N

0   0.25   0.5 mi

Underground Rome (in geographical order)

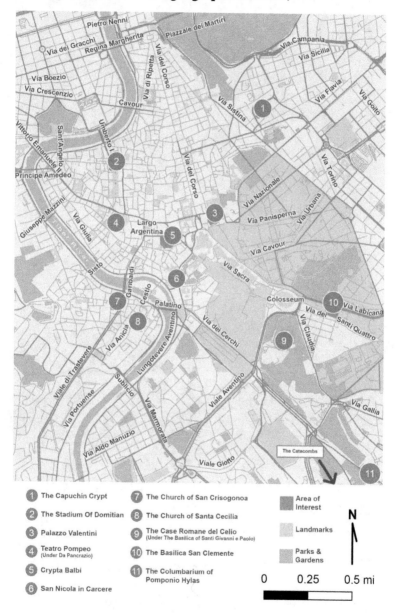

1 The Capuchin Crypt

2 The Stadium Of Domitian

3 Palazzo Valentini

4 Teatro Pompeo
(Under Da Pancrazio)

5 Crypta Balbi

6 San Nicola in Carcere

7 The Church of San Crisogonoa

8 The Church of Santa Cecilia

9 The Case Romane del Celio
(Under The Basilica of Santi Givanni e Paolo)

10 The Basilica San Clemente

11 The Columbarium of
Pomponio Hylas

Area of
Interest

Landmarks

Parks &
Gardens

N

0   0.25   0.5 mi

Ten Fascinating Churches in Rome (in geographical order)

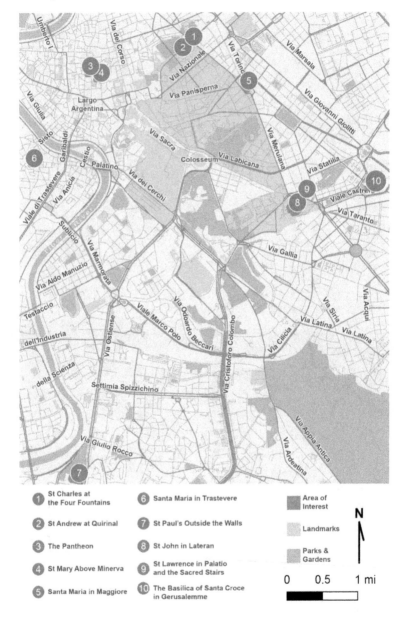

1 St Charles at the Four Fountains

2 St Andrew at Quirinal

3 The Pantheon

4 St Mary Above Minerva

5 Santa Maria in Maggiore

6 Santa Maria in Trastevere

7 St Paul's Outside the Walls

8 St John in Lateran

9 St Lawrence in Palatio and the Sacred Stairs

10 The Basilica of Santa Croce in Gerusalemme

Area of Interest

Landmarks

Parks & Gardens

N

0   0.5   1 mi

Interesting and Unusual Things in Rome (in geographical order)

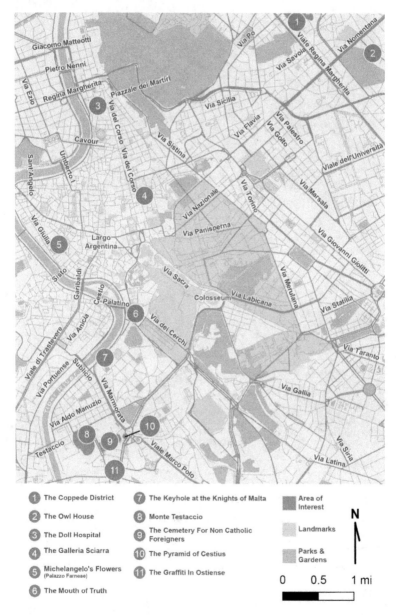

1. The Coppede District
2. The Owl House
3. The Doll Hospital
4. The Galleria Sciarra
5. Michelangelo's Flowers (Palazzo Farnese)
6. The Mouth of Truth
7. The Keyhole at the Knights of Malta
8. Monte Testaccio
9. The Cemetery For Non Catholic Foreigners
10. The Pyramid of Cestius
11. The Graffiti In Ostiense

Area of Interest

Landmarks

Parks & Gardens

N

0   0.5   1 mi

Where to Find Caravaggios in Rome (in geographical order)

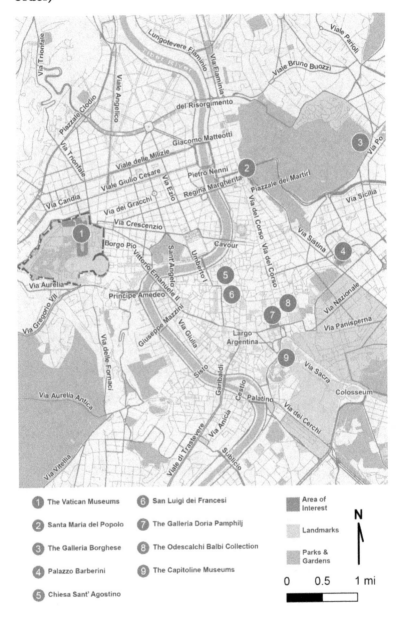

1. The Vatican Museums
2. Santa Maria del Popolo
3. The Galleria Borghese
4. Palazzo Barberini
5. Chiesa Sant' Agostino
6. San Luigi dei Francesi
7. The Galleria Doria Pamphilj
8. The Odescalchi Balbi Collection
9. The Capitoline Museums

Area of Interest
Landmarks
Parks & Gardens

N

0   0.5   1 mi

Twelve Incredible Museums in Rome (in geographical order)

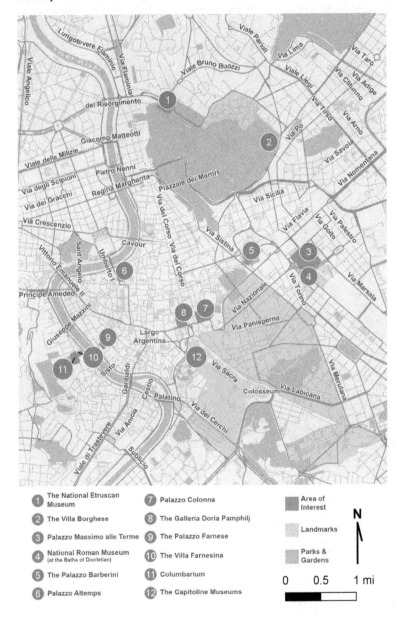

1. The National Etruscan Museum
2. The Villa Borghese
3. Palazzo Massimo alle Terme
4. National Roman Museum (at the Baths of Diocletian)
5. The Palazzo Barberini
6. Palazzo Altemps
7. Palazzo Colonna
8. The Galleria Doria Pamphilj
9. The Palazzo Farnese
10. The Villa Farnesina
11. Columbarium
12. The Capitoline Museums

Area of Interest

Landmarks

Parks & Gardens

N

0   0.5   1 mi

Eight Fantastic Markets in Rome (in geographical order)

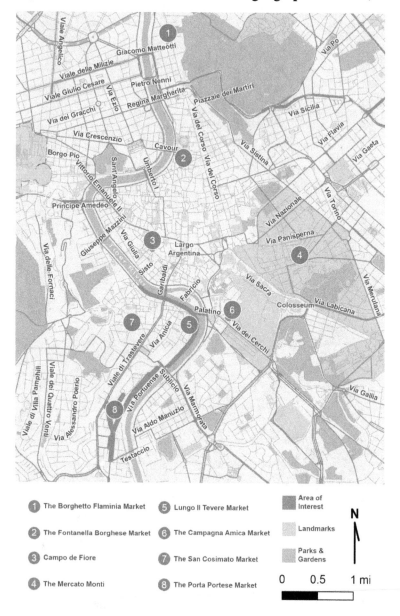

1 The Borghetto Flaminia Market   5 Lungo Il Tevere Market

2 The Fontanella Borghese Market   6 The Campagna Amica Market

3 Campo de Fiore   7 The San Cosimato Market

4 The Mercato Monti   8 The Porta Portese Market

Area of Interest

Landmarks

Parks & Gardens

N

0   0.5   1 mi

Watch the Sunset in Rome (in geographical order)

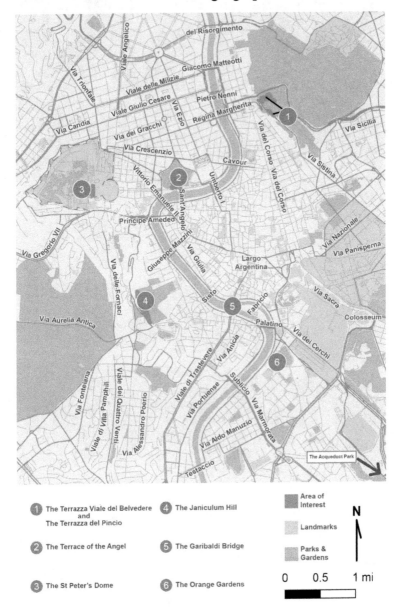

1 The Terrazza Viale del Belvedere and The Terrazza del Pincio

2 The Terrace of the Angel

3 The St Peter's Dome

4 The Janiculum Hill

5 The Garibaldi Bridge

6 The Orange Gardens

Area of Interest

Landmarks

Parks & Gardens

N

0   0.5   1 mi

The (Abbreviated) History of Rome

I'm not a historian — I'm just a girl who loves Rome. However, when I am in Rome, looking at ruins and statues and incredible monuments of history, there are some things that I can immediately put into a timeframe: I know when Caesar was around; I know when Augustus was in power and when Tiberius ruled the empire. I remember them mostly because of things they built or interesting aspects of their lives. But there are plenty that I can't place off the top of my head. If I am looking at something Commodus built, I have to Google to see when he was in power. If I am going to the Baths of Caracalla, I hope that I have WiFi or data so I can Google who came before and who came after so I can put it all in context.

With that in mind, I felt it was important to offer you a list of Roman leaders in order of succession, with the approximate years that they were in power.

Rome was a turbulent place politically and many of its leaders weren't around for very long. If you were an emperor, the chances of you being assassinated were high. There were emperors who were prolific builders and who left behind stadiums and buildings and triumphal arches, and there were others who left nothing much to remember them by.

As you explore Rome and see its staggering history everywhere you turn, this list is designed to help you put things into historical order. You might want to know if a monument is pre-Caesar or post-Caesar. Was this built before the Colosseum or after it? When was the Republic and when was the Empire?

Some emperors were fascinating, others weren't around long enough to do much more than just try to stay alive. I toyed with the idea of only including the emperors and rulers who left buildings that I knew you had a good chance of stumbling upon as you explore Rome, but that left large gaps in the time line. It also meant that you wouldn't see the head spinning madness of the revolving door of Roman rulers. So I've included them all.

The Story of Romulus and Remus (the very short version)

The story of Rome begins with twin boys, Romulus and Remus. The baby boys were released into the Tiber River in a basket, saved from death by the river god Tibernius, and then found and suckled by a she-wolf. A shepherd discovered the wolf and babies and took the boys home where he and his wife raised them.

The boys grew up, and discovered their mother was a Vestal Virgin priestess and her father a deposed king. They killed the usurper king, put their grandpa back on the throne and then, rather than sticking around to inherit the kingdom, they decided to go and found one of their own.

The boys scoped out the general area where they wanted to set up shop, but when it came time to nail down the exact location, they quarreled. Romulus wanted it to be the Palatine Hill and Remus wanted the Aventine Hill. Unwilling to compromise, Romulus murdered his brother and became the first king of Rome. From that day (around 753 BC), the Palatine Hill became the address for kings, and later emperors. Palatine is the origin of the words "palace" and "palatial".

As you explore Rome you will see imagery of a she-wolf suckling babies. Now you know what it means!

Some of the rulers and emperors in this book were incredible visionaries, great leaders and brilliant innovators. Others were just plain nuts. Some I talk about because I love their stories, others because they pertain to a building I want you to see. The men I refer to appear in **bold** in the table below so that you can check back, easily find them, and put them into context across roughly 600 years of the Roman Republic and Empire. I hope you will enjoy their stories as much as I do.

The Republic

The Republic ran from around 509 BC until 27 BC.

After being ruled by autonomous kings, Rome got itself a new improved system whereby power was shared across a senate. The size of the senate grew from 100 to 300 during Sulla's time, and to 900 during Julius Caesar's time. There were consuls who held additional powers, but everything was in a state of flux so it's difficult to get a clear timeline of who was leading the show.

Below are four names you will read about in this book, listed in chronological sequence, so you can place them in context when you hear their names and stories.

Sulla	was a general and a consul and was lived from 138 BC until 78 BC.
Pompeo	(of the Teatro Pompeo) lived from 106 BC until 48 BC. In the mid-60s BC, he joined Crassus and Julius Caesar in a military-political alliance they called the First Triumvirate. Pompeo married Julius Caesar's daughter Julia, but when both she and Crassus died Pompeo and Caesar battled to become leader. This caused a civil war. Ultimately Pompeo was defeated and went to Egypt where he was assassinated in 48 BC.
Julius Caesar	became dictator in 49 BC. He ran the everything until 44 BC when he was assassinated on the Ides of March. As his successor, Caesar named Octavian, who would go on to take the name Augustus and is first on my list of emperors, below.
Marc Antony	lived from 83 BC until 30 BC. Along with Octavian and Lepidus (who died in 13 BC) Marc Antony was part of the Second Triumvirate.

The Empire

| Augustus | ruled from 27 BC to 14 AD. He was the first emperor of Rome, grand-nephew of Julius Caesar, and a prolific builder, so you'll see signs of him all around Rome. He was born Gaius Octavius, was adopted by Julius Caesar and became Gaius Julius Caesar Octavianus. He went by the name |

	Octavian until he became emperor, at which point he was renamed Augustus.
Tiberius	ruled from 14 to 37 AD. He was the stepson of Augustus.
Caligula	ruled from 37 to 41 AD. He was the grand-nephew of Tiberius.
Claudius	ruled from 41 to 54 AD. He was Caligula's uncle.
Nero	ruled from 54 to 68 AD. He was Claudius' stepson.
Galba	was proclaimed emperor by his soldiers and ruled from 68 to 69 AD.
Otho	ruled in 69 AD, military commander.
Vitellus	ruled in 69 AD, military commander.
Vespasian	ruled from 69 to 79 AD. He was a military commander and built the Colosseum.
Titus	ruled from 79 to 81 AD. He was son of Vespasian and much loved emperor in his own right.
Domitian	ruled from 81 to 96 AD He was also a son of Vespasian. He built Domitian's Stadium and Domitian's Palace.
Nerva	was elected interim ruler and was in charge from 96 to 98 AD.
Trajan	ruled from 98 to 117 AD. He was Nerva's adopted son and became one of Rome's greatest emperors.

Hadrian	(aka "the gay emperor") was Trajan's ward and ruled from 117 to 138 AD.
Antonius Pius	was adopted by Hadrian and ruled from 138 to 161 AD.
Marcus Aurelius	was adopted by Antonius Pius and ruled from 161 to 180 AD.
Lucius Verus	was also adopted by Antonius Pius and ruled jointly with Marcus Aurelius from 161 to 169 AD.
Commodus	was son of Marcus Aurelius, ruled from 180 to 192 AD. He was a maniac — you may know a bit of his craziness from the movie *Gladiator*. In reality he was much crazier than in the movie.
Pertinax	was proclaimed emperor by the Praetorian Guard in 193 AD.
Didius Julianus	bought the office from the Praetorian Guard in 193 AD.
Severus	was proclaimed emperor and ruled from 193 to 211 AD.
Caracalla	was the son of Severus and ruled from 211 to 217 AD. He was another maniac whose killing sprees numbered tens of thousands.
Geta	also a son of Severus, ruled jointly with Caracalla from 211 to 212 AD, but was murdered by his brother.

Macrinus	was proclaimed emperor by his soldiers and ruled from 217 to 218 AD.
Heliogabalus	a cousin of Caracalla, ruled from 218 to 222 AD.
Alexander Severus	a cousin of Heliogabalus, ruled from 222 to 235 AD.
Maximin	was proclaimed emperor by his soldiers and took power from 235 to 238 AD.
Gordian I	was made emperor by the senate in 238 AD.
Gordian II,	son of Gordian I, ruled with his father in 238 AD.
Balbinus	was elected joint emperor by the senate in 238 AD.
Pupienus Maximus	was elected joint emperor by the senate in 238 (a busy year!).
Gordian III	son of Gordian II, ruled from 238 to 244 AD.
Philip the Arabian	assassinated Gordian III and ruled from 244 to 249 AD.
Decius	was proclaimed emperor by his soldiers and ruled from 249 to 251 AD.
Hostilanus	was the son of Decius and ruled briefly in 251 AD.
Gallus	ruled from 251 to 253 AD.
Aemilianus	also ruled for a while in 253 AD. He was a military commander.

Valerian	also a military commander, ruled from 253 to 260 AD.
Gallienus	was Valerian's son, and was co-emperor with his father from 253 to 260 AD, then sole emperor from 260 to 268 AD.
Claudius II	was a military commander and ruled from 268 to 270 AD.
Aurelian	ruled from 270 to 275 AD, and was a great leader and unifier. He built the Aurelian Walls that enclosed the seven hills of Rome, the Campus Marcius and the Trastevere.
Tacitus	was chosen by the senate and ruled from 275 to 276 AD.
Florianus	was Tacitus' half-brother and ruled briefly in 276 AD.
Probus	a military commander, ruled from 276 to 282 AD.
Carus	was proclaimed emperor by the Praetorian Guard and ruled from283 to 285 AD.
Carinus	Carus' son, ruled from 283 to 285 AD.
Numerianus	also a son of Carus, was co-emperor with Carinus from 283 to 284 AD.
Diocletian	was a military commander. Due to the vast size of the Roman Empire, he divided it and ruled jointly

	with Maximian and Constantius I from 284 to 305 AD.
Maximian	was appointed co-emperor by Diocletian and shared power from 286 to 305 AD.
Constantius I	had been co-emperor with Diocletian and Maximian, then succeeded Diocletian from 305 to 306 AD.
Galerius	was co-emperor with Constantius I from 305 to 310 AD.
Maximin	Galerius' nephew, co-ruled from 308 to 313 AD.
Licinius	was appointed emperor of the West by Galerius and later became emperor of the East. He ruled from 308 to 324 AD.
Maxentius	son of Maximian, co-ruled from 306 to 312 AD.
Constantine I (The Great)	son of Constantius I, ruled from 306 to 337 AD.
Constantine II	son of Constantine I, co-ruled with his brothers from 337 to 340 AD.
Constans	another son of Constantine I, co-ruled from 337 to 350 AD.
Constantius II,	also son of Constantine I, co-ruled from 337 to 361 AD.
Manentius	took over from Constans, co-ruled from 350 to 353 AD.

Julian the Apostate	nephew of Constantine I, ruled from 361 to 363 AD.
Jovian	was elected by the army, ruled from 363 to 364 AD.
Valentinian I	was put in place by the army, ruled the West from 364 to 378 AD.
Valens	brother of Valentian I, ruled the East from 364 to 378 AD.
Gratian	son of Valentinian I, co-ruled the West with Valentinian II from 375 to 383 AD.
Maximus	took over the West from 383 to 388 AD.
Valentinian II	son of Valentinian I, ruled the West from 375 to 392 AD.
Eugenius	a usurper, took over the West from 393 to 394 AD.
Theodosius I (The Great)	was appointed ruler of the East by Gratian and ruled 379 to 394 AD. He was the last emperor to rule over the East and West, from 394 to 395 AD.

The Fall of Rome

In the end, the Roman Empire collapsed under its own weight. There wasn't just one reason contributing to the fall of Rome, a multitude of things coincided. By the end of the third century the empire had a major cashflow problem. Constant wars and overspending, as well as running out of slaves, lead to a financial crisis.

The Empire had grown so vast that it had split into two, which worked well initially but as time wore on became fractious. The Greek-speaking East, which had its headquarters in Constantinople, was really prosperous whereas the Latin-speaking West fell into an economic downturn. The two parts no longer worked well together defending the empire militarily, and the strength of the East diverted the Barbarians' attention westward.

Interestingly, some of the Barbarian forces were ex-members of the Roman army. They were well trained and had a great understanding of the culture and people of the Western Roman Empire. They waited in the wings as Rome weakened. In 455, they invaded in what became known as the Sack of Rome. A Roman mob killed the fleeing emperor, leaving a power vacuum. The Barbarians looted, pillaged and moved on, and Rome fell into its dark ages.

Living History

The lives and accomplishments of some emperors, like Trajan and Hadrian, were magnificent and you see signs of them all over the city. Others were literally only in power for a few weeks or months and many of those I hadn't heard of until researching this list (such as Philip the Arabian, who assassinated the last Gordian). The job of emperor had to have been one of the most dangerous jobs in the Empire. They kept killing each other, adopting other people's sons to succeed themselves, marrying other men's wives — if you wrote it as a movie or as a soap opera no one would believe it! When you consider how few leaders were in power for more than a couple of months at a time, the accomplishments of the Roman Empire become even more staggering.

If you have the time and the opportunity to have a guide in Rome, I highly recommend it. Their encyclopedic knowledge of all of these characters is fantastic, and I personally love hearing the stories behind the emperors and learning about daily life in those years. If you don't get a guide, I recommend doing a quick Google search on the various emperors as you come across their buildings. Some context will add excitement to your experience.

Ancient Rome

1.

Thirteen Places to Discover Ancient Rome

1. Teatro Marcello

2. The Porticus of Octavia

3. The Forum Boarium

4. The Ara Pacis

5. The Mausoleum of Augustus

6. Largo Argentina

7. Domus Aurea (Nero's Golden Palace)

8. Hadrian's Mausoleum/Castel Sant' Angelo

9. The Baths of Caracalla

10. The Baths of Diocletian

11. The Appian Way

12. The Tomb of Caecilia Metella

13. The Villa dei Quintili

One of the things I love about Rome is that every minute of every day you are surrounded by thousands of years of history. The renaissance and medieval parts are cool, but this city was hustling and bustling 2000—3000 years ago!

I still find myself completely awestruck every time I look at ruins and statues and frescoes that are older than Jesus. The way Rome was planned and laid out, the focus on beauty, the dedication to the religions they held for a thousand years before Christianity — I find it all fascinating!

Obviously one of the best places to experience ancient Rome is at the Roman Forum. It is impossible to narrow down the various sites at the Forum to just a few — the Forum is more than an entire book on its own. By my calculations I have been there with my local guide Daniella more than 17 times, and each time she has shown me something new. There is just so much to take in, crossing so many centuries, I couldn't possibly do it justice here.

I am assuming you will make your way to the Colosseum and Forum, so instead of talking about them now, I want to tell you about 13 other sites that belong to ancient Rome.

Sites you may not already know about or may not have on your itinerary yet, but that are some of my favorites to take people to see. As with everything else in this book, almost everything on this list is right around the corner from something else you are planning on visiting. Some of these items will only take a few minutes to have a quick look at, others need a couple of hours, but any of them will add extra flavor to your experience of Rome!

PUTTING EVERYTHING IN ORDER

When trying to put these ancient sites into some kind of sensible order I experimented with ordering them geographically, chronologically, and finally by trying to tell a cohesive story of the people involved. In the end I opted for following the stories of the people behind each building.

1. Teatro Marcello

The Monumento Nazionale Vittorio Emanuele II (also known as the wedding cake building) is at the bottom end of the Forum, the opposite end to the Colosseum — you can't miss it. There is invariably a ton of traffic buzzing around the square in front of it. If you walk along the sidewalk in front of the wedding cake and then follow the wall there are ancient treasures to be found. The road you are on is called Via del Teatro Marcello, and it will lead you to a wonderful monument and a treasure trove of antiquity with very few tourists.

You could be forgiven for thinking this building looks like a smaller knock-off of the Colosseum, but in fact it may have been the design the Colosseum was modeled on. Teatro Marcello pre-dates the Colosseum by 83 years. It is smaller than the Colosseum, round where Vespasian's amphitheater is oval, and was an open sided semicircle where Vespasian's is closed. It is one of my favorite places in Rome.

After defeating Pompeo and taking control of Rome, Julius Caesar wanted to build a theater to rival the one his enemy had built (the Teatro Pompeo). He made plans and cleared ground to build the

Teatro Marcello, but was assassinated in 44 BC before the project was begun. In a detail I found interesting, he was killed in the toilets behind the curia at Pompeo's theater.

Augustus became the first emperor of Rome and in 22 BC he took over the project and built the theater, dedicating it to his nephew Marcus Claudius Marcellus, who up and died at age 19, before its completion and inauguration in 12 BC. It may be the oldest standing theater in Rome. Teatro Marcello was in use as a theater until the late fourth century.

With a diameter of 111 meters and a height of around 30 meters, this was both the largest and the most important theater in Rome. It is thought to have been able to hold between 14,000 and 20,000 people. Originally sheathed in travertine it was gleaming, white and spectacular. The open side of the amphitheater afforded spectators a view of the Tiber island, while giant sails provided shade from the hot Roman sun.

When you look up you will see a more modern building built into the theater. In the early middle ages the Fabii family took over the Teatro Marcello and turned it into a fortress, the fortification quite possibly saving the building.

In the mid fourteenth century the Savelli family had architect Baldassare Peruzzi transform the fortress into a palace, which then became the property of the Orsini family in the seventeenth century. In 2012 the palazzo was put up for sale for 26 million pounds sterling (roughly $US 36 million today).

Can you even imagine living on top of an ancient Roman ruin like this? I read that the palace wine cellars are down in the actual theater ruins. I would love to walk through the palace and have a look! The top level is now a series of multi-million dollar apartments.

Teatro Marcello is not open to the public so you can only view it from the outside. There is a lot to see though, so you will be glad you came.

WHAT'S NEARBY

Teatro Marcello is the gateway to the **Jewish Ghetto** (well, one of them anyway).

Immediately in front of you is the **Porticus of Octavia**, beside the theater are the remains of the **Temple of Apollo Sosianus** (431 BC) and the **Temple of Bellona**.

Head toward the river and you will find **San Nicola in Carcere** (see Underground Rome), the **Foro Boario** and the **Bocca della Verita**.

At the river you can cross over to the **Tiber Island** and then into the **Trastevere**.

2. The Porticus of Octavia

From Teatro Marcello as you walk toward the Jewish Ghetto you will find yourself in front of another fantastic ancient ruin (actually it is a combination of several, built upon and next to each other). As with much of the living museum that is Rome this is an ongoing archaeological dig encompassing a couple of millennia of history.

About 2200 years ago a fellow called Lepidus was consul of Rome. He had avowed a temple to the Goddess Juno during the last

Ligurian war in 187 BC and it was completed and dedicated to her in 179 BC. In 146 BC Quintus Macedonicus built the temple of Jupiter Stator right next to it and enclosed them with the Porticus Metelli. Roughly 120 years later Emperor Augustus decided this portico was due for a rebuild and created what we see now, the Porticus of Octavia. Octavia was Augustus' sister, the mother of Marcellus for whom the theater mentioned above (which is less than 200 feet away) was named. Augustus built this for her around 27 BC.

So you are standing in front of some very, very old ruins!

To the left you will see two marble columns and to the right, a brick archway. As you look though the archway you will see this facade makes up the gateway to a large rectangular piazza with three more columns.

Honestly, I *love* this stuff, but it can be tricky to discern what you are seeing because there are remnants of multiple ages here. As with so much of Rome this place has a huge wow factor, made more so if you have an idea of what is going on and what you are looking at. So I want to point out a few items for you to look at and identify.

- Look up at the arch itself and you will see that although it was made from Roman bricks it was originally finished with marble edging, a tiny portion of which remains. The original facade of this portico had been all columns, but after an earthquake in 442 AD some of them fell and were replaced by the arch.

- As you look through the archway and the columns you will see a green door built into the back wall. This is a doorway into the church of Sant'Angelo in Pescheria, an eighth century church. While you are in the vicinity it is worthwhile heading around the corner and popping in for a look.

- Look at the pediment above the green door. You will see a jumble of stones and sideways chunks of columns that look odd and out of place. This building had several rebuilds over the centuries and this is evidence of one of them. Augustus' building was damaged by fire in 80 AD and was rebuilt, probably by Domitian. This was followed by another fire which was repaired by Septimius Severus in 203 AD. We know this from the inscription on the pediment of the front wall of the porticus. There are chunks of it missing but if you look along the top line of the inscription you will see Septimius Severus and his son Caracalla (the homicidal maniac who built the baths) and their titles, which enabled the dating of the inscription to 203 AD. The bottom line of the inscription reads *Incendio Corruptum Rest* (or close to it) which means they restored the building after it had been ruined by fire.

- When you look at the Corinthian columns there is another clue that indicates they were part of the rebuild done by Severus and his crazy son. The capitals on the columns are elongated, with the leaves drawn out. This style was typical of the second and early third centuries. (I get a huge kick out of little details like that!)

- We know from Pliny The Elder's book, *Natural History*, that the Porticoes of both Octavia and Metelli as well as the two temples were full of incredible art, from frescoes to statues to other decorations. There is a fantastic story about a mix up with the art. The movers got the two temples confused and put all the woman-related artwork and statues in Jupiter's temple, and all the guy stuff in Juno's. Then, rather than move all the artwork to the temple in which it belonged, it was decided that the gods had spoken and that each had chosen the other temple! And you know you gotta keep the gods happy…

- Between the Teatro Marcello, the Porticus of Octavia and the two temples, this stretch of land you are standing on must have sparkled in the sun. The theater was travertine, the temples and porticoes were marble. It must have been beautiful.

Although you can't walk inside the ruins there are walkways that allow you a great view of it all. It is really quite fascinating, and everyone I have brought here with my tours has walked round and round looking at everything for the longest time. Sometimes it's hard to comprehend just how much history you are standing in the middle of, and it's not in some remote area, it is in the heart of one of the coolest areas in Rome!

WHAT'S NEARBY

You are now at the **Jewish Ghetto** so, before you leave, walk along the main street, stop for a glass of wine and some *carciofi* (artichokes). This street is world famous for its Jewish Artichokes, deep fried and crunchy like potato chips. There are some very famous restaurants along here too, from **Nonna Betta**, Anthony Bourdain's favorite spot for artichokes, to **Ba' Ghetto**, to **La Reginella**.

Another incredible eatery on this short street is the **Pasticceria Boccione**, a Jewish bakery that you would walk past if you didn't know where to look (you can read more about it in the *What to Eat* chapter of this book).

From the Boccione end of the ghetto (opposite end to Teatro Marcello), turn right and walk two blocks to the **Largo Argentina**. Turn right again and walk a block to **Crypta Balbi**.

Or turn left at the Boccione end of the ghetto and walk a couple of blocks to the river and the **Garibaldi Bridge** that takes you into the **Trastevere**.

3. The Forum Boarium

Sitting near the Tiber River between three of Rome's seven hills (Palatine, Capitoline and Aventine) this is the oldest forum in Rome — the cattle market.

In the sixth century BC one of the Etruscan Kings, Servius Tullius, built a port here, the **Portus Tiberinus**. Barges would come up the river carrying vegetables for the nearby **Forum Olitorium** and cattle for the Forum Boarium. It was a busy commercial area and the mercantile center of Rome.

There are two significant temples here that, although don't take much time to have a look at, are worth the visit. These are the best preserved religious temples from the Republican era (509 to 44 BC).

TEMPLE OF HERCULES VICTOR

This lovely little circular temple is considered to be the oldest marble temple in Rome. It is in incredible condition, especially considering it dates back to the end of the second century BC.

Twenty Corinthian columns form a circle around an inner chamber that once held a statue of the god Hercules. I have dropped by here many times when walking from the **Trastevere** over to the **Testaccio** area, either to dine out or to visit the **Pyramid of Cestius**, and I don't think I have ever seen anyone here. It is small and to a degree out of the way, but if you are in the vicinity it is worth seeing.

TEMPLE OF PORTUNUS

The other temple here is the Temple of Portunus. Portunus was the god who protected sailors and harbors. The original temple was built here in the sixth century BC, but the current temple is a restoration and rebuild done in around 80 BC.

Freestanding Ionian columns make up the front of this small temple while the remaining columns are part of the walls. Steps take you up to the portico and the small chamber behind. It was built from tufa stone and travertine instead of marble.

The reason these two temples survived and are in such great condition is that after the fall of the Roman Empire they were converted into Christian churches. Many temples were demolished or fell to ruin, but those converted into churches and kept in use seemed to endure the ravages of time.

While at the Forum Boarium make sure you see the **Bocca della Verita**. (Read about the Bocca della Verita in the *Interesting and Unusual Things* chapter of this book.)

WHAT'S NEARBY

From the Forum Boarium you are just a few minutes walk away from **Teatro Marcello** and the **Jewish Ghetto**.

Walk along the **Via dei Cerchi** to the **Circus Maximus** and then head up the **Viale Aventino** to the church of Saints John and Paul (**SSGiovanni e Paolo**). Keep walking and you will see the back side of the **Colosseum**. From here you are close to **Basilica San Clemente**.

In the opposite direction walk to the river and cross over to the **Trastevere**. You are close to the underground crypt at the **Church of Saint Cecilia**.

4. The Ara Pacis

When in Rome I am guilty of walking past anything that looks new in lieu of discovering something ancient (which is not difficult since ancient treasures are hiding around every corner). As this monument is housed inside a modern-looking museum, I was somewhat late to the game in finding it. And I only found it by accident.

The Ara Pacis was an outdoor altar dedicated to peace and the accomplishments of Emperor Augustus. Augustus was a great politician and leader, designer of Rome as we know it, a towering figure in history, and a spin-master. This guy understood the power of propaganda, Ara Pacis being testament to that.

AUGUSTUS'S STORY

Augustus was the first and the greatest Roman emperor of them all.

Born Gaius Octavius, he came from a prosperous family, but a family that was a step or so below senatorial importance. His father was successful but died when Gaius was four years old. He did however leave young Gaius with two important things. One was a voracious ambition, the other was an incredibly fortuitous marriage.

Gaius' father had married Atia, the daughter of Julius Caesar's sister. Caesar had a shortage of male relatives to mentor, and took notice of young Gaius when he reached his teens. With no male heir to leave his wealth and his estate, Caesar adopted Gaius Octavius posthumously, which was a shock to everyone, including young Gaius himself who was away at school in the east with his loyal buddy Agrippa. On his return to Rome to claim his inheritance, Gaius changed his name to Gaius Julius Caesar Octavianus.

Rome had been in a constant state of war, both from foreign enemies and from enemies within, (as in the senators who had assassinated Uncle Caesar), and it was a dangerous time for him. However, he was a crafty politician and a great tactician. He played the game of pretending to consult the senate on important matters and they played the game of pretending to work with him.

Gaius achieved the highest level of power ever achieved by anyone. The senate realized they were beaten and gave him the name *Augustus* or "revered one".

QUIRKY FAMILY BUSINESS

Augustus understood the importance of the line of succession, and that he needed an heir. He met and fell in love with Livia in 39 BC while his current wife Scribonia was pregnant. Augustus divorced Scribonia the day their daughter Julia was born so that he could marry the already married Livia — he even had her husband give her away at their wedding! You just can't make this crazy stuff up!

When, after a decade of marriage, there was still no heir he decided to marry off his then 14-year-old daughter Julia and get some grandkids instead. Julia's first husband was Marcellus, of the Teatro Marcello fame, but he died at age 19 leaving her a widow. Augustus had been mentoring Marcellus and it is suspected that Livia, as evil step-aunt, poisoned Marcellus to make room for her own sons from her first marriage.

Augustus decided he needed a real man to produce some heirs so pulled in his sidekick, the greatest right hand man of all time, Agrippa, to marry his daughter. Agrippa had been by Augustus' side since school and all through his rise to greatness. He was also a great politician, military figure, architect and statesman. Together, he and Augustus rebuilt Rome, worked on the city's infrastructure, and made her beautiful. Augustus liked to say, when he arrived Rome was a city made of brick and he turned it into a city made of marble.

Marriages amongst the nobles at that time were about political alliances, not love and happiness, but Agrippa and Julia, 25 years his junior, were truly happy and produced several children. The first two were boys: Gaius in 20 BC and Lucius in 17 BC. Before Lucius was even a year old Augustus adopted them both, making his grandsons his sons and taking them from Agrippa's home into his own. Agrippa was cool with it. Because he was the greatest right hand man of all time.

All five of Julia's children died young. Livia was thought to have been behind the deaths of Gaius and Lucius and Julia's last son, named for his father Agrippa, clearing the path for her own sons. Augustus was forced to adopt her first born son from her previous marriage, Tiberius, who would go on to become emperor on Augustus' death. Who knows for sure, but there seem to be plenty of people who suspect she poisoned Augustus so that her own son could become emperor.

CONSTRUCTING THE ARA PACIS

Augustus ended two decades of civil wars in Rome, was triumphant over his external enemies and brought peace to the empire. The doors of the Temple of Janus were closed (see below).

He had created a succession plan that would theoretically keep the empire prosperous for centuries to come, so on the face of things everything was looking good.

Augustus commissioned the Ara Pacis, an altar to celebrate peace.

The Ara Pacis is majestic and beautiful. It is a set of stairs leading up to an altar, all of which are encased inside marble walls that are covered in carvings. The lower half the entire way around is carvings dedicated to nature and more than 50 species of plants. Look closely and you will see frogs in the leaves, and lizards and birds. The carving is quite deep, so you see a wonderful contrast between the white marble and the shadows, making the carvings look as if they are reaching out to you.

The altar is positioned in such a way that at sunset on Augustus' birthday the shadow of the point of the obelisk in Campus Martius would fall onto the Ara Pacis, symbolizing that he had been born to bring Rome to peace.

The upper panels are thought to tell allegorical stories of the history of Rome, but there is much dispute over them — research it enough and your head will spin. But look at them carefully, they are exquisite.

Along the side, moving from the back toward the stairs is a truly remarkable carving of a procession. Although it is not known specifically what this procession was you can see Augustus (missing his body) and his family including Livia, Gaius and Lucius, Agrippa and Julia, and even Tiberius. Agrippa is in a hood — by the time the Ara Pacis was completed he had already died, age 51. When you look at the procession, notice how some figures are carved more deeply, thus standing out more, while others are carved more shallowly, looking like the crowd in the background. It is just spectacular.

Centuries later when the Tiber river was expanded, the Ara Pacis became submerged in mud, where it remained for more than 1000 years. It wasn't until the sixteenth century that some of the remains were discovered, and then in 1938 Mussolini had it reconstructed.

The Ara Pacis is now housed in a bright and airy Richard Meier designed museum, built specially for it. You can walk up Augustus' steps and be inside this incredible piece of history.

THE TEMPLE OF JANUS

Rome's second king, Numa Pompilius (715 - 673 BC) built the Temple of Janus in the Forum, to celebrate peace. The rules were that during times of war the doors to the temple would remain open and during times of peace they would be closed. They remained closed until the next king came along, Tullus Hostilius, who threw them back open. They stayed open for 400 years, closed again for eight years, then back to war Rome went and the doors were opened again. They were hardly ever closed. Augustus ordered the doors of the Temple of Janus be closed and built the Ara Pacis.

WHAT'S NEARBY

The Ara Pacis is open daily from 9:30am until 7:30pm. The address is Lungotevere in Augusta, along the Tiber river between Ponte Margherita and Ponte Cavour. It is opposite the **Mausoleum of Augustus** on the Tiber. It is in walking distance to **Castel Sant'Angelo**, **Chiesa San Luigi dei Francesi** (for the Caravaggio's)

Piazza Navona and the **Pantheon** in one direction, in the other it is just a few minutes walk up to **Piazza del Popolo** and the **Borghese**.

I love to walk along the river through this area, especially on hot Roman summer days when the trees provide gorgeous shade.

5. Mausoleum of Augustus

"Have I played the part well? Then applaud as I exit."
~Augustus

The Mausoleum of Augustus has been closed for years, so I haven't yet been inside it. However, restorations on the mausoleum began in January 2017 and are expected to be complete at some point in April of 2019, which means that shortly after this book is published travelers to Rome will be able to visit it. I can't wait to see it myself!

In its time, the Mausoleum of Augustus was a spectacular and important monument and it housed the bodies of the who's who of ancient Rome.

Augustus was in his thirties and was running the Roman Empire, making him the most powerful man in the world, when he decided to build his final resting place. It was only fitting that he would build a spectacular family tomb that would reflect his importance.

The mausoleum was completed in 28 BC. It was magnificent and it was massive, easily the biggest tomb ever built throughout the entire Roman period. Standing 45 meters tall and 90 meters in diameter, the structure was dome shaped, covered in white travertine, surrounded by trees and topped with a huge bronze statue of Augustus himself. So it wasn't just huge, it was *impressive*.

There was only one entrance, a doorway facing the field of Mars. From there a short corridor lead to an inner circular corridor which in turn had two entrances leading to another circular corridor which lead to a small burial chamber. It too was circular but had a central column with a recess built into it, no doubt for the ashes of Augustus. The burial chamber also had recesses built into the walls for other funerary urns.

It was built to be a family tomb, so it housed several notable names prior to Augustus himself arriving in 14 AD. First in was his nephew and son-in-law Marcus Claudius Marcellus (first husband to Augustus' daughter Julia) in 23 BC. He was followed in 12 BC by Agrippa, Augustus' sidekick, architect of ancient Rome and second husband to Julia. Next came his stepson Drusus the Elder in 9 BC, followed by Augustus' two sons (grandsons really — see *Ara Pacis*) Lucius and Gaius in 2 AD and 4 AD. Augustus himself was the next to take up residency in the tomb in 14 AD. He was followed by Drusus the Younger, wife and evil step-mom/murderer Livia, the next emperor, Tiberius, who happened to be Livia's first son, then Agrippina, Nero, Caligular's brother Drusus (couldn't they have come up with more names?), Germanicus, Caligula, Claudius, Poppaea Sabina (Nero's embalmed wife) and a bunch of others too, with Nerva being the last emperor to populate the mausoleum.

When Augustus died a bronze plaque was placed on either side of the entrance, inscribed with the list of the first emperor's achievements. In (or around) the fourth century AD two red Aswan obelisks were also placed on either side of the entrance to the mausoleum. These later were moved, one to the outside of the **Church of Santa Maria Maggiore**, the other to the horse fountain in **Piazza del Quirinale.**

So What Happened To It?

In 410 the Visigoths came plundering, stole all the treasures and scattered all the ashes. Then in the middle ages the Colonna clan turned the mausoleum into a fortress, which was subsequently broken down in 1167-ish, with many of the stones and the big travertine blocks carted off elsewhere and recycled into other buildings.

In the sixteenth century the Soderini made the now-flattened rooftop into an ornamental garden, which became a bull fighting arena in the eighteenth century. In the twentieth century the building was converted into a concert hall, but when the fascists came to power Mussolini's interest in ancient Rome lead to all the later additions being stripped back.

The Restorations in 2019

I don't know how much they will be able to restore, but what I have read about it so far indicates it will be pretty special. In the last few years Rome has been doing lots of multimedia installations, which bring everything back to life and let you see how things looked back in their time. The Mausoleum of Augustus is apparently going to have a multimedia installation inside, which alone will make it worthwhile seeing.

The last time I saw the mausoleum it was a sad-looking building, in ruins, with equally sad-looking cypress trees surrounding it. I am looking forward to seeing the restorations when they open in 2019. No doubt some of the early readers of this book will get there before me, and I hope they will enjoy seeing this incredibly important and once glorious monument from ancient Rome, that closes out the story of the greatest emperor of them all and his crazy family and descendants.

Before you leave for Rome you may want to check whether the mausoleum has reopened yet. The forcasted opening at the time of writing this is April 2019, but of course it could run behind.

WHAT'S NEARBY

The Mausoleum of Augustus is directly across the street from the **Ara Pacis**, on the Tiber.

6. Largo Argentina

When you are walking around the heart of Rome, this fantastic set of ruins is in the middle of everything.

I am always amazed when talking to people who have been to Rome that hardly anyone knows this place, even though they have been past it or near it a hundred times. Once you know it, it becomes a central compass point, a place to measure the distance to and from anywhere, and a site that is always fun to stop and look at.

SANCTUARY

Before I tell you about the ruins themselves I need to tell you about the cats. You see this is one of Rome's cat sanctuaries. If you find a stray cat in Rome you can bring it here. There is a veterinary office in the bottom of the south side of the site where they sterilize, medically treat, debug and heal the cats. Once in good health they are released into the ruins where they run around and live what must be a dream life. There is a low, glassed wall around the site, so the cats can escape but they don't. They love it here. Look over the low wall (it's just past waist height) and you will see cats playing chasing in the tunnels and around the 2000+ year old columns, sunning themselves on the temple podiums and strolling around, with a staggering history below their paws.

THE TEMPLE RUINS

Ancient Rome sat meters below current street level, so you will be looking down into these ruins. Largo Argentina is a series of four ancient temples positioned remarkably close to one another, and all facing east. They date back from the third or fourth century BC to the first century AD. Much is unknown about the temples so some of the information we have is speculative.

The temples themselves are named A, B, C, and D, with A being the northern-most and D being the southern-most. If you are anything like me and are compass-challenged, look to the staircases, they face east. The Tiber river will be on your left, which is south. So the temple closest to the south edge is Temple D.

- **Temple C** is an Italic temple and is the oldest of the four, dating back to the third or fourth century BC. It is thought that it may have been devoted to the goddess of fertility, Feronia. It was originally built of tufa and if you look around the base of the temple you can see giant tufa blocks that date back to at least 300 BC. Steps rise up to the podium, but were built over later.

    At the end of the second century this area was repaved to help prevent flooding from the nearby Tiber river. At this point all the temples were put on the same level. You can see the paving at Temple C, and how the steps are below it.

- **Temple A** was built next, in the third century BC, possibly by Gaius Lutatius Catulus after he beat the Carthaginians in 241 BC, and possibly as a temple to Juturna (lots of *possiblies*). It was also an Italic temple. This one is the best preserved of the four, because it was later converted into a church, San Nicolo Cesarini. Most of the church was demolished but two apses containing frescoes still remain, along with the altar. You can see the two apses built on top of the podium if you walk around and look from behind. In the front of the temple look to the right and you will see two of the columns are white, while the others are brown. The white ones are travertine and were replacements for the originals. Original columns stand behind the white ones and were made of tufa, fluted and stuccoed.

- **Temple D** is the largest and has only been partially excavated, as most of it is below the street. Built nearly 200 years after Temple C it is a little confusing, because all we can see are the steps and the podium from a first century BC remodel and the travertine paving which was put in in 80 AD. What we do know is that it was devoted to *Lares*, the god who protects sailors. It was vowed by Lucius Aemilius Regillus during a naval battle in 190 BC and was dedicated in 179 BC by the censor M Aemilius Lepidus.

- **Temple B** is the most recent, built in the beginning of the first century BC. It was a circular temple that once had 18 Corinthian columns around the podium, of which six remain. It would have looked almost exactly like the Temple of Hercules Victor in the Forum Boarium. Except that the temple Hercules Victor was Greek-style with the columns standing on three steps, whereas Temple B is Roman-style with the columns standing on the podium itself.

Roughly 50 years later Temple B got a remodel. The columns were walled in, the podium enlarged, and it got new facing and moldings. Then, after a fire in 80 AD the facing was replaced with travertine and the steps were rebuilt with a new altar. The height of the podium was reduced and a new travertine molding was added to mark the new lower edge. If you look to the left of the stairs you can see remains of the new molding.

As if the details weren't fascinating enough, while you are taking it all in, cats pop up out of nowhere, or go lie in the sun on the podium of the temple you are looking at. Recently I was showing one of my tour groups the temples and we got completely distracted by a three legged little cat trying to join in a game of chasing with a group of big old cats. They kept stopping and waiting for him rather than leaving him behind.

THERE'S MORE...

If you walk around the back of Temple A you will see another building built right up close, running behind temples B and C. This is the edge of the Teatro Pompeo — Pompeo's huge theater, the one that Julius Caesar built Teatro Marcello to outdo (read more about this in the *Underground Rome* chapter of this book). Teatro Pompeo had a *curia* at this top end, which became a place where senators would have political discussions and meetings, outside of which were the public latrines that backed up to Largo Argentina. This is the place where Julius Caesar was killed, and from the back of Temple A you look right at it!

WHAT'S NEARBY

From the **Trastevere** cross the Garibaldi Bridge and walk north for two or three blocks and you will be at the **Largo Argentina**. Between the river and Largo Argentina on the east side of the street is the entrance to the **Jewish Ghetto**.

Immediately east of Largo Argentina is the **Crypta Balbi**, then a couple of blocks further is **Piazza Venezia** where you will find **Palazzo Valentini**, **Trajan's Column** and market, the **Roman Forum** and just up the street, the **Colosseum**.

West of Largo Argentina it's a five minute walk to **Campo de Fiori** and **Piazza Navona**.

If you use Largo Argentina as a center point, almost everything you want to see is within a mile radius (or close to it).

7. Domus Aurea (Nero's Golden Palace)

If you asked me to describe the Domus Aurea experience I would say that *this is the best thing I have ever done, anywhere in the world!* Then I would tell you that if there is any way on earth you can make this happen, do it.

WHAT IS THE DOMUS AUREA?

Shortly after the great fire of Rome in 64 AD, (rumored to have been set by Nero himself, but who knows?) Emperor Nero took a giant chunk of the land left behind for himself (as much as 300 square acres) and on it he built his huge golden pleasure palace, the Domus Aurea.

Filled with gleaming white marble, mosaic floors and some mosaic ceilings (he started a craze that later appeared all around the world), hallways with flowing fountains, and a room with a domed ceiling that rotated, powered by slaves. This 300 roomed palace had no bedrooms — it was built for entertainment only. There was a rotating dining room with an incredibly clever underground mechanism making it turn, and frescoes covered every inch of the walls that weren't otherwise embellished. The walls of the great hallways stood more than 11 metres tall and were frescoed from ceiling to floor. This was excess beyond your wildest dreams.

Nero died in 68 AD. Thirty years later, when Trajan became emperor, he decided that Rome didn't need this golden monstrosity so had it filled with rocks and sand, covered over completely, and built public pools on top of it — the Baths of Trajan. The world forgot about the golden palace until the late fifteenth century, so roughly 1400 years later, when a young man fell through a hole in the ground and found himself inside a "cave covered in frescoes".

Intrigued by this sensational discovery, artists such as Raphael and Michelangelo made their way inside and scratched their names into the frescoes. *Can you even believe it*??? Of all people, you would think they would have more respect for art.

Fast forward a few centuries and archaeologists have excavated much of the golden palace, turning into another living museum. Domus Aurea is inside a hill, the gardens on top of the hill are an important part of keeping the structure standing. In fact, the replacement gardens are costing millions of dollars, but are crucial to keeping the roof on the palace.

Most of the ruins we see in Rome are open to the elements, but this one is completely enclosed, giving you a different perspective of how massive, how over the top and how completely glorious it was.

TOURING NERO'S GOLDEN PALACE

The only way you can see Nero's golden palace is to book a tour lead by an archaeologist who works there during the week. The site is a live archaeological dig Monday through Friday, but on Saturdays and Sundays they do small tours in English, French and Italian. Each tour only takes around 15 people, so you have to book ahead of time — and book as far ahead as you can.

Bring a jacket and don't plan on working a fabulous hairdo because you will be donning a hairnet and a hard hat before going inside the mountain. As your guide takes you through, you will pass scaffolding, rooms where frescoes are being restored, areas only excavated a month before you got there. It is truly astounding.

In one of the hallways we walked through with impossibly high vaulted ceilings, our archaeologist-guide pointed to a square of fresco up on the wall. It was maybe 18 inches tall. She told us it took six months to restore this small piece with a laser, and millions of dollars to do it. The entirety of the hallway was frescoed from floor to ceiling, but the frescoes now sit under a gray calcium deposit.

Believe it or not, moisture and water dripping down the walls from Trajan's Baths and, centuries later, the gardens that still sit on top of the hill covering the golden palace, have actually saved the frescoes. The moisture created a calcium deposit that sealed the frescoes underneath. The walls look gray and concrete-like, but when you get a glimpse of any of the brightly colored frescoes underneath it takes your breath away. Looking at that one 18 inch square fresco stopped me in my tracks when I thought of how much money it will take to eventually release all of the frescoes from the calcium, and the realization that it won't be completed in my lifetime.

The archaeologist-guide who took me through was emphatic as she talked to me about Nero. She thinks most of what we have been told is based upon lies, as history was written by senators and political pundits who hated him. I am hoping to find her when I get back to Rome to hear the next installment of her Nero story. If nothing else, she tells a compelling tale and is incredibly passionate about this place, as is everyone who works here.

"Everything you know about Nero is wrong. I *know* him. I am down here with him all day, every day, and I *know* him."

VIRTUAL REALITY

Part way into your tour you will find yourself in one of Nero's 300 rooms, putting on a virtual reality mask and experiencing the palace during Nero's time. It is completely amazing!

The virtual reality show started with the walls to either side and behind me all lighting up in their frescoed beauty. Even though in my brain I knew it wasn't real, my head was whipping around from side to side as each wall lit up, and I couldn't believe I wasn't seeing it in its actual form. Who knew V.R. could be so real-looking??

Then the craziest thing happened. The voice in the virtual reality gizmo told me to look in front of me at the one remaining concrete wall, which then dissolved away leaving a re-creation of how the palace looked in Nero's day. White curtains were moving in the breeze and we were transported out onto the terrace of the palace where we could look over the balcony out at the sheer majesty and beauty of first century Rome. In virtual reality land this happens on a hot summer's day, and you quite literally feel the sun on your skin. I can remember touching my bare arms and my face, feeling the sunshine on them, but it was all in my imagination. I was actually inside a mountain, freezing cold because I forgot to bring a sweater or jacket.

I promise you will feel the heat of the sun when you do it, albeit all in your mind. At the end of my tour as I was tiptoeing back through, I watched another group in the virtual reality room. Their bodies were weaving around as mine had, as they spun around looking at the walls, and although I was shivering cold, they were all touching their faces and arms, feeling the imaginary sun on their skin.

THE GREATEST THING I HAVE EVER DONE

The volume of treasures you see inside Domus Aurea is incredible. I was really taken with the mosaic floors in some of the rooms, as well as the revolving dining room. There was honestly just so much to take in — I will keep coming back here over and over.

Once again let me just say *this is the single greatest thing I have ever done,* anywhere in the world, and I sincerely hope you can make it here yourself.

When I came back outside at the end of my tour I felt shell-shocked. I sat there in the little garden for ages, looking through the trees at the back of the Colosseum and just trying to wrap my head around what had just happened. The various archaeologists working there stopped and chatted on their way by, recognizing how totally blown away I was by the experience, and telling me stories of coming out of the mountain after a long day's work and doing the same thing. Just sitting there in a stupor, not quite believing where they had just been and what they had just seen.

I texted my friend Daniella, a walking talking encyclopedia on Rome and the Rome tour guide for all my Glam Italia Tours. She also totally got it, and told me that she has been to Domus Aurea at least 50 times, and each time it's the same when she comes back outside — she too sits there just spellbound.

I hope you will make your way to Domus Aurea. If you find yourself sitting in the garden afterward, unable to leave and trying to come to terms with what you have just seen and experienced, and you happen to see a pony-tailed redhead doing the same, it's probably me so come say hi!

What's Nearby

Domus Aurea can be a little tricky to find. GPS will send you all the way around the back, but it makes for a lovely walk and a great opportunity to see the Rome the Romans live in, just a stone's throw from the **Colosseum**. From the outside of Domus Aurea you can see the Colosseum just a few meters away.

There is a little cafe up in the park on top of Domus Aurea where you can sit outside with the locals and enjoy an inexpensive cappuccino and a pastry.

Domus Aurea is only a stone's throw from **Basilica San Clemente** and about a five minute walk from **St John in Lateran**. In the opposite direction you have **Trajan's market** and the **Monti** district. Once again you are in the heart of everything, and no one knows about it!

8. Hadrian's Mausoleum & Castel Sant'Angelo

Normally everyone refers to this as the Castel Sant'Angelo. (You will find plenty of references to it in this book, especially in the *Ghosts of Rome* chapter!) It is a great landmark to have up your sleeve if you tend to get turned around a bit — I have a horrible sense of direction and can get lost in my own back yard, so I find my way around the world by going from from one landmark to the next. This one is a huge round castle/fortress-looking building that sits on the Tiber river, almost directly in front of St Peters. It is on the same side of the river as the Trastevere, so in my first forays into discovering Rome I would walk along the river to Castel Sant'Angelo, then cross over the bridge of angels (Ponte Sant'Angelo), then either wander down the other side of the river if it was a hot day and I needed shade from the trees, or duck down into the magical Roman streets that would take me from Piazza del Popolo in one direction to Campo de Fiori in the other. On a map it can look like a great distance, but in real life it is all very close and makes for a lovely walk. In those early days if I got lost I would just head back to the river, look for the Castel Sant'Angelo, and then know exactly where I was.

If you read Dan Brown books or watch the movies made from them, you will recognize this building from *Angels and Demons*. When tooling around Rome and also Florence, I have had no end of fun making walks of the Dan Brown sites. Sometimes my tour travelers have been big fans of his and have geeked out at doing Dan Brown walks as much as I do…

Anyway, we are talking Ancient Rome in this chapter, and this building had huge significance in Ancient Rome. Castel Sant'Angelo began its life as the mausoleum for another incredibly interesting emperor, Emperor Hadrian. I knew a little of Hadrian from his wall in the UK and had heard about his villa in Tivoli, but it wasn't until I actually *went* to Tivoli that I discovered just how fascinating he really was.

HADRIAN'S STORY

Hadrian was born in 76 AD in Italica, Spain. His parents died in 86 AD and the orphaned Hadrian and his sister were placed under the guardianship of their second cousin, Trajan, who was at that time an important army officer in Rome.

Trajan's wife Plotina was also Spanish, and took special care of Hadrian after his parents' death. Childless herself, she is said to have raised him as her own. She was his protector and also influenced him in his love of Greek culture, which she considered to be superior to Roman culture.

Trajan was a successful and popular military man, known to spend time out in the field traveling with his troops. An emperor's safety and success was directly linked to his relationship with the army, so when Emperor Domitian died in 96 AD and was replaced with the old and childless Emperor Nerva, Nerva knew he needed a man like Trajan on his team and took him on as co-emperor and successor. Nerva didn't last long and before you know it he was dead and Trajan became emperor.

Under Trajan's guidance, Hadrian became a seasoned military man himself, immensely popular with the Roman army. He traveled with his soldiers, ate the same rations as they did, and through his first-hand knowledge of day to day life of the Roman soldier was able to keep them on his side. By his early thirties, he was a high ranking general as well as a very talented administrator and politician.

Trajan died in southern Turkey in 117 AD, on his way home from war. Plotina produced a document, thought to be a fake, saying that Trajan wanted Hadrian as his successor. So in 117 AD Hadrian became emperor of Rome.

Hadrian was considered to be one of the five great Roman emperors. He didn't sit back and luxuriate in palace life, preferring instead to travel to all the provinces. He emulated the great Augustus, spending equal time at home and on the road. He saw the value in peace over endless expansion and wars, but knew he had to keep his army busy, so when they weren't running drills and war games he had them building. They fortified the empire with projects such as Hadrian's Wall, which ran for 73 miles along the border with Scotland.

He also promoted culture and the arts and the creation of beautiful buildings. Sometimes he was thin-skinned and petty (read more about this in the chapter about the Pantheon) He did his fair share of killing rivals and family members, some of which was completely crazy. He was the first emperor to sport a beard, and he was gay. Although married to Plotina's grand-niece Sabina, it is said that he was a cold and distant husband, saving all his loving for his Greek boy-toy, Antinous. (I will fill you in on that story when we get Tivoli in the *Day Trips* chapter. It is *quite* the story!)

HADRIAN'S MAUSOLEUM

In 135 AD Hadrian began building his mausoleum. Designed to rival Augustus' mausoleum just along the river from here, Hadrian's was massive. At 50 meters tall, it was the tallest building in Rome, higher than Trajan's Column and higher than the Pantheon.

Hadrian chose his location on the uncluttered west bank of the river so that its complete grandeur would stand out and dazzle everyone. Originally the building was covered in white marble and had trees (probably cypress) growing on the dome. Its shape, size and color made it not only distinct in a city full of amazing marble buildings, but incredibly impressive too. The mausoleum was completed in 139 AD, a year after Hadrian's death.

For the next century it held the remains of Hadrian's successors until 271 AD, when Emperor Aurelian turned it into a fortress.

Over the following centuries it remained an important building. In addition to being a mausoleum and a fortress, it also served as a refuge for popes, a prison, and a castle — the Castel Sant'Angelo.

The very beautiful bridge of angels (Ponte Sant'Angelo) ensured a clear channel for communications with the city of Rome, as well as a key strategic defense. Today the bridge has statues of angels over each of the eight arches, totally gorgeous to walk along and if you are like me, photograph madly.

Inside the castle today you can visit the Papal Apartments, replete with incredible artwork. In the Middle Ages it was used as a hideout for popes during times of danger. Pope Nicolas III had an underground passageway built connecting the castle to the Vatican.

Also, look at the marble chapel built by Pope Leo X (a debauched Medici pope), the facade of which was designed by Michelangelo.

The current entrance to the castle is in the same place as the original entrance to the mausoleum. As you walk in there is a circular ambulatory/walkway that lets you walk around the ancient walls before taking you to a staircase leading down to an atrium where there was once a giant statue of Hadrian. It leads back around a spiral ramp that completes the circuit of the castle.

If you visit the inside of the Castel Sant'Angelo make sure you stop in the Courtyard of the Cannonballs and see the piles of projectiles that still remain. These were used with the catapults nearby through the fifteenth, sixteenth and seventeenth centuries. It must have been horrific (and deadly) to be on the receiving end of one of those!

WHAT'S NEARBY

Hadrian's Mausoleum/Castel Sant'Angelo sits on the Tiber river close to **St Peters**. Directly in front of it is the beautiful bridge of angels, **Ponte Sant'Angelo**. Cross the bridge and turn left and you are only a few minutes walk from **Augustus' Mausoleum** and **Ara Pacis**. Just a few minutes further and you will be at **Piazza del Popolo** where you can pop in to see the Caravaggios before heading up to **Galleria Borghese**.

Cross the bridge of angels and turn right and you are only a few minutes walk from **Campo de Fiori** and **Piazza Navona**.

If you don't want to cross the bridge you can put your back to Castel Sant'Angelo and walk straight ahead to St Peters, or turn left and wander along the river to **Villa Farnesina** and then on to the **Trastevere**. From Castel Sant'Angelo to the Trastevere takes me between 20 and 30 minutes to walk, depending on how much I dawdle.

9. The Baths Of Caracalla

CARACALLA'S STORY

Caracalla was a bad, bad man. It is hard to believe something as majestic as these baths was the brainchild of a crazed mass killer, but there you have it.

In 193 AD, Rome moved into The Year of Five Emperors. When Commodus (who you may be familiar with from the movie *Gladiator)* was killed, after a bizarre 12 year reign (during which, amongst other crazy things, he renamed the months of the year after himself), instead of a new emperor taking power, the Praetorian Guard took over. They would hold auctions to choose the next emperor by asking how much each would pay them to be chosen. Loyalty was paid for with bribes. At the end of this year, one man was left standing — Septimius Severus; soldier, politician, bureaucrat. Severus would go on to build a family dynasty that would leave behind a building so grand it was the talk of the ancient world.

Severus got rid of the Praetorian Guard and replaced them with his own men, ensuring that he was protected by a loyal army. Then in 198 AD he named his ten-year-old son Caracalla co-emperor. In 209 AD he named his other son Geta as a second co-emperor. His system could have been fantastic except that Caracalla and Geta were arch enemies. Severus built a triumphal arch (at the north end of the Forum) to commemorate the three of them, although one would have his name chiseled off before long.

In 211 AD Severus died and the boys came to power. Caracalla tried to have Geta assassinated and failed, turning their rivalry into absolute hatred. Caracalla decided to host a dinner to be attended by only his mother and his brother. No guards were to be present and the family was to sit down together and hash the situation out. It sounded good, but it was a trap. No sooner had they sat down to eat, than one of Caracalla's guards burst into the room with a knife and hacked poor Geta to death. He died in his mother's arms. Caracalla had Geta's named removed from the triumphal arch and then rounded up anyone associated with Geta and had them killed (something in the vicinity of 20,000 people!).

In Alexandria no one believed Caracalla's "self defense" version of Geta's death, so Caracalla went to Alexandria to have dinner with the city elders, played nice for a moment, and then had them all murdered. Riots followed, so Caracalla had all the young men of Alexandria rounded up (25,000 of them) and had them slaughtered too, in an event known as the Rage of Caracalla. He was a maniac.

He was hated in Rome too. Loathed, in fact. He knew he needed to do something to make them like him. Vespasian had already built the Colosseum, giving people a place to watch sports and killing, his dad had made a triumphal arch, but there was one other thing that Romans loved — public baths.

And so to work he went. From around 211 AD to 216 AD, Caracalla built the baths to appease the people of Rome. (They were completed by 235 AD) Crazy, murderous, genocidal Caracalla made the people of Rome the greatest baths ever built. They were enormous. And grand. There was a cold pool (frigidarium), a medium temperature pool (tepidarium), and a circular hot pool (caldarium). A hypocaust (below ground fire) burning coal and tons of wood each day heated the pools and the steam room (yes, they had one of those too.) There were massive gardens to stroll in, two gyms to work out in, even a library for scholars to work, read and study in.

The floors were marble, with intricate mosaics, there was art everywhere, from the magnificent frescoes to exquisite statues, this place was beautiful! And the best part? The cost of admission was free.

Rome's class system disappeared at the public baths. Everyone came, everyone mixed, everyone mingled. They cooled off in the heat, warmed up in the cold. They had massages, listened to lectures, sealed business deals. The public baths in ancient Rome were the absolute hub of social life.

The Baths of Caracalla took up approximately 25 hectares/62 acres. The main building was 214 x 110 meters (yards are close enough) and the ceiling was 44 meters (144 feet) high. The Olympic sized swimming pool was 50 meters by 22 meters. Around the complex there were more than 250 columns, 16 of them more than 12 meters tall.

They would host up to 8,000 people per day, although apparently around 1600 was the maximum at a time. An entire aqueduct had to be brought in to provide the water. (The baths were in use until 537 AD when the Ostrogoths invaded and cut off the water supply.)

The Baths of Caracalla are well worth visiting just to get an idea of their imposing size and of how opulent and exquisite they must have been. Can you even comprehend that they were in use for over 300 years? The treasures are all gone, some of the mosaics are now in the Vatican museum. Two giant bathtub fountains that were originally here now live in the Piazza Farnese (beside the Campo de Fiori).

GETTING THERE

You can buy a single ticket, which is valid for seven days and gets you into the **Baths of Caracalla**, the **Villa of the Qunitili** and the **Tomb of Caecilia Metella**.

WHAT'S NEARBY

The Baths of Caracalla are on the south side of town, about a 10 minute walk from **Circus Maximus** and a 20 minute walk from the **Colosseum**.

10. Diocletian's Baths

DIOCLETIAN'S STORY

Personally, I find Diocletian fascinating. Just between you and me I knew nothing about him until I started googling his namesake public baths and pool. Partway down my neverending list of things to do in Rome was an visit to Diocletian's Baths and I decided to read up on them before visiting them on my next trip to the Eternal City.

So, old Diocletian was a Dalmatian military guy who rose to power towards the end of the Crisis of the Third Century (said "Crisis" was caused by invasions, civil war, economic depression and the plague). The reign of Diocletian stabilized the empire and ended the crisis.

Diocletian became emperor in 284 AD. He realized the empire had become too huge and too far-reaching to be successfully governed by just one person, so in 286 AD he made Maximian his co-emperor. He ran the eastern empire himself and had Max take care of the west.

In recent years, the empire had had a revolving door of emperors, some only lasting weeks or months. In order to ensure smooth succession for himself and for future emperors, Diocletian instated two competent, experienced administrators as *junior emperors*, who would learn how to run the empire so that when the time came for a transition, it would be seamless. (Unfortunately, greed and a hunger for power meant this system would be short lived, even though it was a brilliant idea.) The government, which had been on the verge of collapse during his youth, was reformed and restructured by Diocletian, essentially keeping it intact for the next 150 years.

All went well for Diocletian until 305 AD when in poor health, he decided to become the first emperor to abdicate. He moved back to the Dalmatian Coast and retired to a palace in a Croatian town now known as Split, living out the rest of his life growing cabbages. Years after his abdication when his system of co-emperors and junior emperors collapsed and the empire returned to chaos, Rome asked him to come back, be emperor again and fix everything, but he was happy with his tomatoes and cabbages (or whatever vegetables he was growing) and chose to stay in Croatia.

THE BATHS

Emperors left their mark on the empire by building structures designed to last the test of time. The third century was to a degree a building wasteland, so it was time for something huge.

And so the Baths of Diocletian, the largest of all the imperial baths in the Roman world, was commissioned. They were commissioned by co-emperor Maximian in 298 and completed in 306, by which time neither was still emperor. Maximian named them the Baths of Diocletian. Diocletian himself never saw them, as he didn't go to Rome.

The Baths of Diocletian are gargantuan. They take up 130,000 meters (or 32 acres) between the Viminal and Quirinal Hills. They were designed to be public baths/pools for the people living in the Viminal, Quirinal and Esquiline quarters of the city.

Supposedly large enough to accommodate 3000 people at any time, the complex was made up of a cool water pool (frigidarium), medium temperature pool (tepidarium) and a hot pool (caldarium), as well as a 4000 square meter outdoor pool. There was an open air gym (palaestra) on either side of the pools, as well as libraries and beautiful walkways.

Today the ruins of the baths are still enormous. As you walk through the ruins, the size and scope of the project is overwhelming. You can almost hear the patter of Roman sandals ambling through the common areas nearly two millennia ago. How incredible it must have been for the people of Rome to stroll these giant walkways on their way to the pools, how sensational the beauty must have been!

For two centuries, water was supplied to the pools via the Aqua Marcia aqueduct, until the siege of Rome in 537 AD when Ostrogoths had the water supply cut off.

Even if the shell of the building and the pools were all there was to see I would recommend you add this stop to your Rome itinerary, but there is more.

THE STATUES

Throughout the complex, everywhere you turn there are statues. Spectacular, awe-inspiring statues of gods and kings, beasts and beauties. Statues and artifacts that will take your breath away.

(Sometimes I think they must dig up so many treasures in Rome that there is no place to put them. But the Baths of Diocletian are as good a place as any to line up endless treasures from antiquity!) Walking through the cloisters, looking at them lined up throughout the inner courtyard is just incredible.

Some date back to the first century BC. Plenty are dated to the first century AD. From Nero's head, to a bust of beautiful Antonia Minor (mother of Emperor Claudius) dated to around 18 AD, which stands taller than me! Sarcophagi from 160 AD, water nymphs from second century fountains – there is so much here to look at!

I spent a small amount of time exploring the pools and an enormous amount of time walking around and around all the areas with statues. And here is what I found even more astonishing: once again I had the whole place almost entirely to myself.

My first trip to the Baths of Diocletian was in June of 2018. That day Rome was packed to bursting point and stiflingly hot. I had initially been going to tackle some items on my list that were close to the Colosseum, but the crush of tourists in the area forced me back out of there as fast as I could go. On the map, Diocletian's Baths didn't look far so I decided to walk, which wasn't an entirely brilliant idea on a day so hot and humid. A taxi would have only cost a few euros and buses run right up to the Piazza della Repubblica which abuts parts of the walls.

The entrance is beautiful, with trees and a huge fountain, a lovely place to escape the heat, or if not visiting during the middle of summer just a lovely place to sit and enjoy the scenery. The cost of entry was around 10 euros and was worth every penny. There were other people visiting that afternoon – I wasn't the only one, but I might as well have been. Everywhere I went I had a clear, uninterrupted view. I could look at the statues from every angle, I could see it all unimpeded.

I think my favorite part was walking round and round the cloistered internal courtyard, cool and shaded from the heat of the day. I remember a few artists were scattered around sketching, but when I look at all the photos and videos I took, I can't see them.

This, to me, is part of the incredible magic of Rome. There is so much to see and do, most of which is far from the tourist crush.

THE CHURCHES

Diocletian was said to be the most ardent persecutor of Christians. He killed more of them than any other emperor. I have read that the Baths of Diocletian were built by 10,000 Christians. Whether that number is true or not, suffice to say it was a rough time to be a Christian. This wasn't based on theology so much as it was based on continuity, obedience and legitimacy. Emperors presented themselves as semi-divine. The concept of aligning yourself with "one true God" was a direct challenge to that legitimacy.

In the end, though, the Christians got the last laugh. In 1562, Pope Pius IV commissioned Michelangelo to build a church on the ruined site to commemorate the Christians who died building the baths. **Santa Maria degli Angeli e dei Martiri** (St Mary of the Angels and Martyrs) was built using the frigidarium and tepidarium structures, and a small cloister was built using part of the natation (outdoor pool). This church is a must-see while in the area.

In 1598 a second church was built nearby, **San Bernardo alle Terme** (St Bernard of the Baths). This one is quite remarkable in its own right. Similar to the shape of the Pantheon this church is cylindrical, has a dome and an oculus. There are statues of eight saints in wall niches, by Camillo Mariani.

You could spend a fabulous afternoon exploring the Baths and these two churches, away from the crowds while still in the heart of the city.

THE NATIONAL MUSEUM OF ROME TICKET

The Baths of Diocletian are on the *National Museum of Rome* ticket, along with **Palazzo Massimo**, **Crypta Balbi** and **Palazzo Altemps**. Tickets are valid for two or three days (check when you purchase), so you can see all of those sites for one purchase price.

WHAT'S NEARBY

The church of **Santa Maria Degli Angeli e dei Martiri** and the **Piazza della Repubblica** are immediately there as well as **Palazzo Massimo alle Terme**. It is a close walk to **Santa Maria in Maggiore** and you can follow Via Nazionale down through the Monti district to **Trajan's Column** (about a 30 minute walk).

11. The Appian Way

ALL ROADS LEAD TO ROME

Actually, at one time they pretty much did! Via Appia Antica (the Appian Way) is not only one of the greatest testaments to the brilliance of Roman construction, it was Europe's first super highway. It may be the world's oldest road still in existence, and it was Rome's most important road.

Originally built by Appius Claudius Caecus (hence the name "Appian") in 312 BC, the Appian Way connected Rome to Capua, near Naples, then across to Brindisi in Puglia. More than 300 miles long, it was the widest and longest road in the world. This artery provided an excellent new way to move Roman soldiers across the country with ease.

CONSTRUCTION

I don't know about the roads where you live, but in my city they are always working on the roads. Modern technology seems to be perpetually failing, yet much of the original Appian Way is still intact.

It started as a dirt road, then a layer of small stones and mortar was added, followed by a layer of gravel, before the top layer of tight fitting interlocking stones completed it, giving the road a flat, smooth surface. It was slightly raised in the center so that water could drain away into the ditches that were dug along either side of the road, which in turn were secured by retaining walls. Most of the road was completed the same year as it was started. Centuries of armies marching and carriages rolling over this road have held all the stones in place.

MULTIMEDIA DISPLAY AT PALAZZO VALENTINI

If you go to Palazzo Valentini (see the *Underground Rome* section of this book), their multimedia display lights up the large stones in the ancient Roman road beneath the palazzo. A laser shows you how they weren't random shaped stones placed in random order, but instead a series of stones interlocked and repeated in a pattern. It is brilliant! It also helps make sense of the stones along the Appian Way.

Walking along the Appian Way you are quite literally walking in Julius Caesar's footsteps, as well as those of ancient Rome's most illustrious military leaders and emperors. I have read that St Peter walked this road too, in fact not far from the Porta San Sebastiano entrance (two miles from the Colosseum) you will find the ninth century Domine Quo Vadis church. Legend has it that in 64 AD Peter was fleeing Nero's persecution along this road when he saw a vision of Jesus. He asked him *"Domine, quo vadis?"* ("Lord, where are you going?"). Jesus told him he was heading to Rome to be crucified again, which made Peter decide to turn around, go back to Rome, accept his fate and be martyred. (I, on the other hand, might've said *"Sorry mate - I'm off."* and would have run down the Appian Way towards Brindisi!)

Inside the church there is a fresco of St Peter on the left wall and a fresco of Jesus on the right wall, as well as a stone that supposedly has the footprints of Christ.

HOW TO EXPERIENCE THE APPIAN WAY

A really fun way to enjoy the Appian Way is by bicycle. You can rent them outside the shop at the beginning of the Appian Way. This is a lovely area to enjoy a picnic and to take some really amazing photos! You will see local Romans also on their bikes and picnicking by Caecilia Metella's tomb. So long as it's not too hot, it makes for a really lovely day. You can walk or bike for miles around here, there are ruins and tombs and open fields, and almost everything is at it was built in the fourth century. On Sundays the Appian Way is closed to all traffic other than bikes.

The Appian Way starts at the **Porta San Sebastiano**, which is roughly two miles from the **Colosseum**. You can get here by taxi, or you can take the metro to the **Circo Massimo** stop and then get the #118 bus, which comes every 40 minutes.

WHAT'S NEARBY

There is lots to see in this section of the Appian Way. The first ten miles are part of the **Parco dell' Appia Antica**, and the road itself as well as the monuments through here are protected.

Christians were buried all along here. The **San Callisto and San Sebastiano Catacombs** are here, as well as the **Circus Maxentius**, one of the best preserved Roman circuses, an arena where chariot races were held. The ruins of **Emperor Maxentius' Villa** are here too.

12. The Tomb Of Caecilia Metella

If you're in this neighborhood, you can't miss the Tomb of Caecilia Metella — it looks like a giant, round castle. It is one of the best known and best preserved monuments on the Appian Way. And of course, like everything in Rome, it has a great backstory

Caecilia Metella's Story

This particular Caecilia Metella (there were several) was born into one of the wealthiest families in ancient Rome. The wealth and power of the Metella family dated back to the third century BC and lasted until the end of the Republic. The family held both political power and important military seats.

During that time, female names were often derived from their father's, so the Caecilius Metellus clan had multiple Caecilia Metellas. Every daughter in the family had the same name, (as if they had no importance at all and were just human chattels — can you imagine being of so little value that you weren't even worthy of having your own name??) The Caecilia of this mausoleum was born around 100 BC and was married off to a powerful Roman general and politician, named Marcus Licinius Crassus, who was instrumental in the conversion of the Roman Republic into the Roman Empire.

Surprisingly little else is known about this Caecilia. We know neither the reason for her death, nor even exactly when she died. Her mausoleum gives us no clues either. Which is a little odd. Positioned as it was on the highest and most prominent point along this stretch of the Appian Way, this glorious structure could be seen for miles. You could be forgiven for thinking it was built as a testament to a husband's inconsolable grief at the loss of his beloved wife. But it wasn't.

We know two things about Caecilia from the inscription on the wall. But I'll get to that in a moment.

The Mausoleum

Caecilia's mausoleum is made up of a rotunda sitting on top of a square podium, with the Cetani Castle attached to the back. The podium is 8.3 meters tall and the cylindrical drum rotunda standing on it is another 12 meters tall. The diameter of the drum is 29.5 meters (or 100 Roman feet).

Her sarcophagus originally sat on a funerary sill inside the wall of the massive tower, facing the Appian Way, but now it calls the Palazzo Farnese home. But there is some dispute as to whether that is in fact her sarcophagus. At the time of her death cremation was the norm, so her ashes would more likely have been placed in a funerary urn. Also a study done on the sarcophagus suggests it dates to 180 AD. So who knows?

The exterior of the mausoleum was made of travertine. The upper level of the tower was decorated with a marble frieze depicting wreaths and the skulls of oxen, both of which were references to sacrifices made to the Roman gods. Quite a masculine motif, don't you think? Not really imagery we would expect to see for a tomb dedicated to a woman. The relief in the center is also very masculine, depicting a helmet, shields and a prisoner. The only nod to Caecilia is on the inscription:

CAECILAE Q CRETICI F METELLAE CRASSI

Translated, this reads *Caecilia, daughter of Quinicus Metellus Creticus and wife of Crassus*. (The Creticus part refers to her father having conquered Crete.) No references to beloved wife, dear daughter, loving mother. Just an indication that she was the daughter of one man and the wife of the next, like a possession with transferred ownership.

So why build this huge, spectacular mausoleum for a woman not important enough to have her own name? It is thought to have been built towards the end of the first century BC, sometime after Caecilia's death, but in all likelihood NOT to celebrate her. More likely, her death provided an opportunity to show off the wealth and power and greatness of this eminent family, and to celebrate the glory of the men named on the inscription (her father and husband!).

THE FORTRESS

Skipping over centuries of history, the fortress was built in the middle ages, eventually becoming the Cetani Castle. The rounded, earth-covered roof of the mausoleum had battlements built onto it and it became an important fortress, guarding the Appian Way and the southern entrance into Rome. The castle now houses a museum and ancient statues throughout the courtyards.

GETTING THERE

You can buy a single ticket, which is valid for seven days and gets you into the **Baths of Caracalla**, the **Villa of the Qunitili** and the **Tomb of Caecilia Metella**.

13. The Villa dei Quintili

You made it to the three mile marker on the Appian Way to visit Caecilia, now just two more miles down the road there is something else truly remarkable to see. Being that this one takes a little more work to get to, it gets comparatively few tourists. I read somewhere that around thirty million tourists go to Rome each year, but only ten thousand or so make it out here to the Villa dei Quintili, which in my opinion is reason enough to pay it a visit!

Have you seen the film *Gladiator*, with Russell Crowe? I normally try to get all my Glam Italia travelers to watch it before they come to Italy, because there are so many places we visit and so many references to things we see in Rome in the movie. Also, it's hard to explain to anyone how crazy Emperor Commodus really was, and this film gives you an inkling.

Commodus was the son of Emperor Marcus Aurelius, the last of the Five Good Emperors. The previous four had each adopted a good heir to become their successor, but unfortunately Marcus Aurelius decided to go with his lunatic son, Commodus. In *Gladiator* you get to see him portrayed as being relatively nuts, but in real life he was worse. (I spoke of him in an earlier chapter on the *Baths of Caracalla*, but he's present at Villa dei Quintili in all his crazy glory too.)

Villa dei Quintili was the most massive, most amazing residence in the outer suburbs of Ancient Rome. It was built by two brothers, Sextus Quintilius Valerius Maximus and Sextus Quintilius Condianus. Both were consuls (the highest political office) in 151 AD, so were rich, powerful, and apparently very cultured.

Built during the reign of Hadrian, the villa included thermal baths fed by their own aqueduct. It even had its own hippodrome, a Greek stadium used for horse and chariot racing. The buildings were enormous and gleamed bright white with travertine and marble friezes. Until you stand there, it is almost impossible to really understand how huge this place really is.

In its day, the Villa dei Quintili was not only magnificent but also incredibly beautiful. So magnificent and beautiful and celebrated and coveted that crazy Commodus decided he wanted it. So being the madman that he was, he created a phony plot to have himself killed, made the Quintili brothers the fall guys and had them put to death.

Then he confiscated the property and moved in himself. But you know how karma is — only ten years later a real plot was successful, and Commodus the Crazy was murdered.

You can walk through the ruins and see mosaic floors still intact and perfect after 2000 years of exposure to the elements, wars, and the pillaging of the dark ages. They are amazing! There are also patches of marble, marble floors, columns, and the shells of these giant, giant buildings. The thermal baths and sauna area are open to walk through as well. Some of the exquisite marble sculptures that were part of the original villa are in the small museum on site. (Many were sold off when they were discovered.)

The villa compound was so enormous that while they were excavating it they called it "Old Rome" thinking it must have been a town! Excavations are still going on here.

GETTING THERE

You can buy a single ticket, which is valid for seven days and gets you into the **Baths of Caracalla**, the **Villa of the Qunitili** and the **Tomb of Caecilia Metella**.

Forum & Palantine Hill

2.

Five Things to Look For at the Forum & Palatine Hill

1. Domitian's Palace

2. The House of Augustus

3. The House of Livia

4. The Temple of Caesar

5. The Mamertine Prison

I really didn't want to get into the Forum or the Palatine Hill in this book, because there is far too much to see there to be able to do it justice. I must have been through both places at least 17 times with my private guide Daniella. She has a masters degree in Roman History, and is a walking, talking encyclopedia of knowledge to do with everything Roman. Even with the huge amount of time we have spent there together, with me making her talk non-stop, I feel as though there is still so much that I don't know. If I could convince her to do a book with me about the Forum I highly doubt we could narrow it down to 101 things. But rather than skip the Forum/Palatine Hill altogether, there are five places I want to direct your attention to.

1. Domitian's Palace

I first stumbled upon this amazing place years ago when I was in Rome with my 10-year-old son. We had walked into the Palatine Hill from the Circus Maximus side, and were wandering around and exploring with no specific agenda. The masses all turned right and we turned left, and suddenly we were at this incredible site (it blew the WOW factor right off the charts) and, unlike at the Forum below us which was absolutely teaming with people, there was barely anybody up here!

Over the years I have come up here often. Every time my tour guide Daniella shows me new things, explains more of the story and I become more fascinated by the place. I also have become more and more fascinated by Domitian. In many ways he was a great emperor (see Domitian's Stadium in the *Underground Rome* chapter of this book), but he became an autocrat and had a really bad side. (Maybe that's what makes him so interesting?) Anyway, nothing says "I'm successful" quite like a truly bombastic super-palace. So he built one.

The size and scope of Domitian's Palace are jaw dropping. This place is HUGE! The bulk of Domitian's Palace remained intact from its completion in 92 AD throughout the empire, and was the official residence of the emperor until the fall of the Roman Empire in the fifth century. This area was always the home for the elite, all the way back through the Republic. There was some building over top of prior structures, much is gone but there remain three notable homes you can visit that date back to the Republic: The House of Augustus, The House of Livia and the House of the Griffins.

HOUSE OF GRIFFINS

Although I haven't been down to see them yet there are significant frescoes and incredible floors in the House of Griffins, dating back to 100 BC. They haven't been open to the public when I have been there, but one of these days I will get to see them! When I do, you'll be able to read all about it on my Corinna B's World blog.

Domitian's Palace is also known as the **Flavian Palace** (because others from his dynasty had a hand in building it). The palace is in three parts, separated to allow business and political life to exist parallel to the private dwelling.

DOMUS AUGUSTANA

The Domus Augustana, which is the center of the three parts, was built on top of previous dwellings: Nero's Domus Transitoria and the aforementioned House of the Griffins.

STADIUM

If you are in the center of Domus Augustana, facing outward, looking toward the Circus Maximus, to your left is the third part of the complex, known as the Stadium. This was the equivalent to a modern day man-cave. Domitian (and the emperors who followed him) could hang out here and watch private sports, have outdoor meals under the porticos, and do whatever Roman emperors did in their downtime. The Stadium has a stadium shape: a long oval. From the central Domus Augustana to your right is the first section of the palace, the Domus Flavia.

DOMUS FLAVIA

Walking up to the palace from the Forum along the Clivus Palatinus, the road that connects the Forum to the Palatine Hill, try to imagine how overwhelming it must have been for foreign leaders, diplomats and business people coming for an audience with the emperor. The palace just explodes up out of the ground, huge and imposing. And in its day, gleaming, sparkling white. They certainly would have felt insignificant and small.

The first structure you see is the Basilica, where legal work happened. This is the northeastern corner of the Domus Flavia. Below the Basilica excavations have been done on what was probably part of the Domus Augusti (The House of Augustus) with frescoes dating back to 30 BC. Although now in ruins, you can still see how tall the basilica was. While reduced to its brick core, the whole palace was once bright white travertine and marble.

The different parts of the palace are well marked, so find your way to the center front entrance. This main entrance to the palace takes you through the *Laraium* (below which are the excavations of the House of Griffins) and into the *Aula Regia*, a massive room with 30 meter high coffered ceilings (back in the day). This was a greeting place for the emperor and a place where he would hold banquets. The Lararium, Aula Regia and the Basilica make up the front of the Domus Flavia.

Beyond the Aula Regia you walk into a giant garden dominated by a pool with an octagonal island. Beyond this is the *cenatio*, the official banquet hall.

The Domus Augustana was technically the domestic section of the palace, but the residence was probably just the southern section, with the front section being for entertaining and the middle section being another giant pool, equal in size to the one in the Domus Flavia. You have to wonder if it was just for show or did they actually swim in it? Did the kids do cannonballs off the sides? Were the ladies swimming around, trying not to get their hair wet? I wish I could have been a fly on the wall here back in Domitian's time just to see it all in action.

You can stand at the southern edge of the building and look down into what was the residence, 10 meters below. It is just staggering! There is another pool down there too. Is that the one they swam in? Did they swim??

The *excedra* is or was a long, curved arcade gallery which linked the two wings of the palace and overlooked the Circus Maximus, so the emperor and company could watch races from up here, or go down to the emperor's box.

The hippodrome (stadium) stretches along the entire eastern wall of the Domus Augustana wing of the palace. At 160 m x 48 m it was too small for chariot races, so was probably a sunken garden. Around the perimeter a two story portico with slim columns made of expensive marble made for a sheltered walkway. The garden was full of statues that are now in the Palatine museum.

I can spend an entire morning just wandering around up here, taking it all in. This is one of those places that is even better to see with a guide if you possibly can. I have done it both ways and been totally wowed either way, but there is so much more you can find out when a guide is answering all of your questions.

ABOUT TOUR GUIDES

In Italy being a licensed tour guide is a serious career. It is really hard to get a tour guide license in Italy. You have to have a degree in art history, history, archaeology or other related field. They have to sit comprehensive exams, both written and oral. In most places they have to be fluent in at least three languages. Many people try to get licensed but only a few make it through, and those who do get through have worked incredibly hard for it.

I am a huge advocate of licensed guides in Italy. I hire them everywhere for all of my tours. Most of them have masters degrees or PhDs in their field. They really, *really* know their stuff and they are happy to share it with you. They are really passionate about what they do.

If you are booking a guide, do so ahead of time either through a reputable agency or by searching them on Trip Advisor. Look for guides with excellent ratings — I have found the best private guides that way. Don't pick up guides who are standing outside tourist sites trying to find work — chances are they're not legit and you don't want to be paying for a scammer.

Not being licensed is a crime in Italy, and police are always on the lookout for scammers. Sometimes real licensed guides will tip them off, other times they can tell by watching that someone is doing guide work, and if they don't have the official credentials they get arrested and fined. Don't get caught up in that — do the right thing and only hire licensed guides.

2. House of Augustus

These next two are adjacent to Domitian's Palace. Domitian knocked down and built over parts of the House of Augustus when he built his mega palace.

When walking into places like the House of Augustus and the Case Romane, and basically everything in this book, I am *still* constantly overwhelmed with how lucky we are to be able to see these places and *experience* them. Most people coming to Rome just want a photo at the Colosseum, a whip through the Vatican, a couple more photo ops and a bowl of pasta. They either don't know about places like this or they don't care, which is why I want to share them with you, my friend, because if you are this far into my book then you clearly care about having a different experience in Rome.

In the chapter about *Ancient Rome,* we talked about the first emperor — political shark, master of spin and brilliant leader, Augustus. He who arrived to a city of brick and left us with a city of marble. He was the grand-nephew of Julius Caesar and was named his heir. He took on Antony and Cleopatra, changed Rome from a Republic to an Empire, became its first emperor (and probably the greatest) while creating the constitutional framework, building infrastructure, strengthening the borders and leading Rome into an unprecedented era of peace.

Augustus was not only a great leader, he was adored by his people. So much so that when his house burned down the people of Rome, rich and poor, all donated money to rebuild it without being asked. Augustus showed his gratitude by only accepting one coin from every donation, no matter how huge or small the donation was. Which of course only endeared him to his people even more!

You would expect a leader so great and so powerful to live in an opulent mega-palace, perched up high so everyone could see just how important he was, but not Augustus — he opted for a considerably more humble abode. Instead of building something ostentatious, the emperor chose an existing house on the Palatine Hill, the house of an orator named Hortensio. In 36 BC the senate had it updated for him and he lived there until his death in 14 AD.

The house was modest, set on two floors, with no marble and with short arches (which means a low roof compared to the grander homes of the time). Apparently he didn't even use all the space he had there, and for 40 years slept in the same bedroom no matter the weather and regardless of how it ultimately damaged his health.

His house was situated on the most sacred part of the Palatine Hill, next to the Temple of Apollo and beside the hut of Romulus, the place where Romans came to honor the city's founder, and supposedly above the cave where the she-wolf suckled the twin babies Romulus and Remus. All of these things didn't just add to his popularity, they elevated him beyond sainthood.

Although his home was considered simple in size and style for a man of his stature, Augustus really knew how to decorate! He had the best painters in all of Rome create some of the greatest Roman wall paintings anywhere is the world, and they are still in their original location. As you stand looking at them, you are standing in the footsteps of the greatest leader in Roman history, seeing what he saw each day as he went about his work changing the world.

His home was painted in Pompeii style and colors: reds and blues and yellows. Some of it is beautiful, some of it (the mask room) is (in my opinion) scary. I would have nightmares if I had to look at those scary mask faces every day! You can walk from room to room and even see the beautiful and refined room he used as his study, and where he retired to do his thinking. It's just incredible! One thing that amazes me is the painted coffered ceilings. He of all people could have afforded real coffered ceilings, but instead just had them painted on.

The House of Augustus is a relatively recent discovery. It was unearthed during excavations in the 1960s. Pollution, exposure to biological organisms and harsh weather had all caused severe damage to the frescoes that cover the walls, ceilings and pillars, while seeping water caused damage to both the paintings and the structure. Restorations have included stabilizing the structure, installing protective roofing, conserving and restoring the paintings.

The House of Augustus was an immensely important archaeological find. It revealed what was going on when Rome transitioned from a Republic into an Empire, and when the Palatine Hill was evolving from an elite residential area to the seat of imperial power, which it remained for 500 years. It provided so much insight into the life of Rome's greatest emperor and about life and art in that time. Honestly it is just astounding.

It opened to the public in 2008.

GETTING THERE

The House of Augustus is next to Domitian's Palace on the Palatine Hill, so is part of the whole Colosseum/Forum area. Your best bet is to ask directions when entering the Forum gate on Via dei Fori Imperiali — I find that a little less confusing and there are normally fewer people at that entrance. There is also the Via di San Gregoria entrance to the Palatine Hill.

This one may take some planning to see. The rules seem to change every year, from it being open on alternate days, to only being open if you take a tour, to no tour required. The website gets a bit glitchy and sometimes lets you get all the way to hitting the purchase button to get a ticket and then nothing happens. Don't get frustrated — this site is well worth whatever frustration it takes to get there. (Now watch you all get tickets seamlessly!)

To buy your ticket, my best advice is to go through the Coopculture website or to use the Walks of Italy tours. The tours are around 75 minutes long. You can sometimes do a combination tour with the House of Livia, but when I tried to book it they were doing an alternate day thing where Augustus was open Monday, Wednesday and Friday and Livia was open Tuesday, Thursday and Saturday. Regardless, if you have the option of going with a tour or going alone, take the tour. There is so much to see here, you don't want to miss a thing!

3. The House of Livia

We also talked about Livia in an earlier chapter, but here is a refresher: Augustus met and fell in love with Livia when they were both married to other people. His wife Scribonia was pregnant with his daughter Julia and Livia was pregnant with Drassus, having already given birth to Tiberius, with her first husband. On the day that Julia was born, Augustus divorced Scribonia so that he could marry Livia. Livia wanted her son Tiberius to become the next emperor, and everyone in line for the job started dying off mysteriously, until only Tiberius was left.

Upon the death of Augustus (which she may have had a hand in), he was elevated to god status, making her a high priestess. She was evil, scheming and a murderer, but she was also a wily and clever survivor.

Prior to becoming emperor, Augustus had a small house on the Palatine Hill. He bought up several others and when he became emperor turned them into a little compound. His house faced the Circus Maximus and got the sunshine he craved. The House of Livia, his wife's house was like an annex to his house, connected by a walkway. Although it is referred to as a separate house it was probably more a case of being her apartments as part of the main house. She also had a villa on the Via Flaminia.

This house was excavated in 1839 and was attributed to Livia because her name was stamped onto a lead pipe which is on display in the Tablinum section of the house.

IVLIA AVGVSTA

Translated this means Julia Augusta, which is what she called herself after Augustus became emperor.

If you ever wonder how and why these Roman buildings have managed to survive two millennia it could well be because they were built to last. Factories had to stamp their products both with their own name and with the name of the person it was for, so when we see her name on the pipe we know that pipe was intended for her home. And that if anything went wrong with it they would know who to hold accountable. The building itself dates to the first half of the first century BC then went through some alterations around 30 BC, which is the time the frescoes are dated to.

Livia's was a two-story house built around a central atrium. It was decorated with magnificent Pompeii-style frescoes and wall paintings. The floors were of a simple black and white mosaic, possibly because the walls were so busy. From the rectangular atrium there is a *tablinum* with a room on either side.

In Livia's house the *tablinum* is the best preserved room. It is also known as the Room of Polyphemus due to frescoes telling mythological stories including one of the earliest known depictions of the story of the monster Polyphemus and the sea nymph Galatea.

Off to the side of the atrium is the *triclinium* (dining room). This room also has really remarkable frescoes. Each wall has painted architectural illusions — painted columns with a landscape in the center.

It is amazing to be able to walk through the home of the empire's first First Lady. If you are a history buff or if you just enjoy Roman history, *you will love this.*

As with the House of Augustus, the schedule seems to change around as to when and how you can see it. My best recommendation is to try to get on a tour. The tours have to be booked well in advance. They keep them small, the largest I have seen is for 20, and there are only one or two of them per day in English. (Although who knows how they will do it this year?) There is so much information here that I think you run the risk of missing too much by doing it alone.

4. The Temple Of Caesar

If I were to ask you who is the most famous Roman of all time, I can pretty much guarantee you would answer Julius Caesar. And I think you would be right. He was the catalyst that moved the Republic to the Empire. He was a great politician, military man, and by all accounts a *great man*. He was a man of the people, he loved them and they loved him right back. And yet as we walk around Rome we don't see great buildings attributed to him. He is always there, yet he's not.

CAESAR'S STORY

Julius Caesar was born in 100 BC, into a family that was both distinguished and broke. He grew up amongst the poor people and throughout his life identified more with the common man than the nobles. His early years read like a wild adventure, hiding from the bad guys who were out to kill him. At one point he was captured by pirates and ransomed, and then once freed he turned around, attacked those same pirates, got the ransom money back and crucified them all!

He attained military glory, and he fought for the poor and landless against the members of his own class, only endearing himself more to the citizens of Rome. After years of battles and civil wars Caesar eventually became the leader of Rome (I've skipped a lot of his story here). Unlike his predecessors he wasn't about bloody purges and savagery, instead he brought about peace, pardoned enemies instead of crushing them, and always, always maintained a fantastic relationship with the people of Rome. They *loved* him.

But the Senate didn't. He was blowing their game on enriching themselves at the expense of the poor, and he held far too much power. So they decided to assassinate him.

It nearly didn't happen. On that fateful day, the Ides of March 44 BC, Caesar woke up not feeling well. He was due to head out on a military campaign the next day, and his wife had had a nightmare that he was murdered, so he sent a message to the senate that he wouldn't make it to their scheduled meeting. The senate was desperate — if they didn't kill him today he would head out on his military gig and come back even more glorious. So they whipped up a master plan, sending someone he would trust to get him, Decimus Brutus, knowing that Caesar loved Decimus like a son.

The Senate house had been damaged by fire so the meeting was held at the Teatro Pompeo. (we talk about Teatro Pompeo in the chapter on *Underground Rome* at the da Pancrazio restaurant, and in *Ancient Rome* at Largo Argentina, right beside where all of this went down.) One of Caesar's friends heard about the scheme and sent a messenger to warn him. The messenger slipped a note into Caesar's hand, but he wasn't able to step aside and read it. Caesar sat down, the meeting began, and dozens of senators pulled daggers from their togas and set upon Julius Caesar in a stabbing frenzy. When it was done everyone fled, leaving him to bleed to death alone on the cold marble floor.

The senators thought they had liberated the republic. They saw themselves as heroes. The people saw otherwise. Enraged that their beloved leader had been taken from them they took to the streets and rioted. The conspirators who killed Caesar locked themselves inside their homes or fled. It got worse. Caesar's funeral took place in the Forum and the masses who loved him came to pay homage. Their fury at his murder was at boiling point when Marc Antony took advantage of an incredible opportunity. He got up in front of the people and spoke of all the great things beloved Caesar had done for them. A politician to the core, he got them whipped into hysteria. He held up Caesar's blood stained toga and pointed out all the stab wounds. Right when the crowd was about to explode, Marc Antony read them Julius Caesar's will: Caesar had bequeathed his estates, his gardens, his art collections (which were pretty sizable) and a huge sum of money to the people of Rome. His people. The people he loved more than anything. What could possibly show the people of Rome more clearly that he wasn't the oppressor the senate accused him of being? This proved that his assassination had been a crime. They had been robbed of this great man. And so they rioted. They raged through the Forum smashing stuff, throwing everything that could be burned onto the funeral pyre. Fire tore through the Forum and the mob went wild.

The murderous senators didn't achieve their goal. In fact, instead of strengthening the Republic, this was the end of it. Caesar had named Octavian as his successor, and Octavian went on to amass the most power any man had ever had. He created the Empire and renamed himself Augustus.

Augustus was clever. He built a temple to Caesar, both so that the people had a place to celebrate his greatness and also to remind them he was the heir and the closest thing to Caesar in the world.

There is not much of Caesar's temple left to see, but what is there remains under a canopy, covered from the elements. This is the spot where Caesar's pyre burned, where the anguish of the people of Rome spilled out and burned down the Forum, toppling the Republic. This is the place in Rome where you can stand with Caesar, the most important man in Roman history.

GETTING THERE

It is quite easy to find the Temple of Caesar. Walk along the Via Sacra from either direction and you will find it in the middle of the Forum. It is easily identifiable by the modern metal roof sheltering it.

CAESAR'S ASSASSINATION

Keep your ears open while you are at the Temple of Caesar. You will hear people, including some fake tour guides (the ones I warned you about) saying that this is the spot where Caesar died. This drives me crazy!

He did not die here! This is the place of his funeral pyre. Julius Caesar was murdered at the curia of the Teatro Pompeo, which is immediately behind the Largo Argentina (read more about this in the chapter on *Ancient Rome*).

5. The Mamertine Prison

At the north west end of the Forum by the Arch of Septimus Severus stands an unassuming church that you would walk right past if you didn't know what was going on beneath it. It has special significance for Christians and also for folks interested in how miracles work.

The church is closed to the public, but it's not the church that we have come to see, it's what's underneath. This church, **San Giuseppe Falegnami**, was built on top of another building with a dark and gory history. Find the church, find the side entrance, and then descend down into the bowels of ancient Rome into the Mamertine Prison.

In ancient Rome prisons weren't really a thing. They specialized more in executions, exiles and hard labor. This one is not only special because it was rare or because it survived so many centuries, it was also the lock up of two of the Bible's favorite saints.

The story starts somewhere between 600 and 500 BC when this little jail was constructed as a cistern for a spring that ran under the floor. It was called the Tullianum. Then in 449 BC the Roman elders created a law code known as The Twelve Tables. The Twelve Tables set out specific rules to live by, creating a system of law and order and giving Romans the right to a trial by a jury of their peers. (These were the most sophisticated law codes of the ancient world and still influence laws today. They pretty much set the basis of our current legal system — pretty cool, no?)

Now that they had a system of law and order, they had a new problem. When someone was awaiting trial or punishment, or while the appropriate punishment was being decided they needed somewhere to stash them. The guilty would still end up being executed, exiled or put into hard labor — it made no sense to keep them indefinitely at the expense of the state, but where to put them in the meantime…?

So the Tullianum became the jail site, with two cells, one built on top of the other. Horrifically, the entrance to the lower cell was through a small door in the floor of the upper cell (if you read up on it you will see that prisoners were *lowered through the hole in the floor*. Probably they were just pushed down the hole.). These cells weren't roomy either. They were packed with bodies all squashed together in that dark, dank, hellhole of a dungeon. Inmates weren't kept there for long though. For most the walk down the stairs at the Mamertine didn't have a particularly happy ending. So let's just say this place is *atmospheric*.

BE BRAVE!

Regardless of your reason for visiting, you will definitely feel this place. It's eerie. Just as in the *Ghosts of Rome* chapter of this book, when I talk about how the air moves differently below the

Colosseum, which is just down the street, and how the hairs stand up on the back of your neck and you get goosebumps, don't be surprised if you experience a visceral reaction down here. Maybe I've seen too many scary movies, but personally this place gives me the creeps. I tend to get claustrophobic and start thinking I can't breathe, so you won't be running into me in the Mamertine!

CHRISTIAN SIGNIFICANCE

Two events made this a place of significance for Christians, which has a pretty dreadful irony when you consider how many Christians were to be jailed here before too long.

Theoretically, although not known for certain, Peter and Paul were both held here before being executed in the Christian persecution that followed the great fire of Rome in 64 AD. Paul, being a local had the benefit of a beheading, whereas Peter, the non-local, was crucified. He didn't want to go on the cross like Jesus, so took the upside down option. There is an altar down in the jail with an upside down cross on it. This isn't a sign of the occult but rather an altar to commemorate Peter. To the left of the altar is the column to which Peter and Paul were tied, while managing to convert their guards to Christianity.

And now for the miracle. I have heard two versions of this. The first is that a Christian man who was jailed down there magically created a spring in his cell, delivering fresh water. The other is that Peter magicked up a spring so that he could baptize fellow detainees. The problem is we already know that the jail was initially a cistern for the spring below it. However pilgrims still flocked here and apparently believed the spring water had healing properties.

For centuries countless men both good and bad made their final journey down these stairs into deplorable conditions. Some starved to death, some were strangled. No doubt plenty died from illnesses and beatings. One thing is certain though — few made it back to a life in the daylight. Whether you are interested in the pilgrimage or whether you are interested in seeing an incredibly ancient jail you will want to add this one to your Forum visit.

Underground Rome

3.

Where to Find Underground Rome

- The Columbarium of Pomponio Hylas

- San Nicola' in Carcere

- Palazzo Valentini

- Crypta Balbi

- The Capuchin Crypt

- The Basilica San Clemente

- The Church of Santa Cecilia

- The Church of San Crisogono

- The Stadium of Domitian

- The Case Romane del Celio

- The Catacombs

- Teatro Pompeo under da Pancrazio

Rome is a living museum. Literally everywhere you turn there are ruins, artifacts, ancient columns and statues, so you could quite happily stay at street level and still see millennia worth of history. But there is another city (or cities!) below your feet. The streets we walk along now sit as much as 25 meters higher than those of ancient Rome. Twenty centuries of construction and demolition, accumulated dust and dirt, buildings being filled with rocks and sand and then built back over, have raised Rome to new heights. If you stand at street level and look down into the Roman Forum you will see what I mean!

It seems as though every time they try to dig a new road or repair an old building, a new slice of underground Rome is discovered. Some sites have become big tourist attractions, but nine of these ten don't make it onto most travel itineraries or radars, which of course makes me love them even more! It is thrilling to discover some new underground place, be it an old chapel or a Roman house, and even more so when no one else seems to know about it. The tenth site is the catacombs. I couldn't write about subterranean Rome without mentioning the catacombs, though they are well known and well-traveled, because they're so extraordinary.

1. The Columbarium of Pomponio Hylas

This is another of those fascinating treasures in Rome that tourists don't know about and that few travelers find their way to. It is one of Rome's best kept secrets and it is spectacular.

A *columbarium* was a structure that sat semi-underground and had multiple niches to hold the urns of the dead. Where the wealthier, upper class had mausoleums to house the family when they died, the upper middle class were purveyors of columbaria.

This one was discovered in 1831, in incredibly good condition. It gets its name from the beautiful mosaics framed in shells, all of which are still intact. They are the first thing you see when you make your way down the original staircase.

The mosaic inscription tells us that this is the Columbarium of Pomponius Hylas and his wife Pomponia. Pay attention to these two fascinating details: the V above Pomponia's name indicates that she was still alive at the time it was made, and the L (liberated) Vitalinis means they were liberated slaves of Vitilinis. Roman slaves could work through their time and then become free men and women, going on to own businesses and build their own lives. Because of the mosaic we know it as the Columbarium of Pomponio Hylas, but the tomb wasn't actually built for him. He was part of phase two of the building, which took place during the Flavian dynasty (late first century). Keep going down the stairs and you will arrive at phase one of the building, which houses the tombs of Granius Nestor and his wife Vimilea Hedone.

Throughout the columbarium you will see beautiful frescoes dating back 2000-plus years, and urns holding ashes, still in their individual niches. It is staggeringly fantastic.

Another detail I find especially interesting is in the first phase of the tomb where an inscription indicates the presence of Celadius, one of Emperor Tiberius' freed slaves and his wife Paezusa the former *ornatrix* (hairdresser) of Nero's first wife Octavia. This means that phase of the columbarium dates to 14—54 AD.

GETTING THERE

Entry to the Columbarium of Pomponio Hylas is available by appointment only.

Located inside the Scipioni Park at Via Latina 10.

Call for a reservation +39 060608 or go online.

2. San Nicola in Carcere

I found this one by accident while exploring Rome years ago with my then 12-year-old son. We initially went inside to find relief from the scorching heat of summer. Intrigued with the columns outside, my son had gone to inquire while I took a minute to sit somewhere cool. He spoke no Italian but had a huge understanding of cool stuff, so within seconds was back, jumping half out of his skin with excitement telling me there was a downstairs section to explore for only two euros each!

Located just down the street from Teatro Marcello, the church itself is pretty interesting. Originally built in the sixth century and then redone in 1599 it has plenty above ground to keep you intrigued, and that alone is worth the visit, but it is what is underground that fascinates me.

The first clue is visible from the outside. This is the original site of three temples: the **Temple of Spes** built in 250 BC, the **Temple of Juno** built in the second century BC and the **Temple of Janus**, built in 17 AD. The columns from these temples are built into this church, or the church incorporated them into its walls. This makes them extra special because they are Republican era temples, not Imperial era, making them really, really old.

At one point during the Byzantine period the temples were used as a prison, hence the name San Nicola (St Nicolas) in Carcere (incarcerated/ in prison). Pliny's *History of Rome* refers to the tradition of housing jails in the ruins of temples although it is thought this one didn't become a jail until centuries later. San Nicola is a Greek saint so it is believed the church dedication was to the Greek population.

These three temples were at the heart of the **Forum Horitorium**, the fruit and vegetable market. Ancient ships bearing fruits and vegetables would come up the Tiber river which runs behind the temples, unloading their wares at the back of these buildings. This place was the heart of Roman life.

Here is where it gets even more fantastic. When you go downstairs you find yourself at the base of these temples. There are no frescoes or dynamic art pieces, but instead giant tufa blocks make up the temple bases and some walls, and ancient (really ancient) brick walls opposite, with an ancient Roman walkway running through the middle. You can wander along the walkways that ancient Romans used while making their way to and from the market.

There is plenty to look at below ground including a three-sided Byzantine chapel, a roped off section full of bones (my son *loved* that!) and niches filled with more bones.

There is a model of the three temples standing side by side so you can see how it once looked and as you move through the underground there are posters explaining what you are seeing. When you buy your ticket they will give you a sheet in English with more information and there is also the option of having a guide take you through. With a guide you'll get to ask questions and you can get a much better understanding of what is going on, so any time I can get one (budget permitting) I do.

The ruins aren't huge so you don't need too much time there. For most travelers allowing 30—60 minutes will be ample.

GETTING THERE

Address: Via di Teatro Marcello 46.

WHAT'S NEARBY

If you are walking around Rome you can incorporate San Nicola in Carcere with a visit to nearby **Teatro Marcello** and the **Jewish Ghetto**, as well as the sensational **Palazzo Valentini** just up the road. It is walking distance from the **Colosseum** and the **Forum**.

In the opposite direction you can cross the river and be in the **Trastevere**.

Or you can wander up the Tiber river to **Michelangelo's Unfinished Bridge** and loop up through **Piazza Farnese, Campo di Fiore, Piazza Navona**.

3. Palazzo Valentini

I have to confess that this is one of my favorites. You can stand outside the door and see thousands of tourists in the vicinity of the Colosseum, then walk back inside and only have a small group of you waiting to go on the tour of the Palazzo.

Palazzo Valentini is a Renaissance palazzo with an interesting history.

At one point it was owned by an incredibly handsome fellow by the name of Giacomo Boncompagni, Duke of Sora, Aquino, Arce and Arpino. He was a feudal lord and also happened to be the illegitimate son of Pope Gregory XIII. (Those popes were a raunchy bunch — celibate to the world but with mistresses and wives and children behind the scenes!)

So, in 2005 while renovations were being done on the palazzo, the remains of two magnificent Imperial Roman homes and thermal baths were discovered underneath. Archeologists spent years excavating it and now the 20,000 square foot space is open for viewing. Let me tell you, it is amazing!

Buried for centuries under the palazzo, the Domus Romane (Roman Houses) are incredibly well preserved. You will see original ancient staircases, mosaics, frescoes, inlaid marble floors. You walk across a glass floor, with ancient Rome lit up below you, so rather than observing from the sidelines you feel as though you are in it.

The thermal baths give you an idea of how wealthy this family must have been, and the location alone speaks to their importance — right outside the Roman Forum.

There is a glassed-off room full of ancient Roman trash — plates and cups and kitchen gear that had been thrown away.

And it keeps getting better, because this museum has a multimedia element to it. While a taped narration explains what you are seeing (in clear English, over a speaker system so you don't need to wear headphones), the lights go down and the multimedia part lights up, letting you see how it would have been back then, completing rooms and walls and ceilings with their frescoes and all their grandeur.

One part that I really loved was looking down onto the remains of a Roman road. A laser lights up the stones and shows you how clever they were with their construction and how the shapes of the stones were repeated and not random, making strong roads that lasted for millennia, like the Appian Way.

The final part of the tour takes you into a video room where the stories on **Trajan's Column** are explained (it's brilliant). When the video is done they walk you to a private viewing area that looks out at the column, immediately in front of the palazzo.

This is one of Rome's treasures that I will keep returning to. It is truly fabulous.

GETTING THERE

You can only go through the Domus Romane with a guide and they have set times for each tour. The tour lasts around 90 minutes and is in English. The Domus Romane are closed on Tuesdays.

Make sure you book ahead. You can get dates, times and online tickets at the Palazzo Valentini website. You have to arrive 30 minutes before your tour to turn your voucher into a ticket.

Address: Foro Traiano 85.

WHAT'S NEARBY

From Palazzo Valentini you can look out at **Trajan's Column**. You are right there by **Trajan's Market**, so you have the **Forum** and the **Colosseum** in front of you. Keep walking past the Colosseum and you have **Domus Aurea**, **Basilica San Clemente** and a little further along you have **St John In Lateran**.

In the opposite direction walk down to **Teatro Marcello** and the **Jewish Ghetto** before crossing the river into the **Trastevere**.

You are also close to **Crypta Balbi**, **Largo Argentina**, **Campo de Fiori** and **Piazza Navona**.

4. Crypta Balbi

The crazy thing is that Crypta Balbi had been on my Rome list for several years, and *many* Rome trips before I actually went there. I don't remember where or why I heard about it, and for the duration of it being on my list I couldn't remember what there was to see there. I got so used to seeing it on the list as I scrolled through, it almost became invisible. Then one day, walking down a street I've walked along about a thousand times, past blackened windows I had been aware of but not looked at as I would always look to the ruins on the other side of the road, I saw the words *Crypta Balbi*. I decided to pop in for a quick look, and in that moment my world changed. This place is phenomenal. *And no one knows about it*!

This is the least known and most overlooked of the four museums making up the Museo Nazionale Romano. It takes up an entire city block, smack bang in the middle of Rome. And no one seems to know about it.

This is an incredibly modern and efficient museum (upstairs) that is fantastic to walk around. Not too much stuff, and it is all enthralling. If that was all, it would be worth your visit (the ancient frescoes, statues, marble, treasures…), but this place has much, much more. It is built on the ruins of the theater of Lucius Cornelius Balbus, dating back to 13 BC. There is a columned courtyard and lots of ruins to look at on the various levels.

Ground level has some very cool, *really old* buildings, that you will want to wander around, but then you can go downstairs to below street level and walk along the catwalks through the ancient ruins.

Archeologist Daniel Manacorda discovered the crypt in 1981 while digging between the churches of Santa Caterina dei Funari and San Stanislao dei Polacchi. He initially discovered the colonnated *quadriporticus* of the theater of Lucius Cornelius Balbus, then the *statio annona* nearby, where grain supplies were stored. As they excavated it became a layer cake, with 13 BC at the bottom, working its way up through the middle ages and into the 20th century.

The museum is a reflection of this. 'The Path Of Rome From Antiquity To The Middle Ages' on the second floor gives a fantastic visual guide to the history of Rome, but also to where everything is and was. For me it was a visual that finally put everything into place. You not only see Rome laid out as it was, and as it changed, but you can also see artifacts put in context with the changes over time. I found it incredibly helpful to understand the various neighborhoods as they were in ancient Rome and as they changed throughout history. Seeing the angle of Teatro Pompeo with one end in Campo de Fiori and the other at Largo Argentina (where Julius Caesar was killed) butting up against Teatro Balbus suddenly put everything into perspective.

When I ducked in there I basically had the place to myself. I ran into this one couple a few times, and for some reason they thought I was Spanish and I thought they were telling me *they* were Spanish. I kept saying *no habla espanol,* and they kept saying Spanish things to me when we would cross paths in the ruins.

When I was finally done seeing Crypta Balbi I sat in the foyer for a minute, trying to wrap my head around a) what I had just seen and b) he fact that there was *no one here*! The couple came over to say goodbye at which point I found out they were Italians. They live in Rome and like me had Crypta Balbi on their list but never got round to going, and just happened to be walking past and decided to pop in. Like me, they were totally overwhelmed by it. Which goes to show that even if you have lived your entire life in Rome there are still new things to discover!

GETTING THERE

This is not an overwhelmingly large site or museum, you probably only need 60 to 90 minutes to see it all.

Address: Via delle Botteghe Oscure 32.

WHAT'S NEARBY

This is just down the street from **Piazza Venezia**, so you are very close to **Palazzo Valentini, Trajan's Column, Trajan's Market**, the **Forum** and **Colosseum**.

In the opposite direction you are just down the street from **Largo Argentina**, which puts you mere blocks away from the **Jewish Ghetto** and the **Garibaldi Bridge** taking you to the **Trastevere**. From **Largo Argentina** you can wander to **Campo de Fiori, Piazza Navona** and **San Luigi dei Francesi**.

5. The Capuchin Crypt

"I have never seen anything more striking."
~The Marquis de Sade

You know if the Marquis de Sade liked it, it has to be freaky. And freaky it is.

If you want to see something highly unusual underneath Rome, this could be the ticket. Below the church of **Santa Maria delle Concezione** on Via Veneto you will find this creepy crypt, replete with the bones of some 4000 monks who died between 1528 and 1870. They aren't just lying there either — they decorate the walls in some kind of macabre art expo.

In 1631 the Capuchin friars, named after the capuche (hood) they wore, and for whom your favorite coffee drink, the cappuccino was named, moved from the friary at St Bonaventure to Santa Maria della Concezione. The pope's brother told them to bring the bones of the dead friars with them so that all the Capuchin friars would be together in one place.

So far, so good.

However, instead of just burying their dead or re-burying the bones of the monks they transferred to their new digs, they created bone art, not even keeping the bones from the individual monks together. There is a skull crypt, a thigh bone crypt, even a crypt of pelvises. (Who even thinks this stuff up??)

Even more insane, there are also mummified monks dressed as friars hanging from the ceilings and the walls and acting out scenes: lounging in nooks like they are just chillin', stepping out of a pile of pelvises towards you, coming at you with crosses in their hands. There is even a skeleton holding a scythe and scales (made of his buddy's bones), encircled in an oval of yet more bones.

A plaque in the crypt says: *What you are now, we once were; what we are now, you shall be.*

I'm sure religious scholars and the most devout would find deep meaning in the bone art and meaningfully positioned skeletons, but to my untrained eye it is completely freaky — which makes it an interesting spot to visit.

GETTING THERE

Address: Via Vittorio Veneto 27.

Open daily from 9am to 7pm.

WHAT'S NEARBY

You are close to the **Barberini** and all its fabulous art work, walking distance to **Diocletian's Baths** in one direction, and not far from the **Trevi Fountain** in the other.

6. Basilica San Clemente

Think of this place as a layer cake of Roman history! I don't even know how many times I have visited Basilica San Clemente in the last 10 years, but I bring all of my Glam Italia travelers here, and one way or another I seem to find myself in this Basilica at some point every time I am in Rome.

A mere 300 yards or so from the Colosseum and the thousands of tourists amassed there, this feels like one of Rome's best kept secrets. There are usually a few other travelers here, sometimes small religious tour groups or art tours, but I doubt I have ever seen 50 people here at one time. From the outside the building looks quite unassuming, and there is nothing to indicate the magic within.

You enter through the 12th century basilica, one of the most richly adorned churches in Rome. The mosaics in the apse are truly spectacular, and alone are worth coming to visit. Created in the 1130's they were the high point in 12th century Roman mosaic work. While in this part of the church, make sure to look down at the floors. Created by the Cosmati family (a Roman family famous for architecture, sculpture and church floors like these), the swirling inlaid mosaic floors are known as *Cosmatesque*. This particular floor was created after 1190 and is truly beautiful.

You can't take photos in here and you need to be extra respectful because this is a working church. Once you have explored the ground level, go to the far side of the church, buy a ticket at the ticket booth and head downstairs.

Be ready to be blown away.

At the bottom of the staircase you will find yourself in a fourth century chapel. St Jerome wrote of this church dedicated to St Clement back in 392 AD. There is so much to see down here, including pieces of ruins, sarcophagi, treasures, and incredible wall art. The church upstairs is built on the same footprint as this chapel, so it is deceptively large. Second only to the art in Santa Maria in Antiqua, this is the largest group of early medieval wall paintings in Rome.

St Clement's Story

There is one fresco here that I particularly love because it is so funny: it depicts the story of Sisinnius and St Clement. The story goes that a jealous Sisinnius follows his wife Theodora into a church and sees Clement leading the prayer. Sisinnius is struck deaf and blind and is carried out by his servants. Theodora persuades Clement to come to their home and use a miracle to cure Sisinnius who, once able to see and hear again, accuses Clement of being an adulterer and magician. He orders his servants to kill him, but another miracle occurs and the servants confuse Clement with a stone column.

This painting features the first known use of written Italian (instead of Latin), and in one of the sections of the fresco crazy old Sisinnius is shouting to the servants who are trying to pull a stone column, thinking it is Clement, *Fili Dele Pute Traite!* (*Pull, You Sons of Whores!*) The whole thing is complete madness! If you see a tour guide in front of this painting, stop and listen in — it is hysterical! Or even better, book your own guide to take you through.

Clement was a high ranking Roman who helped St Peter with his ministry. He was exiled to Crimea where he was martyred by being tied to an anchor and thrown into the sea. There are varying stories on what happened next, but from what I can figure out a magic tomb ensconced him and the sea later receded or parted (depending on the story) so his body could be recovered. Cyril and Methodius recovered Clement's remains in the ninth century and brought them back to Basilica San Clemente, where they now reside.

The more you look into it though the less it makes sense, magic tomb, receding sea and all. Clement was martyred around the year 100 AD. The imperial government didn't start exiling troublemakers to Crimea until it was in its new base of Constantinople in 330 AD, and Crimea was for the important troublemakers, so Clement wouldn't have qualified. Heaven only knows whose remains are in the basilica. Perhaps one of the subsequent Clements, or perhaps just some random dude.

Walking through the fourth century chapel is pretty amazing. You will see some incredible old mosaics down there including byzantine mosaics of St Cyril.

ANCIENT HOMES

Listen for the sound of running water. Follow the sound down another flight of stairs and you will find yourself in ancient Rome. The bottom level of this layer cake building has remnants of the foundations of a republican era buildings, possibly destroyed in Nero's great fire of 64 AD. Soon after the fire, an apartment building and a Roman home were built on the site. As you work your way through old buildings made of tufa stone, look inside the rooms — they're pretty amazing!

As you walk around down here the sound of rushing water will get louder. The running water has been explained to me as a) one of the first homes with running water, b) part of an ancient Roman aqueduct and c) part of the ancient Roman sewer system. I like to think it was one of the first homes to have running water…

MITHRAEUM

There is more down here too. Keep walking and you will find a mithraeum, a temple made to the pagan god Mithras. This is thought to be from around the year 200. Replete with an altar where sacrifices were made, the mithraeum is long and narrow and exactly how you would imagine a pagan temple to look. The altar which is in the shape of a sarcophagus has the main cult relief of Mithras slaying the bull on its front, and the torchbearers Cautes and Cautopates on either side.

There is also a mithraic schoolroom down here.

If you add Basilica San Clemente to your itinerary I can guarantee that you will be stunned and thrilled. It really is incredible!

MITHRAISM

Mithraism was a mysterious religion practiced in the Roman empire from some time in the first century until the fourth century, when Christianity became the big thing. Mithraism was popular with the Roman military and soldier class, and seems to have had its home in Rome.

The religion was inspired by the Iranian worship of the god Mithra. Imagery shows Mithra born from rock, slaughtering a bull and sharing a feast with the sun god Sol. No written narratives of the religion have survived and there are only fleeting mentions in Greek and Latin literature, so the information we have has been taken from inscriptions at the more than 400 mithraic sites. The imagery of Mithra slaying the bull has shown up more than 700 times, and it is thought that the sacrifices made at the altars were probably bulls.

Stumbling upon a mithraeum is pretty exciting. I first saw one built inside a mountain in Sutri, but there are several in Rome. I read somewhere that there would have been close to 700 mithraea just in Rome itself. They seem to always be underground or hidden, implying that the cult of the mysteries was always kept a mystery, not for public consumption.

GETTING THERE

This is a great one to have a guide for. You can get a guide from the basilica directly (check their website for dates and times), or go in with a local Roman guide.

Address: Via Labicana 95.

Basilica San Clemente is only five minutes walk from the **Colosseum**. You pass **Domus Aurea** to get there, and if you keep walking you will find **St John Lateran** and the **Scala Sancta**.

7. The Church of Santa Cecilia

Across the river from San Nicola in Carcere, in my favorite neighborhood in Rome (The Trastevere), is the church of the martyred Saint Cecilia. Cecilia, an aristocrat, was martyred in 230 AD, allegedly for holding Christian worship in her home. Many of the stories about Cecilia are thought to be fictional but the site of this church is said to be built over her home.

Cecilia is the patron saint of music and interestingly the Accademia Nazionale di Santa Cecilia in Rome is one of the oldest music institutions in the world. The two prominant saints in Western music history are Gregory the Great (namesake of the Gregorian chant) and St Cecilia.

The first church to be built on this site was probably in the third century. Apparently in 545 AD, Pope Vigilius was captured there by Anthemius Scribo, an emissary of Empress Theodora. The church was rebuilt in 822 AD and more restorations happened over the centuries. Since 1527, a community of nuns from the Benedictine order have lived in the monastery next door and have run the basilica. When you visit the church, it will be a nun who sells you your ticket to go downstairs.

The facade of the church is Baroque, built in 1725, and the courtyard in front of the church is lovely. Before going downstairs to the crypt, allow yourself some time to explore the art inside the church, including Pietro Cavallini's *Last Judgement* (1289—93), the ninth century mosaics in the apse, the Cappella dei Ponziani ceiling which was completed in 1470 by Antonio del Massaro and the ciborium which dates to 1293. The church also holds one of the most famous pieces of Baroque sculpture, the achingly beautiful martyrdom of Saint Cecilia by Stefano Maderno. There is a marble slab in front of the sculpture on which Maderno has a sworn statement that he has created the sculpture exactly as her body looked when her tomb was opened in 1599.

Downstairs you can walk through the riotously colorful crypt and an ancient Roman home, said to be the home of Saint Cecilia. You will walk across 2000 year old mosaics on the floor — it is thrilling to wander through an old home like this.

GETTING THERE

The church closes for lunch so you will want to check on the hours prior to going. I recommend going downstairs first, just in case a big group of people come through. Although most of the time when I take my little tour groups through, we are the only ones there. It is fantastic.

Address: Piazza di Santa Cecilia 22, Trastevere.

8. Church of San Crisogono

On the other side of Viale Trastevere, less than 10 minutes walk from Santa Cecilia, you will find an unassuming church exterior, one that almost everyone walks right past — the church of San Crisogono.

Saint Chrysogonus was a Roman military officer who converted to

Christianity. Emperor Diocletian had him beheaded sometime around 300 AD.

One of the first parish churches of Rome, it was initially built during Pope Silvester's time (314—335 AD), was rebuilt in the 12th century and again in the early seventeenth century. The interior of the church is a mish-mash of different eras. The bell tower is twelfth century, the confessio is eighth century, the high altar is from 1127, other parts are from the 1600s. Suffice to say that although not a remarkable church by Roman standards it is still worth a visit.

Walk to the far end of the church on the left hand side and you will find a room with a little old man sitting behind a desk. He will sell you a ticket for two or three euros, unlock a door and turn on the light, and invite you to head down the stairs into the remains of the fourth century church.

Again, you will in all likelihood be the only ones there, which blows my mind because it's tremendous! Sarcophagi, mosaics, 1800 year old frescoes, a tomb full of old bones, ruins — it really is quite something. Regardless of whether I am there with my son or one of my little tour groups, we are almost always the only ones there. Every now and then another family may show up. (I know I am sounding like a broken record here, but remember Rome is *full* of tourists! Luckily they all tend to stick around the same places, so you can have all these fantastic finds to yourself.)

9. The Stadium Of Domitian

To me it's not just seeing the old buildings and ruins that is fascinating, it's finding out the stories behind them, especially the stories of the people who created them. So I want to tell you about Domitian.

TITUS'S STORY

Domitian was the second son of the wildly popular and successful emperor Vespasian, builder of the Colosseum. The people were devastated when their brilliant emperor died in 79 AD, but at least they got a hero to replace him — his much adored son Titus. Titus was a victorious general and a great administrator. He was handsome and charming and clever, and he was also a man of the people. Once when realizing an entire day had passed without him doing anyone a favor he famously said, "Friends, I have wasted a day." He was a really good guy.

In his first year of reign Vesuvius erupted, wiping out the cities of Pompeii and Herculaneum. Rather than sit back and order help for the people down south from the comfort of his palace in Rome, Titus raced down there himself to organize relief efforts.

His caring and genuine concern for the wellbeing of his people didn't go unnoticed. In the second year of his reign, fire ravaged Rome. Instead of heading for the hills, Titus once again orchestrated relief efforts, further endearing him to the people. They loved him.

But then, only two years into his rule he died, leaving no heirs to take over.

The only person left in the Flavian family was Vespasian's second (and neglected) son, Domitian. Vespasian had poured all of his ambition and effort into his first son Titus, leaving Domitian in the fringes, isolated, lonely and with no understanding of how to run an empire.

DOMITIAN'S STORY

What you know is sometimes not as important as *what people think you know*, so with no military accomplishments of his own, Domitian began building, attaining legitimacy by celebrating the greatness of the family members who had come before him. Titus had started building a temple to Vespasian before he died, and Domitian added his now dead brother to the project. In a great PR move he chose to celebrate his family's military prowess by building a stupendous triumphal arch dedicated to his brother — the **Arch of Titus**. He built it in the Forum (the heart of Roman life), in direct view of his family's other massive building feat, the Colosseum.

He kept his PR machine running, building many projects, one of which was **Domitian's Stadium**. Rome already had the **Circus Maximus** and the **Colosseum**, but they were both too large to hold regular athletic games, so Domitian planned a new stadium designed to hold 15—20,000 people. It was Rome's first permanent facility made for competitive sports. Prior to this, stadiums were made of wood and dismantled after the games were over. This was a fantastic move by Domitian, his stadium became incredibly popular as the crowds flocked to see the *agones* (games). Over the centuries, the term *agones* became *in avona* and then somewhere along the line evolved into *Navona*, hence the name of what occupies the space now — beautiful Piazza Navona (find out more in the chapter on *Piazza Navona*).

Domitian modeled himself on the great Augustus. Rather than focusing on expansion, he strengthened the borders and the empire's defenses. He also followed Augustus' lead by strengthening the infrastructure, building and beautifying Rome. However, he failed to tune in to the egos surrounding him, and he became bit of an autocrat, exiling and murdering his opponents.

Augustus' rule had been firm but discreet, making sure he got his way without ruffling too many feathers. Domitian on the other hand lived in fear of assassins. A prophecy said that he would die at noon, so each day he secreted himself away for the noon hour, emerging safe and alive at 1pm.

Before too long there was a conspiracy afoot. One of the palace staff faked an arm injury so that everyone would get used to him having a bandage on his arm. One fateful day he came to the palace with a dagger hidden inside the bandages. A servant lied to Domitian, telling him it was later in the day than the actual hour, so he came out of his rooms to go back to work and was set upon by the assassin and stabbed. He fought valiantly but was overpowered, and eventually bled to death on the palace floor, dying around noon.

The senate, who'd hated him, decided to purge all memory of Domitian. The toppled his statues, melted down coins with his face on them, carted away the stones from his buildings. He had been a competent ruler, his policies had been both good and effective, but they did everything possible to remove him from history.

Piazza Navona

If you look at Piazza Navona you will see that it isn't the shape of a normal piazza, instead is long and oval. What you are seeing is the outline of the running track of Domitian's Stadium. Once it stopped being used as a venue for athletics and equestrian events it still remained a busy, bustling place, used to train and race horses. After the flood of 1476 Pope Sixtus V had the center of the stadium covered with a floor and it became a marketplace. Over time the seating area and support structures became the foundations for shops and homes, a church was added, the floor was paved, fountains and statues were added and the Piazza Navona we know now emerged.

DOMITIAN'S STADIUM MUSEUM

Of course, as with everywhere in Rome, ruins were found underneath the piazza. It became a UNESCO heritage site and in 2014 below Piazza Navona, the ruins of Domitian's Stadium, opened as a small museum. The museum is the bottom layer of the stadium. Down there you get a sense of the grandeur of the original space. Below street level, you can see the arches that made the arcades and passageways leading up to the seating areas and you can see the craftsmanship that went into their creation. Hidden from the world for centuries, they are in pristine condition, only 4.5 meters below the road.

Interestingly, at the rounded northern end of the former stadium excavators have found travertine and brickwork that are thought to make this the only masonry stadium outside of ancient Greece.

It's only little, but Domitian's Stadium museum is really quite cool. This is another great spot where you can escape the crowds and see something fantastic, while the tourist throngs are quite literally less than a stone's throw away.

It doesn't take much time to wander through and there are audio guides available in multiple languages. Knowing the story of Domitian, knowing that essentially he was a good leader living in the shadow of his larger than life father and brother, and knowing the efforts made to delete him from history, I like to think that taking a few minutes to visit the museum while you are in Piazza Navona is giving him the last laugh.

They tried to wipe out Domitian's memory, but he left behind the blueprint for what would become perhaps the loveliest piazza in all of Rome, and his stadium of the people became the marketplace and the gathering point of the people for millennia.

GETTING THERE

It can be tricky to find this little museum. I can seldom figure out north and south even at the best of times. The museum is at the northern end of the piazza, but in case you are compass-challenged like me, look for the Hotel Raphael. The museum entrance is opposite that.

Address: Via di Tor Sanguigna 3.

WHAT'S NEARBY

You are in Piazza Navona, so there is plenty to see within walking distance. The piazza is across the road from **Campo de Fiori** and **Piazza Farnese**, and a stroll through both of these will take you to **Michelangelo's Unfinished Bridge** and then to the river and the **Trastevere**.

From Piazza Navona you have a two minute walk to **San Luigi dei Francesi** and Caravaggio's St Matthew paintings.

It is a short walk to the **Pantheon** and **Santa Maria Sopra Minerva**, from where you can head south and see **Largo di Torre Argentine** (the cat sanctuary), **Crypta Balbi, Palazzo Valentini, Trajan's Column**, and the **Forum**.

Head north from the Pantheon and you will find the **Trevi Fountain** and the **Spanish Steps**.

10. Case Romane del Celio

This is the type of experience I live for. And die over. And almost no one seems to know about it, which makes it even more special!

Case Romane del Celio is a little known museum and archaeological site made up of 20 ancient, underground rooms dating from the second century to the fourth century AD, conveniently stashed under the church of SS Giovanni e Paolo. It takes up several levels and holds the remains of several houses from different periods as well as an *insula* (apartment building) and a wealthy *domus* (home) that was later converted into a church.

It is an extremely important ancient Roman excavation. The rooms are magnificently frescoed and in incredible condition. It is as though time stood still for two millennia.

You can't take photos in here, but the beauty of the frescoes will sear its way into your brain. From the Room of the Genie to the Nymphaeum of Proserpina to the Room of the Orant — it is all just breathtaking. While being mesmerized by the frescoes, you will also get some incredible insight into Roman life during the various periods this site covers.

The *insula* was at once several stories high and housed local artisans. The houses belonged to Christians, notably John and Paul (not the apostles and not the Beatles!). The pair were executed by Julian the Apostate in either 361 or 362 (I have read both dates) martyred and buried at their house, even though burial inside the city was prohibited. The church was built over the house in 398 AD. One of the rooms in the house has a small window called a *fenestrella confessionis* where worshipers could look at the tombs of the martyrs.

There is also a state of the art museum called the Antiquarium, where you will find pots, amphorae, bricks with their imprinted stamps and other fascinating finds.

Although this description is relatively slim I can't stress enough that you should at least try to visit this site. Immediately behind you, at the Colosseum there will be thousands of tourists lined up and waiting to get in, but up here at the church of Saints John and Paul there will be hardly anyone. While here have a look at the church, and also walk around the outside of the building where you will see parts of the ancient walls built into the newer facade. It's fantastic.

GETTING THERE

Case Romane del Celio is closed on Tuesdays and Wednesdays, open Thursday through Monday from 10am until 1pm and then again from 3pm until 6pm.

Address: Clivo di Scauro, Piazza dei Santi Giovanni e Paolo.

WHAT'S NEARBY

Case Romane del Celio sits roughly halfway between the **Colosseum** and the **Circus Maximus**. You can walk to **Basilica San Clemente** and the **Scala Sancta** in one direction, the **Baths of Caracalla** and Circus Maximus in the other direction, and you are not far from the **Palatine Hill**.

11. The Catacombs

There are more than 40 catacombs throughout Rome, five of which are open to the public.

There is a little mis-information about the catacombs, so let's start by getting the story straight (or as straight as I can get it).

DEFINITION

Catacombs are subterranean passageways that were used for burials, mostly of Christians and Jews, from the second century until the fifth century. *Catacomb* means "next to the quarry" and they got their name because the first ones to be used were just outside of Rome, next to the quarry.

Roman law prohibited the burial of bodies inside the city, so these warrens of catacombs made sense — although underground, they were outside the city walls. Another benefit of being under the ground was that they could freely use Christian symbols without fear of reprisal.

Pagans got rid of their dead by burning the bodies, in doing so solving the problem of not enough space and the high price of land. No doubt it was more sanitary than having decomposing bodies in the back yard too.

Christians didn't agree with the burning custom instead wanting to bury their dead, so someone had the great idea of creating vast underground cemeteries in which to stash the corpses. These underground cemeteries are made up of masses of passageways that stretch for kilometers, with rectangular shelf-like niches cut into the walls. Dead bodies were wrapped in a sheet, placed on these shelves and then covered with a baked clay gravestones with the name of the deceased and a Christian symbol. All very efficient.

PERSECUTIONS

The persecution of Christians ended for the most part in 313 AD with the Edict of Milan. From this point onward they were permitted to build churches and own land without fear of confiscation, but they kept burying the dead in the catacombs until the fifth century. Better safe than sorry.

When the barbarians invaded in the eighth century they started looting the catacombs, so the popes had the relics brought above ground and kept in churches. Once the booty had been moved, the catacombs were abandoned and quite literally forgotten for centuries.

GETTING THERE

I'm not much of a fan myself, but I guarantee that if you're traveling with boys they will love checking them out. Be sure to check the opening times. Each of the five sites open to the public is closed one day of the week, but you should be able to find at least one open each day.

- **The Catacombs of Sant'Agnese** (Via Nomentana 349)
  Agnese was martyred because of her faith. After her burial these catacombs were named for her.

  Closed on Sunday mornings and Monday afternoons (check beforehand to confirm), they are otherwise open from 9am until 12pm and then again from 4pm until 6pm.

- **The Catacombs of Priscilla** (Via Salaria 430
  These catacombs have some very important frescoes, including the first representations of the Virgin Mary.

Closed on Mondays, open Tuesday through Sunday, from 9am until 12pm and then again from 2pm until 5pm.

- **The Catacombs of Domitilla** (Via delle Sette Chiese 280) Made up of passageways that stretch for more than 15 kilometers in length, these were named after Vespasian's granddaughter.

  Closed on Tuesdays, open Wednesday through Monday, from 9am until 12pm and then from 2pm until 5pm.

- **The Catacombs of San Callisto** (Via Appia Antica 126) The catacombs of San Callisto were the burial place of 16 pontiffs and many Christian martyrs. The passageways stretch for more than 20 kilometers.

  Closed on Wednesdays, open Thursday to Tuesday from 9am til 12pm and then again from 2pm until 5pm.

- **The Catacombs of San Sebastiano** (Via Appia Antica 126) Along with neighboring San Callisto, I think these are the best catacombs to visit. Named after the martyred Saint Sebastian, these catacombs stretch for 12 kilometers.

  Closed on Sundays, open Monday through Saturday from 9am til 12pm and then again from 2pm until 5pm.

12. Teatro Pompeo under da Pancrazio

I am torn about telling the world about this insanely exciting and brilliant find. On one hand, it is sensational. On the other hand, it is a wonderful old world restaurant and I have been told never to write about your favorite restaurants because you will come back and find tour buses outside and ketchup bottles on the tables.

Also, this restaurant has been around for decades. It is an institution. I would hate for people to show up and try to march downstairs without having a meal, or start behaving like rude tourists — I would be mortified! But if you are a traveler rather than a tourist, and a polite restaurant customer, read on...

A Restaurant with a Secret Below

I actually found this place by accident. I had a small group of my Glam Italia travelers with me in the neighboring Campo de Fiori and saw that a major rain event was about to happen, so needed to get everyone indoors quickly. We were overdue for lunch so I figured I could kill two birds with one stone. I emphatically refuse to eat in any restaurant or cafe that caters to the tourist trade as they are almost always overpriced and unimpressive. So rather than stopping in at any of the eateries that ring the Campo we ducked back into a small piazza that I had never been in before. We ran through the rain to the opposite side of the piazza (it's only tiny) to da Pancrazio and even though they wanted to close up and go home they let us in.

Food First

Let me start out by saying that the food here is incredible. It definitely took the waiters some time to warm up to us, but I think that watching this group of ladies just dying over the food won them over. In the spirit of the madly hungry, we ordered a table full of food — way too much for *four* tables of travelers, more than enough food for a small army. We had plates taking up the entire table and everyone was eating everything, taking a bite of something and making everyone else try it. The rain was pouring down outside, the wine was flowing and the girls were happy.

As I was walking to the restroom the owner stopped me and kept telling me to go downstairs. I wasn't quite sure what was going on but went down there anyway, after all you never know when something completely fantastic is about to happen — there might be a homicidal maniac at the bottom of the stairs, or maybe a more interesting bathroom, or in this case, ruins dating back to 55 BC.

I swear I nearly burst into tears!

TEATRO POMPEO

The staircase took me into the ruins of the Teatro Pompeo, built by Pompeo during his second consulship. This was the first permanent theater in Rome, and for forty years was the *only* permanent theater. During its lifetime the Teatro Pompeo was considered to be the premier theater in the world, due to its vast size and absolute splendor.

There was a massive garden area with statues and fountains, enclosed by large porticos lined with columns and rooms used to display artworks collected by Pompeo. Pieces of these columns are still embedded in the ground under the restaurant.

At the opposite end of the theater there was a *curia*, used by the senate for formal political meetings. To give you an idea of just how enormous Teatro Pompeo was, it stretched diagonally from Campo de Fiori to Largo di Torre Argentina. The curia was where Largo Argentina is now, and was where Julius Caesar was assassinated.

After the wars of 535-554 AD, the population of Rome declined to the point there was no need anymore for a giant theater, so the original marble was taken and used to build churches and maintain other buildings in the city. The theater's ruins were built over in the 12th century. Later that century the Orsini family bought up all the buildings and made them into a fortress, then in the Middle Ages the Campo de Fiori was built on top of the ruins.

And here I was, walking around the ruins, examining niches with statues, remains of frescoes on the walls, columns from the original garden area. Rooms from the teatro have been converted into private dining rooms, dimly lit and full of atmosphere.

I texted my tour group to come down and look and they were as blown away by it as I was — and still am!

One of the things I love so much about Rome is how the city is a living, breathing museum. Furthermore if you act like a nice person instead of a demanding tourist, doors will open to you and the Roman people will proudly show you magical, fantastical pieces of their history.

If you do make your way to Da Pancrazio, promise me you will be polite and kind, order lunch or dinner, don't try to make them change anything on the menu or ask for fat-free ranch dressing on the side, french fries or ketchup (save that game for the tourist restaurants!). Be your best version of you, and then politely ask if you can go downstairs for a look.

GETTING THERE

I'm not giving you the address this time — if you really want to find this one you will seek it out.

WHAT'S NEARBY

Campo de Fiori! Take a walk from here to **Largo di Torre Argentina** to get an idea of the size of this ancient theater — it was huge.

You are also very close to **Piazza Navona**, the **Pantheon** and **Santa Maria Sopra Minerva**. There are multiple Caravaggios within a few minutes walk from here, at **Sant'Agostino** and at **San Luigi dei Francesi.**

Churches in Rome

4.

Ten Fascinating Churches & the Intriguing Stories Behind Them

Rome is a city of churches. Almost everyone who goes to Rome makes their way to the Vatican museums, Sistine Chapel and St Peter's, so unless you have been blessed with a tour before opening hours or after closing, you will be herded through like cattle, at a relatively rapid pace. (When I take my little groups through the Vatican, I plan a very light afternoon to follow it because being in the proximity of such massive crowds can leave you feeling overwhelmed.)

There are more than 900 churches here, and many of them are *breathtaking*. Many, as in hundreds of them. If pressed for time I would recommend skipping the Vatican in lieu of one or more of the other churches in Rome.

I have a personal travel policy of going into every church I stumble across in Rome (and anywhere else in Italy). Just because a church doesn't show up in a guide book doesn't mean it's not worth looking into. I can't even tell you how many times I've been walking past some random church and ducked in just in case there is something to see, and found frescoes or mosaics or other artworks of such absolutely astounding beauty they have made me tearful. (I would have said *brought me to my knees*, but that is a relatively church-y expectation!)

Here are ten churches you may want to add to visit in Rome. Some are placed in close proximity to each other, some are a further afield, but generally close to other places in this book. The idea here is to learn about some you may not have previously heard of and see where they may fit into your trip. Unless you are on a religious pilgrimage you probably won't make it to all ten, but you might take the opportunity to duck into one or two when you are close by.

Regardless of your religious persuasion or lack thereof, I sincerely recommend you add some or all of these churches to your Rome travel itinerary.

IMPORTANT NOTE FOR VISITING CHURCHES

Almost all of the churches in Rome are still functioning as churches, so you need to be cognizant of the fact that you can't always go walking around inside, especially if there is a service happening.Many churches will have signs asking for silence. You need to respect that request. Even if they don't have signs posted, you should only speak in hushed tones — you are after all in a church.

Other churches may have signs asking for no photography. Sometimes this is to protect the art, other times it is because they don't want hordes of tourists stomping around taking photos. Again it is important to be respectful.

Lastly, you must be dressed appropriately if you wish to go inside. No short shorts or mini-skirts — knees should be covered. No strapless tops, tank tops or spaghetti straps — your shoulders must be covered. I always have a scarf tied to my bag so that if I want to go inside a church I can immediately cover my shoulders. If you're dressed inappropriately, some churches will insist that you buy paper capes to tie around your shoulders and waist, others will just deny you entry. A good rule of thumb when traveling in Italy is to leave your mini-skirts and short shorts at home.

1. Santa Maria in Maggiore

Prepare to be completely overwhelmed by this extraordinary place.

This is both the largest and the most important of the churches dedicated to Saint Mary. In 431 AD, Pope Sixtus III built this church to commemorate Mary being named the mother of God. It was built in the fashion of a second century Roman basilica, with a tall, wide and long nave leading to a semicircular apse at the end. Some scholars think the design was to blend the old, Imperial Rome with a future in Christianity.

Entering the church you will find yourself drawn to the apse at the far end. The 40 giant columns lining either side of the nave, guide your eye, your step and your consciousness directly in front of you to the triumphal arch. In turn the height and majesty of the ceiling make you feel small and insignificant and then call you heavenward.

I never had a huge interest in mosaics until exploring the churches of Italy, now they have become an obsession. The mosaics in this church date back to the fifth century and are just astounding in their complexity and magnificence. Santa Maria in Maggiore is filled with art and artifacts, enough that you can visit 100 times and still find new things.

Under the high altar, the crypt is said to hold wood from Jesus' crib. Devotees swear to it, skeptics raise an eyebrow, you can fall where you will in between!

This is one of the seven pilgrimage basilicas in the world and is a UNESCO World Heritage Site.

GETTING THERE

Address: Piazza di S. Maria Maggiore 42.

WHAT'S NEARBY

Piazza Santa Maria Maggiore is walking distance from **Termini** station and is close to **Piazza della Repubblica**. If you love mosaics drop into the **Church of Santa Prassede** a half block away. The **Baths of Diocletian** and **Santa Maria degli Angeli e dei Martiri** are both close by as are the **National Museum** and **Palazzo Massimo alle Terme**.

The Monti district has wonderful places to eat, and leads you to **Trajan's Market**, the **Roman Forum** and the **Colosseum**.

2. Santa Maria in Trastevere

This is my favorite church in Rome. I consider the Trastevere to be my neighborhood, and I can tell you I have never brought anyone to Rome and not taken them to this church. I sincerely recommend you put a gold star by this one and make sure to add it to your itinerary.

Santa Maria in Trastevere is one of the oldest and most awe-inspiring churches in Rome. Constructed on the site of a Christian house-church that had been built in 220 AD under Pope Saint Callixtus I, Emperor Alexander Severus had made the land available to the Christians. Pope Julius I rebuilt the house-church on a larger scale around 340 AD and is possibly the first church in the Eternal City to openly celebrate mass and is also probably the first church in the city dedicated to the Virgin Mary. Lots of possiblies and maybes.

Restorations happened in the fifth and eighth centuries and in 1140-43 it was rebuilt on its old foundations by Pope Innocent II of Trastevere.

The exterior gives no clue to the majestic beauty held inside its walls. Before entering the church take some time to look at the plaques and pieces of stone tablets fixed to the walls. It will give you a sense of how much history is tied up on this piece of land.

THE FLOOR

Walking into Santa Maria in Trastevere, look down at the floor (before everything else steals all of your attention). The floor is a gorgeous work of inlaid tile as well as a purple-red stone you will see all over Rome called *red prophyry*. In ancient times red prophyry was the most expensive stone available and it was always associated with great wealth, power and prestige. Until sometime around 500 AD it was brought in from Egypt and used to make columns, vases, sarcophagi, busts and giant bowls. It wasn't only the most expensive stone, but also the strongest stone, a strength that has withstood the test of time. Literally.

Emperors lived surrounded by red porphyry, were born in rooms with it and buried in sarcophagi made from it. Once you know it, you will see it all over Rome, particularly in floors. On my tours, this is where I introduce my travelers to red porphyry, inside Santa Maria in Trastevere.

When you see red porphyry in a floor, run your foot over it. Even when surrounded by marble you will feel it sitting higher than all the other stones used in the floor, as it wears down much more slowly. Sometimes I wonder if it wears down at all. Through millennia who even knows how many thousands or even millions of feet have walked across these same floors? The other stones have worn down lower but the red porphyry stands resolute.

THE CEILING

Next, look up at the ceiling, created by Domenichino in 1617. I wish I could lie on the floor and look up at it for hours, but even if I had the place to myself, I couldn't do it.

The nave is lined with two rows of 22 columns, re-appropriated from either the Baths of Caracalla or the Temple of Isis. The columns guide you to the apse, a thirteenth century wonder of mosaic. It is truly exceptional. At this point I don't even know how many times I have seen it but it *still* takes my breath away with every visit.

APSE MOSAIC

The mosaics are definitely worth googling so that you can learn the stories behind them, too much detail to go into here, but I do want to draw your attention to the main mosaic in the apse. In a world of gold, Mary sits to the right of Christ on a large throne. It is highly unusual to see her at his right hand. Her scroll connects her to the bride in the Song of Soloman. It reads: *His left hand is under my head, and his right hand shall embrace me.* Christian writers interpret the bride to be Ecclesia, the Church.

The writing on Jesus' book connects her to Mary of the Assumption: *Come, my chosen one, and I shall put you on my throne.* Apparently words Christ spoke to Mary on her arrival in heaven, according to the Golden Legend. This has been interpreted as the bride of Christ being both Mary of the Assumption and the church.

They are flanked by six figures: from the left is Pope Innocent II (of the 1140—43 restoration), St Lawrence (dressed as a deacon), Pope St Callixtus (built the first church on the site in 220 AD), then on the other side we see St Peter standing next to the throne in a toga, Pope St Cornelius, Pope Julius (of the fourth century restoration) and St Calepodius.

I always love learning the stories behind the mosaics and frescoes.

I really hope you will find the time to visit Santa Maria in Trastevere. It is just wonderful.

GETTING THERE

Address: Piazza Santa Maria Trastevere, Trastevere.

WHAT'S NEARBY

You are in the very heart of the Trastevere, in my opinion the most fabulous neighborhood in all of Rome! Take time to wander the streets, look down every alleyway and side street. Marvel in the beauty of old Rome.

If you want to go underground you are close to both **St Crisogono** and **Santa Cecilia**. If you want to see some fabulous art **Villa Farnesina** is just down the road.

The **Janiculum Hill** is a five minute walk, **St Peters** is around a 30 minute walk along the river. You can cross the river at the Sisto bridge and walk to **Campo de Fiori**, **Piazza Navona** and the **Pantheon** (a really lovely walk). Or cross the **Garibaldi bridge** and either walk straight up to **Largo Argentina** or turn right and go to the **Jewish**

Ghetto, Teatro Marcello and **San Nicola in Carcere**. If you cross the Garibaldi bridge and turn left you will arrive at the best gelato shop in all of Rome, **Gelateria del Teatro**.

Most of the things you want to see in Rome are within walking distance of the Trastevere. Sometimes if the weather is too hot or if it is raining I will take a bus or a tram, but whenever possible I prefer to walk as often as I can in Rome.

3. Saint John in Lateran

If I were to ask you which is the official cathedral of Rome, would you answer St Peter's? It is actually St John in Lateran, the seat of the bishop of Rome — the pope.

Originally built in the fourth century but rebuilt after fires over the years, St John Lateran is one of the four major basilicas in Rome and is also thought to be one of the first catholic churches.

The attached palace was the residence of the pope until the French pope of Avignon. When the papacy came back to Rome the palace and the basilica were both in bad repair, so a new papal palace was built adjacent to St Peter's, where it has remained ever since.

EXTERIOR

Before you go inside the basilica there are a couple of things to take note of. Firstly the obelisk that stands outside the northern facade. This is actually one of the oldest obelisks in the world. It originally was at Karnak Temple near Luxor in Egypt, was shipped to Constantinople then made its way to Rome, where it was erected at the Circus Maximus. Pope Sixtus V dug it up and moved it to its current location.

The second thing I want to make sure you don't miss are the giant bronze doors. These originally were in the senate hall in the Roman Forum.

INTERIOR

Prior to entering the cathedral ask yourself what the official cathedral of the pope should look like, and ready yourself for an explosion of art. Nearly every inch of the church is covered in frescoes, mosaics, columns and sculptures.

The altar's tabernacle, built in 1367, is said to hold the heads of Saints Peter and Paul. Of course there is no way to be sure, but the faithful choose to believe it, and who am I to spoil their fun?

The papal cathedral is in the apse and the church also holds the tombs of many popes.

Make sure you visit the *baptistery*, which is the part of the church used for baptism. Built by Constantine in 315 AD, this was the first baptistery in Rome. The baptisteries stand separate from the churches, because you could not enter the catholic church until you had been baptized, even newborn babies. So first there would be a baptism in a separate building, and only then could you become part of the congregation.

GETTING THERE

San Giovanni in Laterano is open daily from 7am to 6:30pm. The Baptistery is open from 7:30am until 12:30pm and then again from 4pm to 6:30pm.

Admission is free.

Address: Piazza di Porta San Giovanni.

The Lateran district is behind the **Colosseum**, in the opposite direction from the **Forum**. If you start at San Giovanni in Laterano you could go next to the **Scala Santa** then walk down the Via di San Giovanni in Laterano to the **Basilica San Clemente**. From there **Domus Aurea** is very close by as is the **Colosseum**, the **Forum**, **Trajan's Market**, the **Palazzo Valentini**, and the entire **Monti** district.

4. Santa Maria Sopra Minerva /Saint Mary Above Minerva

Saint Mary Above Minerva earned its moniker by being built over the ruins of a temple for Minerva, the ancient goddess of wisdom. (The temple had been built in 50 BC by Pompey.) However, the basilica is actually built over three ruins: those of the temple of Minerva, a temple to the Egyptian goddess Isis, and a temple to the Greco-Egyptian god Serapis.

What separates this church from the other amazing churches all over Rome is the architecture: Santa Maria Sopra Minerva is the only Gothic church in Rome. Building started in 1280 spearheaded by two Dominican monks, Sisto and Ristoro, who had worked on the beautiful Gothic church of Santa Maria Novella in Florence. Completed in 1370, it is considered to be one of the most outstanding Gothic churches in all of Italy (along with the Duomo in Milano).

The somewhat bland seventeenth century facade gives no indication of the magnificence behind that front wall. Inside the church you will find the tomb of Italy's patron saint, St Catherine of Siena. Only her body rests here — her head remains in Siena.

Two of the most powerful popes of the Renaissance lie here too, in the choir behind the altar. The hedonistic Medici Pope Leo X (Giovanni de Medici 1513-21) and Pope Clement VII (Giulio de Medici 1523-34), both huge patrons of the arts, humanists and political strategists.

Another Medici connection here is painter Fra Angelico (Fra Giovanni di Fiesole, 1387-1455). In the late Middle Ages/early Renaissance, Cosimo de Medici, ruler of Florence, so loved the Dominican monk's work he commissioned him to paint the entire convent of San Marco. Then another great patron of the arts, Pope Nicholas V, who incidentally was one of the first popes to live in the new Vatican palace, commissioned Fra Angelico to paint his private Vatican chapels. Fra Angelico died next door at the monastery but is buried in the Frangipane Chapel, left of the altar choir. His painting of the Madonna and Child hangs over the altar.

Soaring columns draw the eye heavenward to the bluest ceiling, dotted with golden stars, the overall effect not only mesmerizing but also making you feel a little weightless, a little insignificant.

I sincerely recommend allowing yourself time to really experience this church — don't rush it.

WHAT'S NEARBY

Santa Maria Sopra Minerva sits just behind the **Pantheon**. If not for Bernini's baby elephant carrying a small Egytpian obelisk on its back, you might just walk past it, the facade is so completely unremarkable. Another obelisk stands in front of the church, found in the ruins of the Temple of Isis, dating it back to the rule of Pompey, somewhere around 50 BC.

Tazza D'Oro, a super famous coffee shop, sits diagonally opposite the Pantheon. Stop in for *un caffe* and then head away from the Pantheon to the **Trevi Fountain** and **Spanish Steps**.

In the opposite direction you are less than 10 minutes walk from the trilogy of Piazza **Navona**, **Campo de Fiori** and **Piazza Farnese**.

Facing away from the back to the Pantheon, you are just a few minutes walk from **Largo di Torre Argentina**, **Crypta Balbi** and then **Piazza Venezia**.

5. San Carlo Alle Quattro Fontane/Saint Charles at the Four Fountains

And now for something completely different.

After the overabundance of staggering art inside Rome's greatest churches let's have ourselves a new experience. One of light and white and wonder. It is time to check out Borromini's incredible church of San Carlo Alle Quattro Fontane.

In the Borromini/Bernini rivalry Borromini is my favorite, so let's look at his church first.

To me, the fascination with an artist or sculptor or a piece of art begins always with a story; the story behind who they were, what motivated them, what made them tick. (There is more about the rivalry between Borromini and Bernini coming up in chapter *The Battle of Bernini and Borromini*, but for now let's just talk about this one church.)

Borromini essentially built this church for free. In 1634 the religious order of the Trinitarians gave him this, his first commission in Rome, so in gratitude he waived his fee, but only with the understanding that he would retain complete creative freedom. Building began in 1638 and ended in 1646.

He found beauty in the pure science of mathematics and the harmony he found when geometry meets nature. All of these elements can be found in his architecture and inside San Carlo. From the outside the Baroque church looks like an undulating wave, a wave that ebbs and flows with perfect balance between the convex and the concave, mathematics and beauty intertwined.

On entering the church you almost feel as if you are floating. San Carlo Alle Quattro Fontane is actually built with very limited space, but rather than feeling cramped Borromini lets your spirit soar. The inside of this church is bright white, and uses geometry paired with nature to create air and space and light. Sit in a pew and feel your mind clear. The play of light and whiteness will make you feel as though it is lifting you.

At first impression you think you are looking at a swirling oval interior, but it is in fact built using triangles and lines. (A little disclaimer here — I would never in a million years have figured this out by myself. An architect showed me and now I can't un-see it.) The Trinitarians are a religious group who base their beliefs in the Holy Trinity, which can mathematically be a triangle. As you look at the shapes inside you will start to see Borromini's triangles emerge.

The central oval shape is not really an oval, it is two triangles back to back, making a diamond.

Borromini's love of mathematics also extended to the way geometric shapes can be interconnected and all fit together. If you look upward to the ceiling you can see these shapes. Squares and crosses, hexagons and octagons, all fitting together perfectly. The church of Santa Costanza Outside The Wall has the same series of interconnected shapes.

I wonder how freakishly zen-like this place must have felt to the parishioners in the mid 1600's. All the other churches were filled to exploding point with art, overwhelming the senses. Life and clothing and politics must have felt so heavy during that time, so sitting in this church must have felt ethereal.

GETTING THERE

Address: Via del Quirinale 23.

WHAT'S NEARBY

Just up the road you can visit **Santa Maria degli Angeli e dei Martiri** and the **Baths of Diocletian**. In the opposite direction **Sant'Andrea Al Quirinale**.

You are in the Monti, so endless great options to eat, the **Palazzo Colonna Art Gallery** is just down the street, as is **Trajan's Market**, **Palazzo Valentini** and the Roman **Forum**.

6. San Andrea al Quirinale/Saint Andrew at Quirinal

And this one is Bernini's.

In 1658 the Jesuit order commissioned Bernini to build this church, just down the street from his nemesis Borromini's church. It was bankrolled by the Pamphilj family. As with the church of San Carlo, there was only a small plot of land to build on, and so rather than build a box Bernini also chose an elliptical shape. Arch rival Borromini had built an oval that went from front to back, long and clear and white. Bernini built his from side to side, a horizontal ellipse, and unlike Borromini's ode to pure white light, Bernini's church was pure theater.

First there was a master illusion outside. Steps work their way up to a single, tall entrance flanked on either side by a single pilaster and topped with a triangle, drawing the eye inward and upward. The steps themselves descend from the doorway and spill out to the street in a series of concentric rings, almost like waves, spreading out as they go. From the wide steps at the bottom looking up to the doorway, he has made a small space look massive.

Walking into the church can be a little disorienting as it swirls past you in a horizontal oval with the altar directly in front of you, not at one of the ends. Bernini used color to make us feel earthly in the bottom half of the church. Columns described as *prosciutto* in color keep us grounded in the sorrow of the passion of St Andrew.

Architectural molding separates the bottom from the ascent skyward up to heaven. As we move upwards the colors change to white and gold, the colors of paradise.

THIS SEQUENCE

Had I not been shown this sequence I probably would have missed it, so although there is much else to see here I want to make sure you know to look for it. I find it completely genius.

Start with the altar directly in front of you. Centered above it is a painting of the passion of St Andrew (the brother of St Peter), nailed to his X-shaped cross. The frame of this painting is built into the wall and is of the same prosciutto marble as the columns around it. A hidden light spills down from above, illuminating bronze and gold cherubs falling from the heavens to collect him. There is actually a secret window hidden above that shines this natural light down on them. It is very theatrical!

Next, a perfect ring of molding runs around the church separating the earthly from the heavenly. It is broken above the altar by a bright, white statue of St Andrew bursting toward heaven. There is energy in his movement as he vaults upward.

From the suffering below he is now released and shoots up to heaven. As he is making that transition we get another optical illusion as the color changes dramatically into the gold and white. Inside the golden dome, cherubs tumble to meet him and guide him upwards. An oval of yellow stained-glass tops the dome, shedding a golden, heavenly light, the spirit watching from above as white stucco figures of men and boys populate the upper tier. These are cherubs and fishermen calling him upward. Andrew was a fisherman.

It was explained to me that it must have been very comforting to the congregation. There is much strife and sorrow down here where we live, but death is inevitable and you too will shoot up to this magical, golden place when you die.

There is much to see here, and in fact Bernini considered this his perfect work. Apparently towards the end of his life he would sit here for hours admiring its brilliance.

I think it's pretty fantastic.

GETTING THERE

Address: Via Del Quirinale 30.

WHAT'S NEARBY

You are just down the street from Borromini's **San Carlo Alle Quattro Fontane**, so all the same things are nearby.

If you can, take some time to wander the streets of the **Monti**. The area is lovely. Hips and knees allowing (and so long as it's not too hot or raining), walk all over this area and down to **Trajan's Market** and the **Via Fori Imperiale**.

7. San Paolo Fuori le Mura/Saint Pauls Outside the Walls

The four highest ranking churches in the Catholic church are the Archbasilica of St John Lateran, St Peter's Basilica, the Basilica of Santa Maria Maggiore and this one, St Paul's Outside The Walls.

Originally built by Emperor Constantine I, apparently on the site of the grave of St Paul himself, this basilica is the second largest church in Rome. For centuries it was able to maintain its original design, but in 1823 a devastating fire swept through, nearly destroying everything. It was quickly rebuilt thanks to donations of building materials (even lapis) from multiple countries. They kept the refurbishment as close as possible to the original church.

Above the 80 columns in the main hall there is a row of papal friezes (mosaic portraits that had been destroyed in the fire but were reproduced as closely to the originals as possible). The artist made up the faces of the popes whose faces had been lost to history in the fire. There is a frieze for every pope. However, there are only six spaces left, which has some believing that when the space runs out it will signal the second coming or the end of the world. I don't personally believe it but I do *love* a good story! (If you are a believer please don't be offended). Some believe that this church heralds the end of times.

Apart from the artwork and the end of times papal portraits, the importance of the church and its colossal size, there is something else not to miss here. The chains that were used to bind St Paul as a prisoner from 61 to 63 AD are kept here in a golden reliquary close to St Paul's tomb. The chains are taken on a procession around the church each year on June 29, the feast day of St Paul.

GETTING THERE

Address: Piazzale San Paolo 1.

WHAT'S NEARBY

Don't be put off by the *Outside the walls* part, as this just refers to the Aurelian Wall. It is only 7 km/5 miles from the Vatican, which is about 15 minutes in a taxi. Grab a cab from the Trastevere and you will be there in a little over five minutes. From there take a taxi back up Via Ostiense to **Cestius' Pyramid** and the **Cemetery For Non-Catholic Foreigners**, then either walk along Via Mamorata back to the river and the Trastevere, or visit the **Aventine Hill**, which backs onto Via Mamorata.

8. San Lorenzo in Palatio & Scala Sancta/St Lawrence in Palatio and the Sacred Stairs

The Sacred Stairs are stairs that Jesus climbed, but this one needs a little more back story.

CONSTANTINE'S STORY

This story starts in 312 AD on the night before a massive fight over who should run the empire. Maxentius was in charge of the Western Roman Empire at the time and Constantine wanted it for himself. The night before the battle, Constantine had a dream that the Christian God told him that in exchange for protection, he should paint the first two letters of Jesus' name on the shields of his 100,000 men. The shields were painted and Constantine won the battle, with the fleeing Maxentius drowning in the Tiber river.

Constantine concluded that the Christian God was more powerful than all the Roman gods, and that he would help the Christians. In partnership with his co-emperor and brother-in-law, he oversaw the Edict of Milan, a proclamation that ended persecution of Christians.

Constantine then picked a fight with his co-emperor and took over the Eastern Roman Empire in addition to the Western Roman Empire (thus ending the succession system that Diocletian had put in place — see the Baths of Diocletian in the *Ancient Rome* chapter for the rest of his story). He moved home base to the East, to Byzantium, where the new imperial capital was renamed New Rome (but later became Constantinople, now Istanbul).

Meanwhile he had to keep things cool with the Christians and show himself to have a greater tangible connection to God. He had a plan, but was stretched thin running the massive Roman Empire, so he needed someone he could trust above all others to execute his plan. Those were dangerous times, with emperors getting assassinated or toppled. He could trust no one. Except for his mum.

And here's where it gets really good: Constantine dispatched his 80 year old mother, Helena, to the Holy Land to scavenge and loot some Jesus memorabilia and bring it back to Rome. So off she went, all 80 years of her along with her team of imperial raiders, to ransack Jersualem. Helena was a devout Christian herself, and brought back all kinds of swag, but also used the opportunity to forge some healing between Rome and the Holy Land. She commissioned churches at the site of Jesus' birth and at the site of his ascension, and it would appear that her trip was a raging success on many levels. Supposedly she discovered Jesus' tomb, thorns from his crown, pieces of his cross and all kinds of memorabilia, including the staircase to Pontius Pilate's office. These were the stairs that Jesus went up to his fate-sealing meeting with Pilate. Helena had them shipped back to Rome where they still reside. (Bear in mind that this was more than 300 years after the death of Jesus, so who really knows just how authentic these treasures really were?)

Helena lived well beyond the average age for the time, but died shortly after returning from her trip. Constantine by all accounts had a pretty profound impact on Christianity, but only converted to the religion on his death bed, aged 65.

Constantine built the basilica of St John In Lateran and the Scala Sancta were hidden away in the Lateran palace where only popes could see them until the palace fell into disrepair and the popes moved to the Vatican palace. During renovations years later, the Jesus stairs were rediscovered and moved across the street to the church of St Lawrence in Palatio where everyone can see them.

I remain skeptical as to whether these really are the stairs that Jesus walked on, but always have to question what if it's true? What if they really are? With that in mind I think it is well worth the visit to St Lawrence in Palatio.

GETTING THERE

St Lawrence in Palatio and the Scala Sancta are easy to find. Opposite St John in Lateran you will see pilgrims lining up, making their way to the staircase. You can go up the staircase yourself, but you have to do so on your knees. You will see the faithful ascending the Jesus Stairs on their knees, saying a prayer on each of the 28 steps. If that's not quite your thing you can walk up a staircase on either side of the sacred stairs.

WHAT'S NEARBY

The Sacred Stairs at St Lawrence in Palatio are walking distance from the **Colosseum** (south east of it) in the Lateran district. You are close to the **Basilica St John Lateran, Basilica San Clemente, Domus Aurea**, the **Monti** district, **Trajan's Market** and the **Forum**.

9. Basilica of Santa Croce in Gerusalemme

The story behind this church continues the story of the Scala Santa in St Lawrence in Palatio, and marks a pivotal point in the history of Christianity. It all goes back to Helena.

HELENA'S STORY

Constantine's mother Helena came from the most humble of beginnings and is said to have been a waitress working in a tavern when she caught the eye of Constantius Chlorus. She is described as being his consort, so he probably didn't marry her although she bore him a son, Constantine.

To become emperor Constantius married Maxentius' daughter Theodora, and became co-emperor from 293—306 AD. He sent Helena and Constantine off to the court of Diocletian, where Constantine could learn how to be an emperor and where Helena was out of the way.

When Constantine became emperor in 312 AD he had his mother returned from exile and reentered public life in the imperial court. He gave her the Sessorian Palace to live in. Helena was a Christian and used her religious influence on her son. Together they built churches across Rome, including St Peters, St John Lateran, St Lawrence, St Paul's, and St Sebastian.

Emperor Diocletian, less than 24 years prior, had nearly wiped out the religion with the worst and most prolific persecutions of Christians. Now with Helena at the helm a new day dawned for Christianity. She wanted to walk in the footsteps of Jesus and so she went to Jerusalem on Constantine's mission for Christian memorabilia.

The Christians had kept a shrine over the place where Jesus died, but in 130 AD Hadrian knocked it down and had a Roman Temple built over it. Helena had the temple torn down. During the excavations a cistern was found with three upright wooden beams in it, one of which carried the title Pontius Pilate is said to have attached to the cross of Jesus.

Helena wanted to be sure, so did an experiment. She had a dying woman touch each of the three. The first two had no effect but the third miraculously healed her.

She had a piece of the cross enshrined in the church of the Holy Sepulchre in Jerusalem, gave another piece to her son Constantine, and kept a small piece for herself in her private chapel in the Sessorian Palace, along with relics including little oil vials. She also brought back soil from the excavation, which she spread over the floor of her chapel, to feel closer to Jesus. Her chapel became the Basilica of Santa Croce in Gerusalemme. Parts of her chapel still remain, including a sealed off section containing the excavated soil.

Santa Croce in Gerusalemme now has a seventeenth century facade topped with a statue of the sainted Helena holding a cross. The apse of the church contains paintings of the story of her greatest achievement, her trip to the Holy Land.

For the devoted this is considered to be one of the most sacred, holiest churches in Rome and in all of the world.

GETTING THERE

Address: Piazza di Santa Croce in Gerusalemme.

WHAT'S NEARBY

Santa Croce in Gerusalemme sits between **St John Lateran** and **Porta Maggiore**. From the church you can work your way backwards to the **Scala Sancta**, **St John Lateran**, **Basilica San Clemente** and the **Colosseum**.

M·AGRIPPA·L·F·COS·TERTIVM·FECIT

10. The Pantheon

The Pantheon is not only an architectural wonder, it is also the best preserved Roman building, largely because it has been in continuous use since it was built in 113—125 AD. I am going to tell you two stories here. One is a quick description of the building, the other is another foray into the craziness, genius and intrigue of ancient Rome.

THE NAME

Pantheon means "related to all Gods", and there is much speculation as to how this applies here. One theory is that it was a temple built to honor all gods. Another is that the original builder, Marcus

Agrippa, had statues of multiple gods outside his building. A third is that the inside of the dome looked like the heavens. Another is that Pantheon was just a nickname for the building. Ancient authors referred to other temples with the word *Aedes*, but on the architrave this one is inscribed with *Pantheum* not *Aedes Panthei*, which would mean "temple of all the gods".

THE STRUCTURE

Regardless of how it came by its name, the Pantheon is impressive. The first thing you will notice as you approach is the massive portico, lined with eight huge columns in front then two rows each of four columns. Their size can seem like an optical illusion — you don't realize quite how wide they are until you try to join hands circling one. Most of the time it takes three people to link up hands and complete the circle.

These columns originally came from Egypt.

Behind the portico you enter a rotunda, spectacular by itself with its red porphyry and marble floors, niches for statues and unearthly acoustics. (If you have the pure luck to be there when a choir sings and hear the voices swirl around the rotunda you will know what I mean.) But look up and you will see a dome that is testament to the sheer genius of Roman innovation and their ability to achieve the impossible.

Two thousand years later this is *still* the world's largest unreinforced concrete dome. As if an imaginary sphere or ball took up the entire space of the rotunda, the height from floor to the top of the dome and the central diameter are exactly the same, 43 meters (142 feet). Apollodorus, the architect, cleverly created a coffered system of concentric rings of squares within squares, getting smaller each tier upward until they reach the next marvel, the 30 foot wide oculus at the top of the dome. The oculus is both the source of light and also part of the way the dome stays in place, both alleviating and supporting the pressure.

The bottom most tier of the dome was built with travertine and is 6.4 meters (21 feet) thick. As is raises up to the oculus Apollodorus used lighter and thinner rings of stone, each foot weighing less than the one below it, through terracotta to tufa to lightweight pumice stone 1.2 meters (3.9 feet) thick at the very top.

The dome is an incredible feat of absolute genius. Put into perspective, the cathedral in Florence (Santa Maria dei Fiori) sat without a roof for more than 100 years because no one could figure out how to build a dome of that size that wouldn't either crush the walls supporting it or collapse inward on itself.

I have been inside the Pantheon several times when it has rained. It is an absolute marvel to watch the rain come through the oculus and drain away. The floor tilts imperceptibly, but enough to keep the rain water contained and draining. I had never thought about being in Rome when it snows, but after reading Anthony Doerr's book I know that should it happen I will drop everything and run to the Pantheon. To be inside and watch snow come through the oculus has to be one of the most amazing experiences ever!

Art lovers may be interested to know that the Pantheon is the final resting place of Renaissance painter Raphael. His mortal remains — bones and ashes are in a sarcophagus given by Pope Gregory XVI with the inscription, *Here lies Raphael, by whom the mother of all things (Nature) feared to be overcome while he was living, and while he was dying, herself to die.*

To the right of his sarcophagus his fiancé Maria Bibbiena is buried. She died before they could marry, but by all accounts he was being forced to marry her instead of his true love, the baker's daughter.

THE INSCRIPTION

So now let's look at the second part of the story of the Pantheon, a story of architectural brilliance paired with an imperial pettiness that is quite mind boggling.

Stand in front of the Pantheon and you will see a Latin inscription on the front of the temple that reads:

M*AGRIPPA*L*F*COS*TERTIVM*FECIT

It means: *Marcus Agrippa, son of Lucius, made this building when consul for the third time.*

However, Agrippa had been dead for well over a hundred years by the time the Pantheon was built. So why did he get credit for building the Pantheon, and who really built it?

AGRIPPA'S STORY

Marcus Agrippa (64—12 BC) was a Roman consul, general, statesman and brilliant architect.

Born to very humble beginnings, Agrippa served in the Roman army and impressed Julius Caesar enough that he shipped him off to school in Apollonia with young Octavius. The two became great friends. When Caesar was assassinated and Octavius became Augustus, the first emperor of Rome, he had his friend Agrippa at his right hand.

The two embarked upon a goal of making Rome the "City of Marble", creating and constructing some of the most notable buildings in Roman history. Agrippa was a prolific and genius builder. He also renovated the Aqua Marcia aqueduct, bringing more water to the city, became the first water commissioner of Rome, repaired the streets and sewers, constructed baths and porticos and public gardens, and gave Romans of every class access to the best public services. He was also a huge proponent of public art exhibitions.

Agrippa was married to Julia the Elder, was grandfather to Caligula and great grandfather to Nero.

The original Pantheon was part of a complex of buildings he built between 29—19 BC on his own property in the Campus Martius: the Baths of Agrippa, the Basilica of Neptune and the Pantheon. The last two were thought to be part of his private space, not public temples, which could explain how the original designation of the Pantheon was lost after it burned down in 80 AD, 92 years after Agrippa's death. It was rebuilt by Domitian but in 110 AD burned down again.

APOLLODORUS'S STORY

Emperor Trajan, who reigned from 98—117 AD, had his own genius architect and engineer, Apollodorus of Damascus. When Trajan wanted to conquer the lands on the far side of the River Danube, Apollodorus built him a stone bridge 50 feet wide and two thirds of a mile long. This was an amazing feat of engineering — it was more than 1000 years before another bridge that long was ever built.

In Rome the pair teamed up to redesign giant stretches of the city. They built Trajan's Forum and Trajan's Column. They buried

Nero's golden palace and built Trajan's Baths over it. At this time Trajan was undefeated in his battles, so the two decided to build a new temple to the success of Emperor Trajan and to the glory of Rome. They settled on the idea of rebuilding the twice-burnt-down Pantheon. Apollodorus got to work designing the building now known as the Pantheon, one of the greatest buildings of all time.

Meanwhile Trajan decided to conquer Rome's arch rivals, the Parthenians. He was again victorious, however on his way home he suffered a stroke and died. With no heir and no plan for succession in place, his wife claimed that as he was dying he had adopted Hadrian, who was a distant cousin, a well-respected general and clever administrator. Hadrian was a good choice. He was intelligent, cultured and educated. Hadrian was a proponent of peace so he kept his soldiers busy by having them build and build. He was a lover of art and sculpture and beauty.

He was also thin skinned. He fancied himself as an architect, designing the largest temple in ancient Rome, the temple of Venus and Roma. The otherwise clever Apollodorus mocked Hadrian's effort, making fun of the sensitive emperor. Hadrian had Apollodorus first exiled and then executed in 130 AD.

And here is the petty part.

With perhaps the greatest building ever designed finally completed, all that remained was to dedicate it. Emperors would often dedicate buildings to themselves, but instead of naming it for himself, and with everyone involved in the creation of this masterpiece already dead (Trajan, Apollodorus) Hadrian decided to rob Apollodorus of the glory, instead inscribing the building to the long dead Agrippa, who had nothing to do with its design or construction!

So for millennia, anyone who has looked at the front of the Pantheon and read the inscription will have assumed that this was Agrippa's masterpiece, not that of Apollodorus.

In the seventh century it became a Christian church, St Mary and the Martyrs, informally known as Santa Maria Rotunda, and you'll see signs of this today.

GETTING THERE

The Pantheon is located in the Piazza della Rotunda.

You probably won't need more than 30 minutes of your time to visit inside the Pantheon. As of 2018 there is supposed to be a two euro charge for admittance, although it wasn't in place while I was there. Do expect to be turned away if your shoulders and thighs aren't covered.

WHAT'S NEARBY

The Pantheon is situated in the heart of Rome, and from here you can walk to everywhere. You are close to **Piazza Navona** and **Campo de Fiori** in one direction, the **Trevi Fountain** and the **Spanish Steps** in the other. **Santa Maria Sopra Minerva** is immediately behind the Pantheon and from there it is an easy walk to **Largo di Torre Argentina**, **Crypta Balbi** and **Piazza Venezia**.

Caravaggio fans are very close to **San Luigi dei Francesi** and the incredible paintings of **St Matthew**.

Catty-corner to the Pantheon is the world famous **Tazza D'Oro** coffee shop. I don't think I have ever walked past it without ducking inside for a quick *caffe*.

Interesting & Unusual Things to See in Rome

5.

Interesting & Unusual Things to See in Rome

1. The Pyramid of Cestius

2. The cemetery For Non-Catholic Foreigners

3. The Graffiti in Ostiense

4. The Keyhole at the Knights of Malta

5. La Bocca della Verita/The Mouth of Truth

6. Mount Testaccio

7. The Galleria Sciarra

8. Michelangelo's Flowers

9. The Doll Hospital

10. The Coppede District

11. The Owl House

Here is my list of *must-sees* that didn't fit into any of the other categories within this book. You will want to see most if not all of these and you will be glad you knew about them!

Here are eleven quirky, cool and very interesting things to see in Rome.

1. Pyramid of Cestius

Yes, Rome has a pyramid, and this is one of my pseudo-secret, really unusual and totally fascinating places to take people in Rome.

Positioned just beyond the Aventine Hill, in the heart of one of the coolest neighborhoods in Rome (the Testaccio) this is one of those treasures that is easily accessible yet is far from the tourist crowds. You can wander around and explore without being overrun by busloads of people, annoying vendors hawking selfie sticks and pickpockets.

THE ONLY PYRAMID IN EUROPE

Back in around 30 BC give or take a few years Egyptomania was a huge craze in Rome. All things Egyptian were both coveted and cool. Marc Antony had been getting it on with Cleopatra, who was not only a fierce ruler but also chic and beautiful and totally captivating. Obelisks came over from Egypt, copies of all things Egyptian popped up, but only two pyramids were built, and of those two pyramids only one remains: the Pyramid of Cestius is the only pyramid in all of Europe.

Cestius' Story

We don't actually know an enormous amount about Gaius Cestius. He was a magistrate, a praetor and a member of one of the four big religious corporations in Rome called the *Septemviri Epulonum*. Based on the unusual shape of the pyramid, he may have served in the military and been part of the Roman attack on Meroe in Nubia in 23 BC. It would make sense that he built this unusually shaped pyramid as a type of commemoration, or maybe the builders just didn't know any different.

The tomb was ransacked centuries ago, taking away much of the information we could have had about Cestius and his family. Also the landscape changed dramatically in the first couple of centuries after construction, so if there had been family info nearby, it is long gone.

The Pyramid

If you have been to Egypt and seen the pyramids there, you will notice that Cestius' pyramid is unusually narrow, steep and pointy, and at a much sharper angle than the Egyptian pyramids. Also it isn't a series of stepped blocks working their way up the sides, instead it has a smooth, travertine finish.

There are three main schools of thought on this. One is that the Nubian pyramids close to Jebel Barkal (now Sudan) were shaped more like this one, so if Cestius had been part of the 23 BC invasion of the region this is what he would have thought the Egyptian pyramids looked like. Another suggestion is that they just didn't get the right info on pyramid shapes and sizes. The third possibility is that 1000 years after the construction of the Egyptian pyramids there was new building technology. The Roman builders used brick and concrete instead of giant stone blocks, and as such could build it steeper, and then cover it in glowing white travertine.

Cestius' pyramid stands 29.6 meters square at the bottom (100 Roman feet) and is 37 meters tall. The interior of the tomb was decorated with frescoes, most of which have worn away now, but on Sundays (check first) you can go inside and see those that remain.

The guess-timate is that the pyramid was built at some point between 18-12 BC. We do know it took 330 days to build, because it says so in Cestius' will, which also states that it was executed by *L. Pontus Mela, son of Publius and his freedman Pothus.* (A *freedman* was a slave who had completed his slave years and now was a free citizen of Rome.)

AURELIAN'S WALL

At the time the Pyramid of Cestius was built it was outside the city of Rome. We know it was originally surrounded by large, stately columns and two bronze figures which now are in the Capitoline Museums. Building tombs and burying your dead inside the city was forbidden, but the city of Rome underwent massive expansion, it grew and grew and by the time Aurelian built his wall around Rome, the pyramid was at the city limits.

However, Romans appreciated cool and beautiful buildings, especially those built by the Greeks, and didn't like to pull them down for no reason. So when Aurelian's wall was constructed (271— 275 AD), rather than demolish the pyramid they built the wall right up to it and continued out the other side. These fortifications no doubt helped it to survive the next 1800 or so years until today.

Today a major road bisects the wall at the pyramid but the fort-like watch tower still stands on the other side and the wall keeps going. You can get some amazing photos of the pyramid from the next place on this list, **The Cemetery For Non-Catholic Foreigners**.

TWO PYRAMIDS

There were actually two pyramids built at around that time. The other was near Castel Sant'Angelo, and was larger than Cestius' pyramid. It didn't survive all the construction going on in Rome over the next centuries, and the marble from this other pyramid was used to build the stairs of the St Peter's Basilica nearby.

I have read that in the Middle Ages there were stories that the two pyramids were the tombs of Romulus and Remus, the wolf-suckled twins who founded Rome.

The inscriptions on Cestius' pyramid were not rediscovered until tunnel builders found them in the 1600s. The Pyramid of Cestius had restorations done in the 1600s , then again in 1999 and more recently in 2015.

GETTING THERE

The Tomb is open on Sundays (though you'd be wise to double-check this).

You can find the Pyramid of Cestius at the Porta San Paolo, near the Pirimide metro station.

WHAT'S NEARBY

The Pyramid of Cestius is in the Testaccio, one of Rome's best food districts. Time your visit with lunch and your belly will be happy, as will be your wallet!

From the river you can walk up Via Mamorata along the side of the **Aventine Hill**.

Combine a visit to Ostiense and see the pyramid, the **Cemetery For Non-Catholic Foreigners** and the **Keyhole of the Knights of Malta** and end your afternoon with sunset at the **Orange Garden** (see my chapter on *The Best Places to Watch the Sunset in Rome*).

2. Cemetery For Non-Catholic Foreigners

The first time I went to the Pyramid of Cestius, I stumbled on this cemetery completely by accident. I was trying to find an angle to photograph the pyramid that didn't involve me getting run over — the roads around the pyramid are quite busy. I could see what at first looked like a park on the other side of the pyramid. When I looked down to the base of it I spotted some ruins and a bunch of crazy cat ladies feeding giant bowls of tuna to the fattest cats you've ever seen.

I knew there had to be a story here so I wandered around until I found the gate. It is an arched hedge-way, looks a little like an unkempt version of a British garden scene and is the entrance to one of the coolest cemeteries anywhere. Here you will find quite possibly the most diverse and eclectic group of writers, poets, artists, sculptors, painters, historians, archaeologists, architects, scientists and diplomats in perpetual residence. An international who's who of interesting characters of non-Catholic persuasions.

The cemetery is often referred to as the Protestant cemetery (*Cimitero dei protestanti*), but in fact its residents are theologically all over the place. From Jews to various eastern Orthodox, to Muslims to Buddhists, even some of the Confucius gang are here. Tombstones are inscribed in more than 15 different languages, many in their own non-Roman script.

You have to imagine that if they get up at night and socialize the conversation would be incredibly stimulating! If ghosts have dinner parties, the ones here would be fantastic.

TRADITIONAL ITALIAN CEMETERIES

If you are familiar with French cemeteries then you already know they are filled with wailing statues and sobbing angels. They are artsy, often totally over the top, and in my opinion, DRAMA. I love them! Want a really great, moody photo of some cherub statues or wailing women/angels stretched out over a grave stone? Head to a cemetery in France. Initially I had thought the Italians would be the same, so on my first trip back to Italy with my friend Michelle (I talked about it in my first book, *Glam Italia! How To Travel Italy*) we would pull up to cemeteries to see the statues. Only there weren't any. Italian cemeteries are structured and orderly, with graves that are simple and clear and normally have a photo of the guest in the bunk below. Zero drama.

We were *so disappointed*! But that all changed when I discovered this one. It has statues, my favorite of which is an angel on her knees, theatrically draped over a stone with the inscription EMELYN STORY, her face buried in one arm. The statue itself is exquisite, her anguish is palpable, and I would definitely file it under Drama with a capital D.

There is another one that is huge, a full length human-sized statue of a dude lying on pillows, his head propped up on one hand, lounging with a blanket over him, a book in his hand and a puppy against his belly. His name is Devereaux Plantagenet Cockburn. The inscription on his grave reads like a book, easily the most wordy epitaph I've ever seen. Devereaux died age 21, and included in the epitaph is that he was *of rare mental and corporeal endowments.* Really. I kid you not.

The cemetery is beautiful, with towering cypress trees guarding the inhabitants, flowers everywhere, and grassy spaces including a parklike area where you can sit in the shade of more giant trees and contemplate life, death and the giant pyramid in front of you.

It might make one in love with death, to think that one should be buried in so sweet a place, wrote Shelley, not long before he drowned and moved in here.

The Cemetery For Non-Catholic Foreigners was created in 1716. Pope Clement XI donated the land and got things going on account of exiled King James II moving to Italy.

FAMOUS INHABITANTS

So we know that Percy Bysshe Shelley is here, so are John Keats, Joseph Severn and August von Goethe (son of Goethe). You can Google a list of who else made this their final resting place. Many of them although well-heeled and famous are names I don't personally know, from Norwegian sculptors to Russian painters. One of the newer residents is an American named Gregory Corso, a poet who kicked around with the Beat Generation writers, like Kerouac and Ginsberg. The cemetery website gives a mini bio on each inhabitant, and they are really interesting.

Cat Sanctuary

At the base of the pyramid there is another of Rome's cat sanctuaries, this one run by crazy cat ladies. You will not only see the ladies walking around like feline guards, but also the fat cats themselves, sunning their bellies on the gravestones. One time I was walking along one of the lovely pathways inside the cemetery, heading over to the pyramid, when I came upon a cat lady placing a bowl with an entire can of tuna on the low fence beside her for a cat that made Garfield look like the poster boy for a Weight Watchers ad. She shooed me away, convinced that I would disturb fat-boy and put him off his late lunch/early dinner.

What's Nearby

The cemetery is adjacent to the pyramid, so is also close to the **Aventine Hill** with the **Giardini degli Aranci/Parco Savello**, a beautiful place to watch sunset with a view of Rome. It is also close to the next spot on the list, **Ostiense**.

3. Graffiti in Ostiense

I had read about the buildings in Ostiense, entirely covered in artsy graffiti but didn't go see them until I went to the pyramid for the first time.

It started with one of the world's most famous street artists (he made the top 10 list), a thirty-something-ish Italian who goes by the name BLU. His street art highlights political and social issues and is predominantly on buildings used as squats in somewhat forgotten areas. His work is allegorical and full of metaphors and symbols. It's not tagging though, more like murals taking over facades and sometimes entire buildings.

MY FIRST TIME

I had been at the pyramid with a couple of girlfriends. We had walked there from the Trastevere, which had taken a half hour or so. Now done with the pyramid and the cemetery we were heading to the Jewish Ghetto for a glass of wine and three faces full of artichokes. It was a hot day and we were losing steam (I frankly couldn't be bothered walking back), so hailed a cab. I had asked the driver how much it would cost to get to the Ghetto. I think he quoted us 10 or 12 euro, so we jumped in the car. As he was pulling into traffic I happened to mention that I had planned to go see the graffiti building but had run out of time or energy.

Dude looks at me and says *"I vill take you!"*. Next thing you know, as if we were in a spy movie with the KGB hot on our tail, he whips a death defying U turn across I don't even know how many lanes of traffic, (probably only two, but in the moment it felt like 16) and with us hanging on for dear life hurtled like a rocket down the street towards the next neighborhood, Ostiense. I may have some of the details about what he was telling me muddled, because not only was he telling me them in rapid fire Italian as he was weaving at high speed in and out of traffic, taking my "not having time" quip quite literally, but also I was laughing giddily, the way you do after someone has jumped out on you, scaring you half to death. I tried to process what he was telling me while simultaneously being in that hysterical place of gratitude for still being alive and giving thanks for the relative certainty that I hadn't peed myself during the U-turn. I would say *"Sweet Jesus that gave me a fright"*, but as if the situation couldn't get funnier, with the exception of his outfit, the taxi driver looked exactly like Jesus.

Anyway, he pulled in to all the great photo spots so that we got great images and told me (I think!) this: *The building was gray and ugly and depressing, so BLU decided to paint it, even though the city forbade it. So he amassed a huge crew of local graffiti artists and street painters, and in the space of 24 hours, with the police trying to stop them, they got the entire building painted.* Whether that's correct or not, the building is worth having a look at if you are nearby. I have never seen anything like it! The images are incredibly clever and quite brilliant.

Once he had driven us around the Ostiense graffiti buildings and the urgency was gone, Jesus drove us back down to the Jewish Ghetto (at normal speed). We had blown a good half hour of his work day on our little adventure, but he would not accept one dime more than he had quoted for the pyramid to ghetto fare. I couldn't believe it! I tried to reason with him that he was earning a living and had done us a huge favor and should be compensated for it. He wouldn't hear of it. Said that it had been his pleasure to show us this piece of Rome. He even refused to accept a tip.

Assuming that he wasn't in fact the messiah, merely a lookalike, he is a great example of the hospitality of Romans, the pride they have in their city, and their neverending sense of fun. It is also an example of how being open to new opportunities and new experiences, even high speed ones, and choosing to be a traveler rather than a tourist, getting off the beaten path and seeing more than just the main monuments, can turn a good trip into a fantastic one. That's when you get the great stories, meet the amazing folks and get an understanding of a place and its people.

If you want to do a tour of BLU's street art, I suggest you start with the following spots:

Fronte del Porto, Via del Porto Fluviale, Ostiense

The first I ever saw was the former aeronautical barracks building in Ostiense. Depending on where you read about it, it houses somewhere between 60 and 85 families from North Africa and South America, all squatting inside. BLU used the building's windows as eyes, and painted incredible giant monster-people all over the building, such as Banana Man, a monster/man painted entirely in yellow bananas.

Alexia, Via Ostiense 124

This one was a squat for students and temp workers in the former ACEA (power company) building that then became the ATAC (public transport) building. The squat was named after a Greek student, Alexis Grigoropoulous who was killed by a policeman during the riots in 2008. Alexis is painted inside a circle on the right hand side of the front of the building. The entire facade is painted with an intricate chain of cars all held together with a giant lock, apparently referencing the insane traffic in the area.

The squat has been closed down since I was there, so you may want to check ahead of time to see that the art is still in place. It was really cool.

Acrobax

This one was a run down and abandoned dog track that became one of Rome's most popular squats. I should add at this point that I have never been inside a squat, and only know about these because of the art.

Anyway this was BLU's first (or one of his first) in Rome. Unlike his other murals this one is black and white and from a distance looks like yet another ancient Roman building with friezes, reliefs and statues.

Then you get up close and see it is painted and that the imagery is a poignant social commentary. From what looks like a group of huddled klansmen, to attacks on war, politics, religion and consumerism, this one is not only brilliantly executed, but it really does give you pause and makes you stop and think, regardless of where you stand on the issues.

Piazza del Quarticciolo

This one takes over the facade of the former police headquarters in Quarticciolo on the east side of Rome. For two decades the abandoned six-storey building has been the home to 30 squatter families, unable to afford housing in the city. BLU has recreated two enormous vertical images in the Greco Roman style, again using white and black so that at first they look like ancient Roman monuments, but this time offset with a bright golden yellow.

On the left hand side there is a six-storey Venus de Milo and on the right hand side is Michelangelo's David with a twist. These two are a reflection on today's consumer society, both of them adorned with the trappings of modern day greed. She is carrying designer brand shopping bags, wearing shiny, gaudy jewelry that wraps around her neck and trails down her ancient robes. She even has a poodle at her feet. Venus is a little chubby, of course has no arms, and has a slightly shocked expression on her face.

David is quite something with a big fat belly, ridiculous golden Hogan running shoes on his feet, an obnoxious gold watch on one wrist, and a matching chain bracelet on the other. He even has a gold chain with a cross on it around his neck and a bottle of beer in his right hand (this country was built on wine!). In the ultimate nod to crass consumerism he holds up a golden cell phone in his left hand, posing with an arrogant, overly confident face, while snapping a selfie. This work is genius! Between his gut and the look on his face it is priceless!

The two works are surrounded with scenes of war and people with shopping carts, tying in the imagery of greed leading to bloodshed and destroying society.

One thing that immediately grabs my attention with this one is the shade of gold BLU has used. It's that grotesque Vegas-gold, Trump-gold, crass and nouveau and completely tasteless. So clever!

When I saw this building the center panel was unpainted. I don't know if it will remain that way or be filled in.

GETTING THERE

There are more BLU works in Rome too, but I haven't been to see them. If you are interested in street art you could make your own little subway tour of them, or I am pretty certain there are tours you can take. I definitely recommend Googling them first though.

4. The Keyhole at the Knights of Malta

As you stroll up the Aventine Hill, taking the break from the crowds of tourists at the big attractions, enjoying this truly lovely neighborhood, you will eventually find yourself in the Piazza dei Cavalieri di Malta (the Piazza of the Knights of Malta). In this piazza is the small church of Santa Maria del Priorato with a green door. Once you've spotted the green door look for the small brass keyhole. If there is a line of people waiting you won't have to search to find it, but should you get there when there's no one around you need to know exactly what it is that you are looking for.

Shimmy on up and look through the keyhole. You will see perfectly arched hedges, and then as your eye focuses you will see they are perfectly lined up to frame the dome of St Peters in the distance. It is incredibly clever, more so when you stop to consider they achieved this without a laser, a computer, or even a calculator. The precision required to pull this trick off is mind boggling!

Next, try and get that perfect photo of the archway with the dome. I am assuming that if you have a really killer phone then it will be easier. Or if you have a real camera with the right lens. I haven't been up there for a while and haven't tried to take a photo with either my Canon or my iPhone, but it is on my list of things to do this summer. (I'm one of those people who, when facing the choice between getting the latest iPhone or buying a round trip airfare to Italy, will always find my feet on Italian soil — so I never, ever have the latest phone.)

WHAT'S NEARBY

You are very close to the **Giardini degli Aranci**, so just a couple more minutes walk and you will be at one of the bests places to watch the sunset in Rome. You may want to time the keyhole for an hour before sunset in case there is a long line.

You are also close to the Testaccio district with all the great food, so after sunset head down there to eat. The Aventine Hill is close to **Circus Maximus**, the **Pyramid of Cestius**, The **Cemetery for Non-Catholic Foreigners** and **Ostiense**. In the opposite direction you have a short walk to the **Forum Boarium, La Bocca Della Verita** and **Teatro Marcello**.

5. La Bocca della Verita/The Mouth of Truth

If you have seen the 1953 Audrey Hepburn & Gregory Peck movie *Roman Holiday* then you may be familiar with the large stone disc with a mask like face known as *La Bocca della Verità* (The Mouth of Truth).

There is some dispute as to what the Mouth of Truth actually was or why it was created. The huge stone disc has a diameter of 1.75 meters (5 feet 9 inches), is carved into a humanoid face with holes for the eyes, nose and open mouth and has a beard. It dates back to the first century and one thought is that it is the god Oceanus. It actually does have a man-of-the-sea look about it.

There are suggestions that it may have been a manhole cover, a drain cover, or a ceremonial well cover. It has even been said that it might have been a drain for the blood of cattle that had been sacrificed to the god Hercules in the nearby Temple of Hercules Victor.

It was located in the Piazza della Bocca della Verità until 1632 when it was transferred to one of the outside walls of the nearby church of Santa Maria in Cosmedin, where it still resides today.

In the Middle Ages legend said that if you put your hand inside the mouth and told a lie it would bite your fingers off. Because of this you will often find lines of people waiting to take a photo with their hand inside the mouth. (Wouldn't it be hilarious to rig up some kind of snapping device behind the mouth and scare people??)

SAINT VALENTINE'S SKULL

While visiting the Mouth of Truth you may want to go inside the church to see the skull of the patron saint of lovers, Saint Valentine. Now whether this is actually *that* St Valentine is up for debate, as there were actually three Saint Valentines over 1500 years, and their stories seem to converge a little. Also, during the Victorian era there was, according to Atlas Obscura, some rather *enthusiastic redistribution and re-labeling* of body parts going on, so there is every chance it might not be Saint Valentine, it might just be Bob from Accounting inside the glass box. Who knows? I do however quite enjoy his teeth, whoever he is. If you go see the skull try to imagine the owner of it biting into an apple…

What's Nearby

You are close to the **Aventine Hill**, the **Forum Boarium**, **San Nicola in Carcere**, **Teatro Marcello** and the **Jewish Ghetto**. Also the **Trastevere** is just across the river. **Piazza Venezia**, the gateway to **Palazzo Valentini**, the **Forum**, **Trajan's Column** and the **Colosseum**, is only a 15—20 minute walk away.

6. Mount Testaccio

Mount Testaccio is a hill made up entirely of ancient Roman terracotta jars, or amphorae. Basically it was a giant trash heap for broken oil jars. Also known as *Monte dei Cocci* (Mountain of Shards), this one has a really interesting history.

Located next to an ancient port on the Tiber river, the amphorae would have come up the river on barges to the Horrea Galbae warehouses where they would have been stored. Ancient Rome had an appetite for olive oil that surpassed local production volume, so some of the oil they consumed was imported from all over the empire. The amorphae have markings called *tituli picti* that indicate the oil came in from Libya, Tunisia and Spain. Not only that but the jars also show the port of origin, quality control markers and the name of the makers of the jars! Isn't that cool??

Archaeologists have been able to learn all kinds of interesting facts from Mt Testaccio. One thing that I find fascinating is that the cracked or broken amphorae that could not be reused and were therefore heading to the dump, weren't just thrown in a pile like trash. They were cut in half so they could nest into each other, and the pile was planned out into a series of terraces. It is thought that somewhere between 53 million and 80 million amphorae make up the hill, which stands 115 feet tall above ground, and with another 45 feet below ground (which was probably street level when the building of the hill began).

In the 1990s they began excavating the hill and archaeologists examining the jars were not only able to discern their provenance but also their age. The bulk of them date back from 140—250 AD, but they think the earliest layers may in fact date back to the first century, making it one of the largest and best preserved dump sites in all of Italy.

THE LAST 1500 YEARS

After the fall of Rome in 500 AD the hill was pretty much abandoned. It became a terraced, grown over hill, host to many of Rome's celebrations, festivals and pageants. It is often associated with Easter ceremonies, having been used for pre-Lent festivals, and during Easter week Mt Testaccio was the final stage in the Way of the Cross, with parades leading to Mt Testaccio and re-enactments of the crucifixion taking place on the summit, where a cross still stands to mark the spot.

In 1849 Garibaldi tried to stave off the French invasion by mounting guns on top of Mt Testaccio. At some point wine caves were dug into the sides of the hill. In 1931 it became a public park with hedges and a fountain and a semi-circle bench, but as money ran out it couldn't be maintained and before long was abandoned again.

Mt Testaccio is one of those places you would pass by without looking twice. Until you know what it is. I find it completely intriguing. As you walk up the hill what look like broken stones along the path are actually pieces of broken terracotta jars.

WHAT'S NEARBY

Mt Testaccio isn't far from the **Pyramid of Cestius** and the **Cemetery for Non-Catholic Foreigners**. It is quite close to the Farmers' Market but it is perhaps a little far to walk from central Rome.

There will be a bus you can catch, or taking a taxi from the Trastevere area it won't be expensive. The closest metro station that I know of is Pirimide, but you still have a decent walk from there.

7. Galleria Sciarra

Two things I have learned over the years about Rome are that it will never stop surprising me with fascinating things to see, and furthermore some of the most incredible spots are hidden in broad daylight, right under your nose. Like this one.

I would guess that while in Rome most tourists wind up at pickpocket central, the Trevi Fountain. Catch it at sunrise or after sunset when the crowds and the thieves have moved on for the day and it is quite wonderful, but during the day it gets very crowded. Which is fine. Leave the crowds there and slip two minutes down the street to this gem, the Galleria Sciarra, for something completely different.

Hidden in plain view, across the street from McDonalds, is the Palazzo Sciarra. Relatively nondescript from the outside, you walk in through a beautifully ornate entrance arch (look up at the ceiling and take it all in before going further) and into the central courtyard, where color explodes all around you! From the bleached white marble and travertine that covers Rome, you have now entered the brilliantly colored art nouveau world of painter Giuseppe Cellini.

The courtyard walls, all four storeys of them, are entirely frescoed. It is sensational. Pillars rise up to heaven painted in beautiful scrolls of flowers and vines, accenting and framing the body of the building which is painted in a late nineteenth century style with the theme of the glorification of women. So far the frescoes you have seen while in Rome have been from as far back as 2500 BC through to the Baroque era. These ones date to around 1890. And did I mention they cover every surface?? They really are fabulous!

You will also notice a change in the architecture as you walk into the courtyard. This is what is known as *Liberty Style* or *Italian Liberty Style* architecture, and is perfect with this style of fresco, the two being of the same period and the same art nouveau movement. The frescoes are protected from the elements by a vaulted glass and iron ceiling.

Built between 1885 and 1888, the opulent Galleria Sciarra started out as the courtyard for the Palazzo Sciarra Colonna. The Sciarra were a wealthy and influential family. At some point the family had hoped or planned to make this a shopping mall — it would have been the most beautiful shopping arcade, but I'm glad that happen. Now as far as I know, it is currently used as offices.

GETTING THERE

Galleria Sciarra is open to the public during business hours. If you find your way in here you will notice most of those you encounter are local folk using the covered walkway to get from Piazza dell 'Oratorio to Via Marco Minghetti. (Inured to the never ending beauty of Rome, you seldom see the locals look up at the artwork. I, on the other hand am the idiot in the center of the courtyard, slowly turning round in circles, looking up and trying to take it all in.)

Address: Galleria Sciarra, Piazza dell' Oratorio.

WHAT'S NEARBY

You are right by the **Trevi Fountain** and the **Via del Corso**, which is the main shopping street in Rome. Galleria Sciarra is very close both to the **Pantheon** and the **Spanish Steps**. A few minutes walk up the street and you get to **Piazza del Popolo** and then the **Villa Borghese**.

8. Michaelangelo's Flowers

This is one of those Rome secrets that brings me no end of joy and that I get a huge kick out of showing my Glam Italia travelers. You can sit in Piazza Farnese for ages people-watching, and everyone blows right by, not seeing the secret, and none the wiser.

PALAZZO FARNESE

Palazzo Farnese, the big palace in Piazza Farnese that greets you as you walk in from Campo de Fiori, is one of the most important Renaissance palaces in Rome. It is owned by the Italian Republic but is currently home to the French Embassy. You will see armed guards outside, confirming that you are in the right place. Another landmark to orient yourself is the giant pair of bath fountains sitting in the piazza, pilfered from the Baths of Caracalla.

The palazzo was designed in 1517 for the wealthy Farnese family, but was later redesigned and enlarged when Alessandro Farnese became Pope Paul III. (Being that the pope is supposedly the voice of God, or at least his right hand man on Earth, it is astounding how many popes throughout history were not in fact pious men of faith, servitude and sacrifice, but were more or less varying versions of Trump — wealthy and influential men who could buy anything... But I digress.) When Alessandro became pope he brought in other architects to make the palace more magnificent, including Michelangelo, who worked on the redesign and completion of the third floor.

Palazzo Farnese is remarkable on many many levels and it is worth taking a tour of the artwork inside. There is, amongst the many rooms filled with jaw dropping art, something of greater note to be found in the Farnese Gallery: a fresco cycle called *The Loves of the Gods*, by Annibale Carracci. You will want to see it because it is spectacular. (Remember Annibale Carracci? He was the nemesis of our friend Caravaggio and he painted the altarpiece at the Santa Maria del Popolo. Caravaggio painted a giant horse's ass aiming right at it.)

This is also where you'll find Carracci's work, *The Judgement of Hercules*. (That was the painting where Caravaggio made fun of Carracci's ugly depiction of Vice, from Virtue and Vice — in his painting *Rest on the Flight into Egypt*, Caravaggio painted an ass peeping from behind a tree at an angel he had based on Carracci's

Vice. But unlike Carracci's character, Caravaggio made his angel lovely.) These artists were so brilliant but also hilariously *petty*!

MICHAELANGELO'S FLOWERS

From outside, look up to the third floor and you will see a large, deep cornice reaching out from the facade of the building, creating shadow when the hot Roman sun is beating down. Now walk along, following the cornice as it wraps its way around the palazzo and look up. Michelanglo created 220 plaster flowers, each the size of a patio table, and no two alike. These flowers, *Michelangelo's flowers*, look down at you from the underside of the cornice. Everyone walks right on past, not knowing to look up and not realizing they are there.

In his fantastic book *Four Seasons in Rome*, Anthony Doerr ponders how long making something like that would have taken? That question has burned itself into my brain, and on more than one occasion I have found myself standing under the cornice, looking up at the flowers for so long I thought my neck might snap right off, wondering myself, *how long would something like that take to create?*

ILLUMINATING

Before we leave Piazza Farnese I want to highlight one more "secret" sight.

If you walk through here after dark (and I definitely recommend you do), look up. When the lights turn on inside the palazzo and the other buildings in the piazza they illuminate frescoed ceilings that remain hidden during the day.

MICHELANGELO'S UNFINISHED BRIDGE

With your back to the bathtub fountains and Campo de Fiori, walk along the side of Palazzo Farnese under Michelangelo's flowers, along Via del Mascherone towards the river. At the end of the palazzo you will see in front of you a fountain called Fontana del Mascherone, which is a large face drooling water into a tub below it. It's pretty cool. This is at the cross street of Via Giulia and Via del Mascherone. Now turn right and you will see a big archway bisected by the road. This is Michelangelo's Unfinished Bridge.

Back when he was working on Palazzo Farnese, Michelangelo had the auspicious idea to build a bridge from the back side of the palazzo, where the garden area was, across the river, to connect the palace to the Vigna Farnese (Alessandro's property on the other bank). That property was adjacent to the Chigi Villa that Alessandro went on to buy and rename Villa Farnesina. It would have been quite something being able to walk across a private bridge from one property to the next, but the grand plan was never completed. All we are left with is this beautiful arch.

I have taken ridiculous numbers of photos of Michelangelo's Unfinished Bridge and of the fountain and, just as I take endless night time shots of St Peter's Dome from the Garibaldi Bridge (see my chapter on *The Best Places to Watch the Sunset in Rome*), I know I will keep taking more!

WHAT'S NEARBY

From here in the heart of Rome there are endless exciting things to see within a mile or so of where you are standing. Head back through the Piazza Farnese and you will find yourself in **Campo de Fiori**.

Wander to the back end of Campo de Fiori and you will find **Da Pancrazio** for lunch and some ancient ruins, (see the chapter on *Underground Rome*) or walk straight and cross the street into **Piazza Navona**, magnificent in its own right, and only two minutes around the corner from **San Luigi dei Francesi** with the Caravaggios of St Matthew.

From Michelangelo's Unfinished Bridge you have more options. With your back to the bridge stay on the left hand sidewalk and head two blocks to Via Arenula. Before you get there you will pass the best gelato shop in all of Rome, **Gelataria del Teatro**. You have to stop there before turning left on Via Arenula! On Arenula walk straight for another couple of blocks and you will be at **Largo Argentina**, or instead, shortly after turning left on Arenula turn right into the **Jewish Ghetto**.

Want more? Both the bridge that crosses the river by Michelangelo's Unfinished Bridge, the **Ponte Sisto**, and the bridge past the gelato shop that intersects with Via Arenula, the **Garibaldi Bridge**, take you over the Tiber and into the **Trastevere**. There is so much to see and do right inside this relatively small section of Rome!

9. The Doll Hospital

Firstly let me say this is not the kind of doll hospital you want to take your kids to unless you want them to be serial killers. It is however, weird and fantastically creepy and has no doubt been the inspiration for many horror movies! It certainly gives me the screaming heebee-geebees — I've never understood clown-phobia, but I do remember watching the *Trilogy of Terror* with Karen Black when I was in my teens and my brothers scaring me by sliding knives back and forth under my bedroom door like the psycho doll in the movie. I'm blaming that for the creepy effect this place has on me!

The Doll Hospital is literally just that: a family business that specializes in the repair of antique dolls. They repair other things too, but dolls are what they are best known for. This teeny tiny shop is only 15 square meters, although it does have a downstairs storeroom as well. The ancient shop window is suitably macabre, with vacant eyed doll heads, broken and haunting, stacked all the way up to a shelf of evil looking owls (why??). The side windows are full of doll body parts. The outdoor window frames are suitably weather beaten, adding plausibility to the moniker "*Little shop of horrors*".

Its real name is *Restauri Artistici Squatriti* and the proprietors are world renowned restoration specialists. Antique porcelain dolls are sent to them from all around the globe for the painstaking perfectionism of their work.

Inside the store, which smells of glues and solvents, you can find Federico Squatriti and his mother Gelsomina working away, breathing new life into dolls, some of which are centuries old. Every surface in the shop is covered with doll parts, broken figurines and toys as well as vases, antique plates and even ancient Roman platters all waiting for repair.

I haven't seen any younger members of the Squatriti family inside the doll hospital, so I wonder if this master craft will die along with the master-craftsman when Federico becomes too old to work.

GETTING THERE

This is a shop is therefore open to the public.

Address: Restauri Artistici Squatriti, Via di Ripetta 29.

What's Nearby

Via di Ripetta is maybe two minutes walk from **Piazza del Popolo**, where you can drop in at **Santa Maria del Popolo** to see some Caravaggios before heading up to **Villa Borghese** and then to the **Terrazza Pincio** for sunset.

Heading away from Piazza del Popolo you are only a few minutes from **Ara Pacis** and the **Mausoleum of Augustus**. Follow the river a little further and you reach the **Bridge of Angels** and **Hadrian's Mausoleum**, the **Castel Sant'Angelo**. A little more inland from the river it will take you between five and ten minutes to walk to **Piazza di Spagna,** from where you can wander along to the **Trevi Fountain**, the **Pantheon** and **Piazza Navona**.

10. The Coppede District

Welcome to fantasty-land! The Coppede is Rome's smallest district and also its most whimsical. Hidden away behind the main streets of the Quartiere Trieste between Via Tagliamento and Piazza Buenos Aires, this is Rome's secret neighborhood. And it looks nothing like the rest of Rome.

The Coppede is elaborate, bizarre and completely gorgeous. Built between 1913 and 1927, it was the brainchild of architect Gino Coppede using nature as his inspiration. Multiple architectural styles all swirl around in a delirious frenzy: art nouveau, Baroque, medieval, ancient Greek. Frescoed exteriors, exciting colors and unusual shapes mixed up together make these buildings exciting to look at. *And* fantastic to photograph! If you want some Instagram images from Rome that are completely different, this is the place to come.

The closest thing I can compare this to is Gaudi's Barcelona, possibly because of the elaborate ironwork and the swirling, moving lines. Yet it is also quite different from Gaudi.

GETTING THERE

The address for the Coppede is Piazza Mincio, Roma, situated behind Villa Borghese.

I will walk almost anywhere in Rome but this one is a little far. Jump in a cab from Piazza del Popolo or from the Pinciana gate of the Villa Borghese park.

11. The Owl House

If you have had enough of ancient architecture and want to see something completely different while in Rome, the House of Owls might be just your thing. This is best added to your itinerary if you are in the city for more than just a few days and if you have seen the big sites already.

Hidden on the grounds of the Villa Torlonia, the House of Owls was built in 1840 by Prince Alessandro Torlonia as a place for his family to escape and relax with friends for the evening when they didn't want to be formal. It initially resembled a Swiss chalet but over the following 80 years the exterior underwent an endless series of unusual changes. Turrets were constructed, stained glass windows were added on every floor with no two alike, window frames staggered like a staircase up the side of a wall. There are archways and porticoes and quite frankly, no end of oddities. It is very, very unusual. There is a concrete snake coiled and working its way up a wall and windows crisscrossed with what look like petrified sticks from a haunted forest. This architecture looks like mania. It reminds me a little of the Winchester mansion in California.

WHY OWLS?

The building became known as the House of Owls in 1916, partly due to a stained glass window depicting two stylized owls among ivy, and partly because the motif of the owl was also used extensively throughout the house in the decorations and furnishings. The house's inhabitant, Prince Giovanni Torlonia the Younger, was an interesting, mysterious fellow who loved esoteric symbolism. He lived in the house until he died in 1938.

PRINCE GIOVANNI'S STORY

There was more than one prince, actually. The Torlonia were a noble family from Rome who acquired their huge fortune by managing the Vatican finances.

The first Torlonia to 'make it' was Marino, who went from a very humble background in Auvergne, France, to becoming a very rich cloth merchant and money lender in Rome in the mid 1700's. This became the foundation of the family bank established by his son Giovanni.

Giovanni got hooked up with the Vatican, and in return for doing a good job with the cash was named Duke of Bracciano and Count of Pisciarelli by Pope Pius VI in 1794. In 1803 Pope Pius VII made him

Marquess of Romavecchia e Turrita and the first Prince of Civitella Cesi. He was given more titles too. Giovanni built the Villa Torlonia in Rome in 1806.

Villa Torlonia (the main villa here) sits in large park-like grounds under which a large third and fourth century Jewish catacomb was later found. In the 1920's Mussolini rented the villa for one lira per year, and lived there for many years. It was abandoned in 1945, fell into ruin, and sat empty for decades. In 1991 the House of Owls, which is on the grounds of the big villa, was ruined by vandals and fire, but extensive restorations began in 1992 and now both the villa and the House of Owls are museums.

GETTING THERE

If you are in the mood for quirky, for something a little offbeat and different, this one may be right up your alley! Google it first, because unlike most things in this book it takes a little effort to get to, and can chew up a lot of time.

Address: Museum of Casina delle Civette, Via Nomentana 70.

WHAT'S NEARBY

You are quite close to the **Coppede** district and can walk between the two. The surrounding **Trieste** district is one of Rome's loveliest residential areas.

Piazza Navona

6.

Piazza Navona

This is considered to be the loveliest piazza in all of Rome.

I have always adored Piazza Navona but got an entirely new appreciation for it when I went there with my (then) 10-year-old son, Tommy. We were staying in an apartment in the Trastevere, and all day, every day, walked the length and breadth of central Rome. Multiple times per day we would return to Piazza Navona, not only for its beauty and its quintessential Roman ambience, but also because a jazz quartet set up shop every day beside the Fontana del Moro, and would play most of the day. Tommy is a jazz saxophonist and at that time had only been playing for two or three years. He was completely enthralled with this band. It was his first time really experiencing street music, especially street music of his genre. The saxophone player, an older gentleman named Giorgio, saw that Tommy was captivated, and during breaks would come and sit beside him and pat him on the back. Giorgio didn't speak any English, and at the time my grasp of Italian was pretty rudimentary, but he managed to tell me he was a music professor at one of the universities and that playing street music helped supplement his income. He was interested to learn about Tommy's musicianship and tried to give him encouragement to keep at it. I wish the two could meet up again now!

Every evening that summer in Rome, while out strolling we would invariably end up back in Piazza Navona where an entirely different crowd would be out and about enjoying the evening. It really was wonderful.

Piazza Navona had an auspicious beginning. As you now know (it's covered in the *Underground Rome* section of this book), Domitian originally built Piazza Navona as an athletic stadium for running races and sports that didn't require chariots or gladiators. It was known as the *Circus Agonalis*, named for the *agones* (athletic games) that took place there. Over time it evolved into *in avona* and then to *Navona*.

At the end of the fifteenth century Piazza Navona became a public space and the city market was moved there from the Campidoglio. During his reign from 1644 to 1655, Pope Innocent X transformed the market space into one of the leading examples of Baroque Roman architecture, using the skills of Bernini and Borromini. Innocent X's family palace, the Palazzo Pamphilj, faces the piazza.

Some of the rivalry between Bernini and Borromini played out in this very piazza, making the space even more interesting on many levels, including architecturally. The result of their rivalry gave us one of the most beautiful piazzas in all of Rome.

FOUNTAIN OF THE MOOR — *FONTANA DEL MORO*

There are three incredible fountains in Piazza Navona, and each has a story. The first you will see as you come in to the piazza from the south side, or the side closest to Campo de Fiori, is the *Fontana del Moro* (Fountain of the Moor). You will notice as you walk around this masterpiece that it doesn't have a bad angle. It is perfection from every direction. The Fountain of the Moor was originally sculpted by Giacomo della Porta in 1575 and featured a basin with four large tritons looking outward. In 1673 Bernini added the center statue of the moor wrestling the dolphin.

The originals of these three fountains are safe and sound at the Villa Borghese since 1909, and these are actually replicas, which is fortunate as on September 3rd, 2011 a lunatic with a hammer smashed one of the triton faces of the Fountain of the Moor, breaking off the pieces covering the ears. The fountain was drained, the pieces recovered and the mask was repaired.

FOUNTAIN OF NEPTUNE — *FONTANA DEL NETTUNO*

At the opposite end of the piazza, the end that leads to the Pantheon, is the *Fontana del Nettuno*. This was built in 1574 by Giacomo della Porta. In 1878 a sculptor by the name of Antonio della Bitta carved the statue of Neptune which gave it the vertical balance it needed to offset the height of the *Fountain of the Moor*.

FOUNTAIN OF THE FOUR RIVERS — *FONTANA DEI QUATTRO FIUMI*

The center fountain is the *Fontana dei Quattro Fiumi*. This is the largest of the three fountains, and it sits right in the middle of the piazza. Originally the commission was given to Borromini in 1651, but ultimately it was taken over by Bernini (see details of their feud in my earlier section on churches). The rivers represent the four major rivers of the four continents through which the papal authority had spread: Rio de la Plata represents the Americas, the Nile represents Africa, the Danube represents Europe, and the Ganges represents Asia.

A random fact you may find interesting is that my favorite of the old popes, the one with the best name of them all, Innocent X, created a tradition where every summer the drains of these three fountains would be covered, allowing the water to pool so that the people could bathe or at least cool off. This tradition was maintained for two centuries until 1866 when Pope Pius IX put an end to all the fun. What a jerk.

OBELISK AGONALIS

Did you know that Rome is the city with the most obelisks in the world?? It has eight Egyptian obelisks and five Roman obelisks, as well as some more modern ones. There was a time when all things Egyptian were considered madly chic and were much coveted. Think back to Antony and Cleopatra being the most glam couple on the planet and it all makes sense.

The *Obelisk Agonalis* was originally commissioned by Domitian for the temple of Serapis. It was moved to the *Circus of Maxentius* (by Maxentius), and in 1651 Bernini had it moved in pieces to the *Fontana dei Quattro Fiumi* in Piazza Navona.

PALAZZO PAMPHILJ

The Pamphilj Palace is inextricably intertwined with the story of one of my favorite wicked women, Olimpia Maidalchini (she also features in the *Ghosts of Rome* section of this book). She was the Mistress of the Vatican, the Secret Female pope — what's not to love??

Olimpia came from somewhat humble beginnings. She caught herself a wealthy husband who conveniently died quite quickly, leaving her with his wealth and status. At age 20, she remarried one of the wealthiest men in all of Italy, Pamphilio Pamphilj, who was 30 years her senior. Pamphilio was the brother of Cardinal Giambattista Pamphilj, who became Pope Innocent X.

Olimpia and Innocent X became incredibly close, so close that they were rumored to be lovers. Olimpia influenced Innocent X's every move. When she decided that she and hubby Pamphilio needed a palace befitting her new status, she convinced Not-So-Innocent-X to build her one. He decided (or she did, who knows?) to replace a building on their land (on Piazza Navona) with a grand palace built by the leading architect of the time, Girolamo Rainaldi. Deciding that her magnificent new palace needed even more grandeur, Olimpia persuaded lover boy to commission three fountains to occupy space in the piazza outside the front door. Innocent X wanted his favorite architect and sculptor, Francesco Borromini, for the project. He specifically disliked Borromini's arch rival and nemesis Gianlorenzo Bernini for a beautifully petty reason — Bernini had been the protege of the previous pope, Urban VIII, who Innocent X couldn't stand. Bernini however had other plans. He wanted a piece of this action and knew exactly how to get it: he used the influence of Olimpia. At this point you couldn't get to see the pope unless you went through her, so he made her a silver sculpture of the fountain he had planned. She loved it, and next thing you know the pope hired Bernini.

Today the Palazzo Pamphilj is the home of the Brazilian Embassy, as it has been since 1920.

The Church of Sant'Agnese in Agone

We're not quite done with Olimpia just yet.

While her palace was being built, Olimpia decided she needed a family church as well, so Innocent X hired Rainaldi and his son Carlo to build it. The original church on that site had been built in the eighth century, and had been dedicated to Saint Agnes who was martyred on that spot 2000 years ago.

Borromini built the church gallery and took over the design for the facade of the church, which was not only beautiful but clever too. The problem with typical church design is that when you are standing outside, looking up, you can't see the top. So Borromini made the facade of this church concave so that you can stand below and look up and still see the dome.

Borromini lost the commission when Innocent X died and it reverted back to Rainaldi, who kept most of what Borromini had designed. The church was completed in 1670.

PIAZZA NAVONA TODAY

In 1861 the market moved from Piazza Navona across the street to Campo de Fiori. The traditional market that for centuries had serviced the local population has now become mostly a tourist attraction, although it is still a good place to buy flowers, fruit and vegetables.

If you are in Rome at Christmas time, Piazza Navona holds a Christmas market which is a must-see.

Even if you were unaware of its history, Piazza Navona is a special place to spend time in Rome. The long sides of the former stadium are now lined with restaurants where you can sit at sidewalk tables and drink pricey glasses of wine or cups of coffee while watching the world go by.

All summer long the piazza is filled with artists, entertainers and musicians. It looks, sounds and *feels* like your dream of Rome.

WHAT'S NEARBY

Piazza Navona is in the very heart of Rome. It is across the street from **Campo de Fiori**, two minutes from the church of **San Luigi dei Francesi** and Caravaggio's St Matthew paintings. From the north end of the piazza it is just a few minutes walk to the **Pantheon** (follow the signs) and **Santa Maria Sopra Minerva** church with the little elephant statue outside.

From Piazza Navona if you turn left on Via Corso Vittorio Emanuelle II (instead of crossing the street to go to Campo de Fiori and Piazza Farnese) it will take you five minutes or less to walk to **Largo Argentina** and the cat sanctuary, another two minutes to **Crypta Balbi** and just a few minutes to **Piazza Venezia**, gateway to **Palazzo Valentini**, the Wedding Cake, **Trajan's Column** and **Trajan's Market**, the **Roman Forum** and the **Colosseum**.

Also just off the Via Corso Vittoria Emanuelle II you can turn left on Via del Corso and walk up to **Galleria Doria Pamphilj** art gallery and palace apartments.

7.

The Battle of Borromini and Bernini

There's nothing quite like a good rivalry between two major artists!

In the seventeenth century two men completely transformed Rome. They left a legacy of beauty still seen everywhere you look. The most beautiful piazzas, the most beautiful churches the most beautiful buildings are the creation of these two visionary geniuses. Walk through the Vatican and Piazza Navona and you are surrounded by their work, their exquisite Baroque architecture, their beautiful sculptures. And their legendary rivalry!

The Baroque period was a time when the plethora of enormous commissions handed down by popes and cardinals not only created many of the exquisite and clever buildings that still dominate the Roman skyline, but also incited intense rivalries amongst artists and noble families.

Two of these artists embroiled in a bitter rivalry, each trying to win as many commissions as possible and each leaving an indelible mark on history, on sculpture, on architecture and on Rome, were Bernini and Borromini.

Gian Lorenzo Bernini was born in Naples, the son of a sculptor. He lead a huge studio with many employees and became the preferred architect of seven popes. He was popular and built great relationships with the wealthiest and most powerful patrons in Rome.

Francesco Borromini was from Lombardy. He was an architect by profession, preferred to work by himself and work slowly. He was a loner, was quick tempered, impulsive and resentful. He was innovative and eccentric and ultimately overshadowed by Bernini.

Their competition became the stuff of popular legend. The ultimate symbol of their rivalry can be seen in Piazza Navona, which may just be Rome's loveliest piazza. It is also the home of some of Rome's most celebrated ghosts (see the Ghosts of Rome chapter) was the home of a pope with a porn-star name (Innocent X) and a mistress who ran the show - some of the best stories come out of Piazza Navona!

Bernini's Fountain of the Four Rivers in Piazza Navona sits opposite Borromini's Church of Sant' Agnese in Agone. At the base of Bernini's fountain are four allegorical statues representing the four major rivers of the world. Legend has it that the statue of the Rio de le Plata is raising his hands above his head to block the ghastly sight of Borromini's church, and the Nile statue shields itself from it by hiding under a veil. This story although indicative of their ongoing fight is in fact just legend, because the statues were completed years before the church was built.

The two artists fought over the Palace of the Propagation of the Faith. Bernini had been commissioned to enlarge the building but when Pope Urban VIII died the job was given to Borromini instead. Bernini lived next door to the palace, so Borromini had a pair of donkey's ears carved into the side of the building. Not to be outdone, Bernini had a penis sculpted onto the side of his house, pointing at

Borromini and his team. Neither is still visible - deemed indecent both were removed.

The two worked together in St Peter's Basilica and at the Barberini Palace, where Borromini changed and finished work started by Bernini.

Innocent X preferred working with Borromini, but after the pope's death much of the big work dried up for him, with Bernini getting the best commissions.

One of the most incredible examples of Borromini's genius, modern vision and innovative style was the church of St Charles at the Four Fountains (San Carlo alle Quattro Fontane in the chapter on 12 Interesting Churches). He wanted to be buried here inside his masterpiece church but because he ended up committing suicide he was rejected and ultimately was buried at St John of the Florentines.

Bernini lived on for another decade, working up until 2 weeks before he died. He was buried with pomp and circumstance in the church of Santa Maria in Maggiore.

As you explore Rome pay attention to all the Baroque architecture and see more of the rivalry between these dueling geniuses. Walking tours of Baroque Rome are available, teaching you more about Bernini and Borromini, and how they changed the face of Rome.

Caravaggios in Rome

8.

The Caravaggios in Rome and Where to Find Them

1. San Luigi dei Francese

2. Santa Maria del Popolo

3. Galleria Borghese

4. Chiesa Sant'Agostino

5. Palazzo Barberini

6. Galleria Doria Pamphilij

7. Odescalchi Balbi Collection

8. The Capitoline Museums

9. The Vatican Museums

I don't know about you, but I like my artists to be a bit crazy.

I want my accountants and doctors completely sane and structured to the point of being boring. Let them live between two solid lines, eat the exact same meals every day, get up and go to bed at exactly the same time every day of their lives, never deviate. But my favorite artists are more interesting if they are deviants. The more they have suffered, the crazier they are, and the more exciting both they and their art become. I could be wrong but I would imagine more people know Van Gogh than Monet or Renoir? I have seen every one of his works in every city I've been to in the world. I ache for Vincent's beautiful, tortured soul. I have gone to every exhibition of his work in any city I have been even slightly close to, have driven six hours through the night just to have one day with him, then turned around and driven six hours back. As much as I love his art it is also the story of his life that draws me to him. It's a little like that with Baroque artist Caravaggio and me. This cat was a straight up crazy genius.

ANDREW GRAHAM-DIXON

I have to confess that I was really late to the Caravaggio party. My life has been one giant art obsession, I am often deeply immersed in some art movement, the works of some painter or sculptor or sketcher or etcher. Although I knew of Caravaggio, he wasn't really on my radar until a few years ago, when he exploded into my consciousness and became a new art obsession. I lay 100% of the blame at the feet of one man: an art historian by the name of Andrew Graham-Dixon.

Most art historians seem a bit stuffy to me. I wouldn't exactly call them exciting. They have immense knowledge, are great on facts and figures, but aren't really compelling. Then I found this British fellow called Andrew Graham-Dixon. He writes books and does TV shows (which is where I discovered him) and stands out from the others because he tells stories in a way that I can immediately relate to. I found myself really paying attention when he was speaking, and leaning in closer to the TV — I didn't want to miss anything.

He is always excited to talk about any given piece of art but I started noticing this whole different thing happening when he talked about Caravaggio. He wasn't just enthralled, he became *impassioned*. And he made Caravaggio sound so *exciting. A*nd completely crazy. In other words, my kind of artist. So, rather than just look at a Caravaggio in a book I decided to go visit one the next time I was in Rome. I wanted to see for myself what it was all about.

MY FIRST CARAVAGGIO

I found myself trudging through torrential rain in the Eternal City, decked out in an ineffective pink rain poncho, soaked to the bone, on my way to San Luigi dei Francesi, to see Caravaggio's St Matthew paintings. For anything else I would have just added it to the *Things To Do Next Time* list and found somewhere warm and dry to hide out with a glass of wine.

But thanks to Andrew Graham-Dixon I kept going, arriving at the church completely sodden and wondering if I would get pneumonia for my efforts. I was so busy detaching myself from the stupid plastic poncho and wiping water off my face that I didn't get any warning. I was standing at the railing, I looked up and I remember feeling like my brain exploded. There was St Matthew spinning as the angel twirled down from above to see him. It was majestic! There was so much movement in the painting, the look on St Matthew's face, his bright orange robes; it was frenetic, yet calm. It sucked the breath right out of me. My shoes were squishing with water, I was dripping all over the floor and I literally couldn't move. I don't think I could even blink.

A tour guide was explaining the St Matthews to a group of Asian tourists, and as they moved on he walked over to me and said, *I saw how you reacted to the painting. It still hits me that way every time.*

When I got back home to the US, I ordered Andrew Graham-Dixon's book about the artist, *Caravaggio, A Life Sacred and Profane*, which I consider to be the bible on Caravaggio.

When writing a book about Rome, I knew I had to talk about the Caravaggios there. I thought I'd write maybe a paragraph or two on each painting, but the stories got away on me and this section of the book is now much larger than planned. I really hope you will visit at least one of these during your visit to Rome, and that at least one person who reads this book will catch the excitement I feel about Caravaggio and his paintings, and feel the magic I feel when I look at them. Plus some of the stories are hilarious…

CARAVAGGIO'S STORY

Caravaggio is perhaps the most important painter since Michelangelo.

He revolutionized painting with his use of chiaroscuro (an effect caused by contrasting light and dark) and realism and even today, 400 years on, is still influencing art.

Michelangelo Merisi of Caravaggio in Lombardy became known simply as Caravaggio. His paintings, like his life, were dramatic, obsessed with sexuality and sensuality, violence and fear. He lived a low life drama of bars and brothels, and eventually murder. He spent years of his short life on the run with a bounty on his head, went to jail at least twice (in Rome and in Malta) was beaten up and left for dead in Naples, along the way becoming increasingly deranged and dangerous. And through it all he painted some of the greatest art of all time.

Caravaggio was a rebel. At a time when art was about creating ethereal creatures, separate and superior to the average person, he painted with a realism that was considered blasphemous. His subjects were gritty; his martyrs looked and dressed like normal folk. He brought them down to our level to the point they nearly fall out of some of the paintings. While his contemporaries painted peaceful and beautiful figures floating up to heaven, Caravaggio's figures were twisting, heaving, frenetic and coiling, giving you a sense of anxiety and of what was about to happen next. Others were just plain and simple beauty, their naturalism making that beauty tangible and relatable.

One of the things I love so much about Caravaggio is his choice of models. He took people off the street – prostitutes, beggars and street kids, drunks and down and outers, and painted them as religious figures. Mary the prostitute from Piazza Navona, St Peter and St Matthew the homeless drunks from around the corner.

Furthermore, a pioneer of chiaroscuro, he sent beams of light slicing through his paintings, directing your eye where he wanted you to look, adding to the endless drama of his eternal opposites, lightness and dark, violence and beauty, the sacred and the profane.

Caravaggio was an exciting madman. Not someone you would ever want to meet, but someone fascinating to learn about.

The following is a list of places in Rome where you can find the Caravaggios. In each you learn not only the paintings themselves but the crazy stories that go with them, some of which are very funny. I sincerely hope you will visit at least one of these while you are in Rome

1. San Luigi dei Francesi

If you only make time to see one set of Caravaggios in Rome, let this be the one. These three works are simply magnificent.

The Caravaggios at the church of San Luigi dei Francesi were the first that I visited in Rome. I was new to Caravaggio and had made a list of places in Rome that had his work. This one happened to be first on my list. When the heavens opened and I got soaked, I nearly turned around and went home. When I finally got there I found the church was closing for lunch in 20 minutes, I honestly came so close to just giving up on it! Instead, I went in for a quick look.

Ever since that fateful day I have made a point of dropping by every time I am in Rome, even if only for a few minutes. Many say the paintings in the church of San Luigi dei Francesi are Caravaggio's most powerful work. Even if you are soaked to the bone, have squishy shoes and a 20 minute window to see these works, make the effort and give them a chance to take your breath away.

THE CALLING OF ST MATTHEW

The cycle is made up of three stories involving St Matthew and are some of Caravaggio's earliest religious works. They hang in the Contarelli Chapel, and are enormous and compelling.

The first, on your left, is *The Calling Of St Matthew*. I try to look at it without seeing the other two first. In this painting you meet the realism Caravaggio was famous for — his people don't look stylized or other worldly, instead they look like real people. This was unusual — people weren't painted to look flawed and gritty at that time.

If you are new to Caravaggio this is a perfect work to learn about his use of chiaroscuro. Normally the light comes from a specific direction and falls unevenly on the subject. In this case it is light streaming through a window, illuminating St Matthew, the tax collector, counting money at the table. He even has a coin in his hat. The other people at the table are also lit up while Jesus and St Peter, standing below the window are bathed in darkness. St Matthew looks a little unnerved, his finger pointing at himself as if to say, *Who, me?*

This is the calmest and most normal of the three paintings, yet 400 years ago when it was painted it was provocative and modern. St Matthew and his crew are wearing contemporary Roman clothes, while Jesus and St Peter are dressed in biblical fashion.

THE INSPIRATION OF ST MATTHEW

The center painting is *The Inspiration of St Matthew*, also known as *St Matthew and the Angel*. At first glance it is quite simple, only two elements, St Matthew and the angel. But stand and look at it for a moment and you will see swirling movement and a frantic energy to it. There are no absolute verticals or horizontals in this picture. Everything is off kilter. The angel descends at an angle with eggshell robes swirling around her. St Matthew's bright orange robes fall from one shoulder and slip from the other as he spins around to see the angel. One knee lifts away from his prayer stool as his leg leaps up and he seems to hang onto his desk for support. You feel his surprise, and if you are against the balustrade you will find yourself holding on to keep your balance. Genius.

THE MARTYRDOM OF ST MATTHEW

The third painting is *The Martyrdom of St Matthew*. This painting has hung here since 1600. It epitomizes the genius and madness of Caravaggio in that you feel the chaos, the violence, the savagery. It is unsettling and yet brilliant.

The Martyrdom depicts the death of St Matthew, who was murdered on the orders of the King of Ethiopia, Hirticus. Hirticus wanted to marry his niece Iphigenia, the abbess of a convent. St Matthew forbade the marriage and so Hirticus had him killed.

St Matthew lies beside a sunken baptismal font as his near naked assassin grabs his wrist with one hand while swinging his sword to stab him with the other. (In Rome, where Caravaggio was painting, baptism was performed by sprinkling water over the head, but in Milan where he grew up baptism was by immersion, symbolizing death, burial and resurrection.) At first glance it looks as though St Matthew has his hand up to ward off the blow, but look higher and you see an angel reaching down to him with a palm frond. There is some Christian iconography here: the palm branch is associated with the victory of martyrs and the victory of the spirit over the flesh, so perhaps St Matthew isn't cowering in fear but instead acknowledging in triumph that although his body may die his spirit will go on?

Look closer and you will see a trickle of blood coming from his side. He has already been wounded, echoing the wound in Jesus' side. The altar appears to have the symbol of the Maltese Cross on it, the symbol of the Christian Warrior. Malta would feature in

Caravaggio's life just a few short years from this time. Also note the single candle burning on the altar — some say it symbolizes the fragility and inevitable end of human life, others say it is the eye of God, ever-present and witnessing the sacrifice of the martyr.

As the assassination is going on we see everyone around St Matthew panicking and fleeing. No one is moving toward him to help him, they are all scrambling to get away. Behind and to the left of the assassin we see a dark haired, bearded fellow look back in fear. This is Caravaggio himself — a self-portrait. I choose to believe Andrew Graham-Dixon's interpretation of this feature: he says, "If Caravaggio had actually been there, he suggests he would have had no more courage than anyone else. He would have fled like the others, leaving the martyr to his fate. According to the logic of his own narrative, he remains unbaptized and therefore outside the circle of the blessed. He is a man running away, out of the church, into the street." (*Caravaggio, A Life Sacred and Profane*).

I want to leave you with one last, fantastical thought on the Caravaggios in the Contarelli Chapel. The paintings are in darkness inside the church, you have to insert a coin to light them up. Hopefully while there you will experience them without the light. They hang in the dark where they have always hung. In the 1600's they would have been in the same eerie darkness, lit only by a multitude of flickering candles. How unnerving must that have been for the local people? To see the subjects of these disruptive paintings, looking like them, dressed like them, telling their frantic story in the dim, moody light of the candles? Genius.

GETTING THERE

It closes for lunch, so check the hours of opening prior to heading over there.

WHAT'S NEARBY

The church of San Luigi dei Francesi is only a couple of minutes walk from **Piazza Navona**. Combine it with a visit to **Campo de Fiori, the Pantheon, and Piazza del Popolo in one direction, or Largo** Argentina and **Crypta Balbi** in the other.

2. Santa Maria del Popolo

I love the pettiness and snarkiness of artists and emperors in Rome. I think it makes the paintings more fun to see. My first time visiting Caravaggio at Santa Maria del Popolo I was unaware of this fantastic story, and just enjoyed the paintings. After I heard the story I had to go back to the church on my next visit to Rome and see it for myself. Now it is one of my favorites.

CARRACCI & CARAVAGGIO

In July 1600, Tiberio Cerasi (Pope Clement VIII's Treasurer General) bought the patronage rights to the old Foscari Chapel in the left transept of Santa Maria del Popolo. He promptly demolished it and had Carlo Maderno design and build the new Cerasi Chapel. He commissioned Rome's two rising stars to paint works for it — and two rivals.

Annibale Carracci got the coveted center spot above the altar. It's the first thing you see when you enter the chapel. He was commissioned to paint the *Assumption of the Virgin*, and painted it in the style of the time: beautiful, brightly colored; perfect subjects with perfect complexions, a great work but oddly juxtaposed with the dark, moody work of Caravaggio.

Caravaggio was awarded two paintings, one on either side of the altar. He wasn't happy that he didn't get the main attraction. He was commissioned to paint *The Conversion of St Paul* on the right hand side of the altarpiece, and *The Crucifixion of St Peter* on the left. These are the two most important works of art in the basilica and are considered to be unrivaled high points in western art. (Although personally, I prefer the St Matthew works.)

THE CONVERSION OF ST PAUL (SAUL)

His name was Saul but in the tradition of the Old Testament he became Paul. The story is that Saul's job was to persecute Christians, and he was on the road to Damascus when he was blinded by light and heard the voice of Christ say, "I am Jesus who you persecute. Arise and go into the city." The light was so bright that he was blinded for three days, after which he was rescued by the divine and became Paul.

This painting is a prime example of how Caravaggio changed the art world and became the most important painter since Michelangelo. If we think about what art had come before, Renaissance art was about perfect balance, where subjects were set further away from the viewer, to be observed in context of what surrounded them. This separation put them in the realm of the divine and made us, mere mortals, lower in status than the figures in the painting.

Caravaggio's painting of St Paul turns all of that on its ear. There is no wide scene with a background, no landscape, no architecture, nothing to distract us from the power of what is happening *in this moment*. It is immediate. Everything is right up in the foreground and fills the space from top to bottom, side to side. The horse is enormous. He is the biggest thing in this tableaux, and is a testament to Caravaggio's naturalism. He looks real. He is tended to by a groom who is in the shadow and oblivious to what is happening. The groom doesn't see the light of the divine. This makes the moment personal — only you, the viewer, and Saul know what is going on.

Then we have Saul, his back to us, almost falling out of the painting, lit up by God. Everything else is dark. He is on the ground, in the dirt. His helmet has fallen off, his sword askew and his horse is about to stomp on him. He is vulnerable. His body language is interesting in its real-ness. Rather than lying prone, his legs are apart with knees up and his arms reaching up. He looks as though he has just crashed to the ground, landing on his backside and lower back. It is immediate and we witness it as it happens.

In Renaissance art, bodies traditionally formed an ideal pyramid. Think of the shapes in a Madonna and Child painting with Mary's head as the top of the pyramid and the mass and width of the bodies making up the bottom bar of the triangular shape. It creates balance and harmony. What Caravaggio has done here with Saul is turn the pyramid upside down, upending the triangle, so that Saul's head is pointing toward us with the mass of his body as the pyramid base. It's topsy-turvy land. He has distorted the gravity line. Instead of the heaviest things being at the bottom of the painting, Caravaggio has made the horse the biggest feature and placed it at the top of the painting. Following an artistic period of form and balance, this would have been jarring to the viewer and no doubt very exciting.

Now think of the psychology behind this maneuver. Which painting would the people have been drawn to as they entered the Cerasi Chapel? Carracci's lovely but incredibly normal-looking work with all of its pretty colors? Or this crazy, brilliant new idea that almost explodes out of the frame at you?

And Caravaggio gets a last little petty revenge at Carracci. Instead of having the action in his painting directed forward to the altar (and Carracci's piece), he directs our eyes away and aims the horse's butt at Carracci! I love it!

THE CRUCIFIXION OF ST PETER

This subject was especially relevant to the people of Rome as this is where St Peter was crucified.

As with *The Conversion of St Paul,* this painting is cropped and zoomed in. We don't see the crowds of onlookers, we don't see the landscape. We are caught witnessing a moment in time, freeze-framed in a moment of action, weight and counterweight, coiling movement with a powerful sense of gravity. The energy in this picture is uncoiling and moving up and around. It is intensely physical.

Caravaggio loved to use local people as his models. They were no doubt cheap to hire, were probably people he hung out with, and it flew in the face of the establishment. Notice here that St Peter doesn't look serene or beatific, he looks like a crotchety old man with an old man's body. We are reminded that Peter was a humble fisherman before he was found by Christ. The model here was probably some homeless dude.

Renaissance art had no sense of weight or gravity or anything particularly physical, by contrast this is *intensely* physical. Starting with the Roman workman who has dug the hole and is now bent down under the cross ready to hoist it up. We see his dirty feet and the tension in his arms and legs as he is about to push upward, any second now. His backside is pointing right at us, about to push right out of the picture and into our space. (That must have seemed novel and scandalous at the time!) Peter's feet and the bottom of the cross are also about to push out of the picture and into us. Look at the realism in his feet, the way the skin puckers under the nails anchoring him to the cross — does it make you feel squeamish? Also look at the hand clasping at the nail hammered through it. There is more movement in the picture with Peter's knees angling toward us as gravity tips his body away, as if the upward movement of the cross has already begun.

The darkness makes the tension visceral, while God's light beams down on Peter. Notice we don't see any Roman faces — the three men are all looking away. We are left wondering, is that thin rope going to be strong enough? Are the men going to be strong enough to raise up that cross or will they drop it and have to start over?

If they were to have raised the cross, this old, weathered St Peter would be staring at Carracci's painting, upside down. If Caravaggio had painted it facing the other way, the workman's backside would be saluting it. I think Caravaggio got a little revenge here too, don't you?

WHAT'S NEARBY

From the Piazza del Popolo you can walk just a couple of minutes to **Villa Borghese Park**, and the **Galleria Borghese**. Of the streets radiating out from the piazza Via del Corso will take you along the big shopping street toward the **Pantheon** and **Piazza Navona**, Via del Babuino will drop you into the **Piazza di Spagna** and the **Spanish Steps**.

Walk a few blocks to the **Lungotevere** then wander along the river to **Augustus' Mausoleum** and **Ara Pacis**, and the market at **Piazza Borghese**, both of which are a block or so from the river, but the walk is so lovely.

Hips, knees and weather permitting continue along the river to **Ponte Sant'Angelo**, the bridge with the beautiful angel statues that leads you to the **Castel Sant'Angelo**.

3. Galleria Borghese

This gallery in the former Villa Borghese Pinciana, holds what is considered by many to be the greatest single collection of Caravaggios — a group of six paintings spanning his life's work. It's a fascinating look at his career.

It is a good idea to check the paintings are at the gallery before heading there. Several of them were recently at an exhibition at the Getty in Los Angeles, so I assume they travel around a bit.

BOY WITH A BASKET OF FRUIT, 1593-1594

Before we look at the painting itself it is interesting to look at the genre and what it signified. There was a heirarchy in painting genres at this time, with history paintings at the top, landscapes and portraits below and still lifes at the bottom. Caravaggio defied this structure, mixing portrait, still life and mythology into this work. He gave equal importance to the boy, 16-year-old Mario Minniti, and to the fruit. He said that painting still life required as much skill as painting people.

There is a lot going on in this picture. If you start with the basket of fruit, it is almost photographic in its quality, down to the bug-eaten, brown-edged leaves. Now look at the boy and the background. It looks staged and almost artificial, quite different from the fruit. Some have described the boy as talking or being in movement, while others see the open mouth as almost sexual. I look at the wavy hair and the grapes and see an allusion to Bacchus. But then again I see that in every painting with grapes and wavy hair. Regardless of how you interpret it, the painting is beautiful.

YOUNG, SICK BACCHUS, 1593-1594

This is an early self-portrait, also known as *Bacchino Malato*.

Along with *Boy With A Basket of Fruit* and *Boy Peeling Fruit*, this originally belonged to Caravaggio's patron Giuseppe Cesari as part of his extensive art collection. Scipione Borghese (the pope's nephew) coveted Cesari's art, so had him charged with a bogus count of illegal possession of an *arquebus* (a medieval forerunner to the rifle). The pope himself was corrupt and an idiot, forbidding Galileo from saying the earth revolved around the sun. The price of Cesari's freedom was his art, which was seized by Scipione in 1607 and now hangs in the Galleria Borghese.

Bacchus was the Roman god of wine and fertility. He is typically depicted in a scene of debauchery, with grapes and wine and women in a celebration of excess, ecstasy and hedonism. Normally he has luscious thick, wavy hair and juicy lips, golden shoulders and is the picture of health, all representative of a fertility god.

But not this time.

Sick Bacchus is thought to have been painted around the time that Caravaggio had arrived in Rome from Milan, and spent six months in the hospital of Santa Maria della Consolazione. At a glance you can see that he is ill. Although he has well defined musculature, he is ashen and jaundiced, his eyes are sunken and his lips are gray. The body language is that of suffering rather than Bacchus' usual prowess. When you look at the grapes he is holding you can see that they too are turning, about to go bad. Look at the grapes and peaches on the table and you will see by contrast they are healthy and robust.

The more I research this painting, the more conflicting theories I find. Some theorize that this is part of his nod to naturalism, painting real people in real life rather than stylized perfection. Others say that it is an autobiographical piece indicating his own illness. I have also read that this could be testament to the hard drinking, hard partying life that Caravaggio was living, and that this could be Bacchus the morning after a hard night of drinking, hungover and feeling like hell. What do you think?

St Jerome in his Study, 1605

This one is also known as *St Jerome in his Study*. St Jerome was a Roman priest and scholar who translated the Bible into Latin, this version known as the *Vulgate*. In this painting St Jerome sits reading a large book while his arm stretches out across two other books as he works on his own Holy book. With his left hand supporting the open book his right hand holds a quill. The action of the outstretched arm draws our eye across to a skull sitting on top of the books. Jerome is frequently pictured with the skull, symbolizing the inevitability of death and the transience/worthlessness of earthly life.

Caravaggio painted this one for Cardinal Scipione Borghese, which may account for the red sheet St Jerome is wrapped in. The sheet is the traditional clothing of an *anchorite* (religious recluses who were withdrawn from society). Jerome spent time as secretary to Pope Damasus I. The job of secretary was later occupied by cardinals, who wore red robes. Anchorites lived as hermits in small cell-like rooms with little furniture or decoration. We can't see anything much of the room as, with the exception of Jerome himself, everything fades back to blackness.

Knowing Caravaggio, his model for St Jerome was no doubt another homeless friend. Look at the sinewy arms, the scraggly beard and the tufts of white hair on the sides of his balding head. He looks very real. Apart from the halo...

John The Baptist, 1608

This painting was amongst the last he did. It was from his time in exile in Sicily, at this point living in Messina. Scipione Borghese secured him a papal pardon (for murder) and this work was found with his last effects when he died in Porto Ercole in July 1610 on his way back to Rome.

The first thing to notice about this painting is that it is very different from the depiction St John the Baptist we are used to seeing. Like many of Caravaggio's paintings it is borderline sexual. John was Jesus' cousin. He lived in the wilds of Judea between the Dead Sea and Jerusalem, his mission was to prepare the way for the coming of the Messiah. He is easily identifiable in Christian art as he is usually pictured wearing a camel skin, carrying a staff or reed cross, and with a lamb. Here we see John portrayed as a nearly nude adolescent, reclining on a swath of red fabric, staring at us with a sulky, sensual, knowing gaze. This is considered to be one of Caravaggio's more homo-erotic works and, as much as it is exquisitely beautiful, it is a little unsettling.

The best story I have found about this work is in Andrew Graham-Dixon's fantastic biography *Caravaggio, A Life Sacred And Profane* (a must-read for Caravaggio lovers). He tells a story from Caravaggio biographer Francesco Susinno's book, *The Lives of Messina's Painters,* published 1724.

Caravaggio took to following grammar school teacher Don Carlo Pepe when he would take his students to the arsenal in Messina for recreation (similar to our PE). Caravaggio would watch the boys, supposedly to get inspiration for his work, but Don Carlo Pepe became suspicious and questioned why he was always hanging around. Caravaggio was so incensed that he "wounded the poor man on the head" and consequently was forced to leave Messina and move to Palermo. Susinno said, "In short, wherever he went he would leave his mark of madness."

So we have the school teacher perhaps accusing Caravaggio of having an inappropriate interest in his students, Susinno writing it off to more of Caravaggio's madness, but Graham-Dixon wonders if it has some truth to it? Could the boy modeling for this picture be one of Don Carlo Pepe's students? He questions whether this image is of John the Baptist, prophet and holder of secret knowledge, or is it a swarthy Sicilian boy, older than his years and aware of his sexuality? We will never know, but this wasn't a commissioned work, which leads to speculation that it had some extra importance for Caravaggio. Enough importance to take it with him to Rome.

Another theory is that he had the three paintings with him on his final voyage as a gift of gratitude to the pope for pardoning him. It will remain a mystery, but don't you think not knowing makes the painting even more interesting?

MADONNA OF THE PALAFRENIERI, 1606

This masterpiece is also known as *Madonna of the Serpent* or *Madonna and Child With Saint Anne.*

In September 1605 the new pope, (Pope Paul V, uncle of Scipione Borghese) ordered the demolition of the old nave of the old St Peter's church, which was under the dome of the new one. Seven altars had to be moved to the new transept, including the one owned by the Confraternity of the Palafrenieri (the papal grooms), whose patron saint was St Anne. The Confraternity decided to commission an altarpiece for the Altar of St Anne in St Peters. They were steered towards choosing Caravaggio for the job.

The deacon, Antonio Tirelli gave Caravaggio a down payment of only 25 scudi and on completion only 50 scudi more. This was a very low fee for such an important work, but Caravaggio had recently been evicted, was in deep debt, had recently been wounded in a sword fight, and was once again in trouble with the law, so was in no position to complain and no doubt must have been incredibly relieved and grateful to receive the commission.

The completed painting was enormous — 10 feet tall and 6 feet across, and it hung over its altar for only a few days. It was the cause of much consternation and discussion. In the painting we see an incredibly beautiful Virgin Mary holding a four-year-old Jesus by his upper arms as, with his foot on top of hers, they stomp the head of a serpent, while St Anne, Mary's mother, looks on from the shadows.

The serpent is the symbol of original sin and there was debate over who did the actual stomping. The Protestants believed Jesus did it, the Catholics thought it was Mary. In 1569 a Papal Bull declared it was both, so here we have the two feet.

Notice the light slanting down over Mary and Jesus, highlighting her youth and beauty, while in contrast St Anne is in the shadows, her skin old and dry. Rather than lighting her whole face the beam seems to highlight Mary's voluptuous boobs. Have you ever seen Mary depicted as sexy before? This must have been beyond scandalous in 1606 when everyone was to believe she was a virgin, pure and non-sexual. Even more scandalous, the model for Caravaggio's Mary was none other than Lena, Magdallena Antognetti, a prostitute from Piazza Navona who had modeled for him before and who he may or may not have had a sexual relationship with (depending on whether or not you believe he was a homosexual).

Caravaggio delivered the painting on April 8th (we know this because of a dated letter he gave with it). There is record of a carpenter, Pierfrancesco being paid one scudo to hang the painting over the altar on April 14th. Then on April 16th records show it was taken down and moved to storage at the church of the papal grooms, Sant' Anna del Palafrenieri, in the back of a mule driven cart.

Caravaggio must have been devastated.

Records also show that the Palafrenieri sold the painting mid-June 1606 to none other than Scipione Borghese, for a mere 100 scudi. Borghese had managed to acquire yet another painting from the artist he most admired — and for an absolute bargain.

It is not known if the Palafrenieri were more incensed that their patron saint, St Anne, was depicted as old and left in the shadows, or that Mary was painted in a low cut dress, all boobs and cleavage, or that she was a famed local prostitute. My guess is a combination of all three. It is a shame, because the work is sensationally beautiful.

DAVID WITH THE HEAD OF GOLIATH, 1610

This painting is generally attributed to the last part of Caravaggio's life, but Andrew Graham-Dixon thinks it was painted soon after the artist's escape from Rome, possibly around the time he was hiding out at the Colonna Palace in Zagarolo, 20 miles outside Rome. It is the familiar story of a young David killing the giant Goliath, but it is portrayed in an unfamiliar manner.

At this time there was a bounty on Caravaggio's head, a papal warrant for murder. Some think that he painted this work for Scipione Borghese as an act of contrition, asking for forgiveness and pardon so that he could return to Rome. The head of Goliath, dripping with blood, is a self-portrait.

Young David is thought to be Caravaggio's boy-servant/painting assistant/possible lover, Cecco. Notice how he holds the head out at arm's length, as if in disgust. He grips the giant's hair in his hand as light angles down across his face, onto his arm, and to the side of Goliath's face. Instead of looking triumphant or exultant, David looks contemplative, maybe even saddened. But definitely not joyous. He holds a sword with the inscription *H.OC.S.* This is *humilitas occidit superbiam* (humility kills pride).

The head of Goliath/Caravaggio is jarring. He looks as if he is still screaming. His bottom lip is wet, one eye is glazed over while the other is still fiercely outraged. If you didn't know what was going on here you would think he was still alive. Notice the dent in his forehead from the slingshot. The uneven and graying teeth imply he wasn't in good health when he was working on this painting. His use of chiaroscuro directs our eye to exactly what he wants us to focus on — his anguish and fury.

Scipione Borghese, the pope's nephew, was also the chief administrator of papal justice, so in effect held Caravaggio's life (or death) in his hands. I believe this is Caravaggio reaching out to him, begging him to save him, saying *let me give you my head in a painting if you will let me keep it in real life.*

Another school of thought on the timing of this painting is that it occurred after Caravaggio had returned to Naples from his time in Sicily and Malta. Shortly after arriving back in Naples he was savagely beaten, a beating which left his face damaged. When you look at Goliath's eyes it is easy to see that they could have been scarred from being beaten half to death.

GETTING THERE

To visit the Borghese Gallery you must book in advance. Admissions are at every odd hour: 9am, 11am, 1pm.

WHAT'S NEARBY

Wander back down to the **Piazza del Popolo** and see the Caravaggio's inside the church of **Santa Maria del Popolo**. From there follow all the options from the piazza listed above. Alternatively wander over to the **Terazza del Pincio** and take in the gorgeous sunset, then head on to the **Spanish Steps**.

4. Chiesa Sant'Agostino

THE MADONNA OF LORETO, 1605

The thing about Caravaggio is that it's easy to get caught up in the madness and the sideshow of his crazy life, and then out of nowhere you stumble across a painting of such intense beauty it takes your breath away. It was like this when I saw his *Madonna of Loreto* for the first time. And the hundredth time.

Legend has it that Jesus' childhood house flew through the night, from Nazareth to Loreto in Le Marche, Italy, in December of 1294. A Frenchie by the name of Louis Richeome wrote a bestseller about it in 1604, in French, which was later translated into Latin and Italian and several other European languages. The shrine of Loreto was already pretty popular but the book brought thousands more pilgrims to see the Holy House.

There were two main ways the story of the shrine of Loreto was depicted: either Mary and Jesus would be sitting on the roof of the house for their magic carpet ride, or Mary would be shown holding Jesus in a pose taken from a statue supposedly carved by none other than St Luke himself, which resided on the altar of the shrine. (Not having been to the magic flying house myself, I can't say whether or not the statue is still there.)

Naturally Caravaggio defied convention and did something completely different, and of course there was a subsequent outcry about it, which makes this painting all the more magnificent, in my view.

If we think back to the other religious art happening at the time, and all that came before, we can see that the figures telling the religious stories were all recessed into landscapes and scenes that separated them from the viewer. This helped remind us that they were separate from us, better than us, above us.

In Caravaggio's work, we have Mary holding a big, chubby baby Jesus, leaning against an Italian-looking house, while two poor pilgrims, barefoot and dirty, kneel down and pray to her. We see more background than usual but in this case it is there to give us context. The house is old with walls peeling back to brick. It looks decrepit, there are no angels or cherubs hovering. The pilgrims are dressed as peasants from 1604. They aren't idealized and they don't look exultant. Instead they look surprised, thrilled, a little in awe, and as if this was meant to be.

Chubby Jesus holds onto his mother's sleeve as he gazes down at them, to my eye it looks as though he is looking into the face of the pilgrim woman as she looks up into his face. But it is Mary who has me transfixed. She looks like a barefoot Italian girl leaning up against a wall, languidly watching the world go by. As if her doorway is in some dark alley and she just happened to be leaning there holding her baby as this couple came along and recognized her. Her hips and backside lean into the wall, her right knee crosses her left leg as her right foot props itself up on the ball of the foot.

Her splayed right hand indicates the chunky baby is heavy, while her left hand holds a white rag under his bottom. Her lovely neck is elongated as she looks down at the pilgrim woman, who in turn is looking up to the baby, making a gorgeous visual triangle of glances. Some say she is listening to their prayers but to me she looks bored, though not unkindly so. And she is exquisite. No doubt one of Caravaggio's girlfriends or prostitute friends posed for the painting, whoever she was she was powerfully lovely. The makeup artist in me is enthralled with her perfect eyebrow.

As you walk through the church of Sant'Agostino, which is worth a visit even without the Madonna of Loreto, you will notice that the Cavalleti Chapel where this piece lives is quite dark. Caravaggio shines a light across Mary's neck, the baby and down onto the hip of the peasant man, a light that at first makes you think there is a window tucked into the wall of the chapel. The room from which Mary has emerged is in darkness and we look beyond the peasant woman into the shadows.

This is one of my favorite Caravaggios and I try to visit it every time I'm in Rome, even if only for a few minutes. Before you leave, examine Jesus' hands. To me they look all wrong, and I can't stop looking at them!

WHAT'S NEARBY

Chiesa Sant'Agostino is smack bang in the heart of everything. It is right by **Piazza Navona** and **Campo de Fiori**, close to **San Luigi dei Francesi**. From there you can walk up to the **Pantheon, Trevi Fountain** and **Spanish Steps**.

You can wander down to **Largo Argentina** and **Crypta Balbi** and on to **Piazza Venezia** in one direction, or turn the other way and it's only a couple of blocks to the river which you can follow down to the lovely bridge of angels that leads you over to **Castel Sant'Angelo** and along to **St Peter's**.

You can slip into this church at any point during a day wandering in the heart of Rome!

5. Palazzo Barberini

In the upcoming chapter on *Art & Museums*, I'll tell you the crazy story of how the Palazzo Barberini came into my life (and it is worth reading if only for that!). You need to know about the Barberini and its three Caravaggios.

Narcissus, 1597-1599

This painting tells Ovid's story of Narcissus, the boy who fell in love with his own reflection in the water, so much so that he fell in and drowned.

There is so much to take in here.

Notice how the reflection is dimmer than Narcissus himself. Even though the images mirror each other he is able to make us feel water rather than glass, and the earth underneath the boy.

Caravaggio's clever use of tenebrism (the almost violent use of light and dark) has lit up Narcissus's knee, shoulder and sleeve, making it seem as if he is leaning almost out of the painting toward us. The water line, although not dividing the painting quite in half, is nearly so, giving us a balance line to focus on. We see the round shape made by real Narcissus' hands meeting reflected Narcissus' hands, which again pushes the lit knee, shoulder and sleeve towards us. Clever, no?

Look at his hands. His right hand is supporting his weight but his left hand is in the water, and he is so entranced by his reflection he doesn't even notice. As his weight moves to his left hand, or to balance the pressure on his right, he will slip and fall in, face first. We are seeing him right at that moment when he is about to fall in. Brilliant.

Judith Beheading Holofernes, 1598

The basis for this work comes from the deuterocanonical Book of Judith. Our heroine, Judith, a beautiful Jewish widow from Bethulia comes up with a scheme to save her people from the Assyrian general, Holofernes, who was about to destroy their home. She pretends to be fleeing Bethulia and meets Holofernes who is quite taken with her. She tells him he will be victorious against the Jews, so he lets his guard down and either lets her into his tent and gets drunk, or gets drunk and lets her in. Regardless, when he passes out she cuts off his head, which is taken away in a bag by her elderly servant.

There is much to take in here. The heavy red curtain looks like it has just been flung open. Holofernes is naked and appears to still be screaming as she holds him by the hair and slices his throat. Caravaggio shines his light on Judith as if highlighting her purity. She is pictured as a young, renaissance girl wearing a clean white bodice that maybe implies virtue? Her brow is furrowed as if this is so distasteful to her, her skirt swishes as if she is in motion, turning away from the horror of it all. As she moves away, her servant moves in.

Look at the old handmaid. She has been described as a masterpiece within a masterpiece. She is old and leathery, wisps of her hair peeking out from under her cap, large, elderly ears poking out. Her tanned skin identifies her as a servant, rather than another high-bred woman, giving us context and separating her from lovely young Judith. The look on her face is amazing. We see the pure hatred she has for Holofernes and what he has done to her people. She wants to see his blood and her expression is a study both in disgust and fascination as she holds open the bag in which his head will go. I love her.

Darkness surrounds everything, we only see part of Holofernes, coming out of the dark (to his death), the old lady is partially in the dark.

The blood coming out of Holofernes' neck looks odd though. It's like strands of red spaghetti…

St John The Baptist, 1604

Caravaggio painted several versions of St John the Baptist but there is some debate as to whether this one is one of his or not. For the sake of argument let's say it is his.

This is a very different St John the Baptist. There is no camel skin, the bowl for baptism is tucked away in the back, stripped of importance and his cross is barely visible. This is a moment of requiescence, taking place during John's time of penitence in the desert. Without the title would you recognize him? Devoid of iconography I don't know that I would. This John is near naked, a loin cloth of sorts covering his manly bits, a red cloak draped over his right arm and across his left leg. He is smooth cheeked and his chest is hairless, implying he is quite young.

Yes, the work is beautiful and Caravaggio is incredible, but to me this one is more naked-young-boy-with-red-cloak than a significant religious piece. But it is no less genius for that.

What's Nearby

The Barberini is just down the street from Borromini's **San Carlo Alle Quattro Fontane** and Bernini's **Sant'Andrea Al Quirinale**. You are also in walking distance to the **Baths of Diocletian, Santa Maria degli Angeli e dei Martiri, Santa Maria in Maggiore** and not too far from **Palazzo Massimo Alle Terme** Museum of Roman Art.

6. Galleria Doria Pamphilj

PENITENT MAGDALENE, 1594-95

The subject matter of the *Penitent Magdalene* paintings bothers me. The story is that Mary Magdalene, who we are told was a prostitute (although who knows if that is true or not) repenting her "dissolute life". Most often she is depicted naked, and off in the desert where supposedly she did the hermit thing for thirty years after the Ascension of Jesus.

This bothers me because prostitution is not exactly a fun and engaging career chosen by young girls with options. If Mary Magdalene was in fact a prostitute it a) was probably not her fault and not her choice, and b) was no doubt an incredibly unpleasant position to be in, so c) why should she have to repent? I think all the men who used her should be on their knees repenting.

At least Caravaggio didn't have her naked in the wilds. Instead he has her sitting low to the ground on a chair, wearing contemporary clothing. He made her a Roman girl. He didn't idealize her, he made her look normal instead of perfect; she isn't slender, but is a little chubby, and definitely fuller that we are accustomed to seeing Magdalene. She looks as if she might be sitting there drying her hair. He also changed his perspective, making us look down to her as if to signify how humiliating it was for her. She looks away from us, and her head is at the angle of Jesus' when he is on the cross. A single tear runs down the side of her cheek to her nose. You can feel a sense of shame radiating off of her and I can't help but ache for her.

To the side of her are the trappings of a courtesan — jewels that she has cast off, and a stoppered bottle of what is possibly oil, like the oil she used on Jesus' feet.

Historians speculate that the model Caravaggio used for this painting was his friend, prostitute Anna Bianchini. It has also been suggested that there is an allusion to violence in this picture —the pearls are broken and Anna's face and hands are swollen — and that maybe Caravaggio is making some social commentary here about the mistreatment of prostitutes and courtesans by the police at the time. Clement VIII would have prostitutes whipped and paraded through the streets on a donkey as a way of enforcing public morality. So maybe Caravaggio's friend, 17-year-old Anna, had been whipped and the oil was there to treat her wounds? Apparently she and a friend were brought to Rome from Siena by their mothers when they were 13 and 14 years old, and the mothers pimped them out. In my opinion, Clement would have been better to whip the mothers and parade them around on donkeys.

I think it is a very sad painting. Beautiful, but sad.

REST ON THE FLIGHT INTO EGYPT, 1597

This painting is based on folklore that was going around in the middle ages. Not as much fun as Jesus and Mary's magic carpet ride to Loreto, but still worth painting. This story has the Jesus, Mary and Joseph escaping to Egypt to seek refuge after hearing that Herod wanted to kill young Jesus. While pausing to rest, Jesus commands a tree to bend over so that elderly Joseph can pick its fruit, and he also commands water to spring up from the roots so that the family could quench their thirst.

To this theme Caravaggio has added an angel who plays music from a book held by Joseph, while Mary holds the sleeping baby. The music has been identified as *Quam pulchra es et quam decora* from the *Song of Songs*. He painted the musical notes but not the words, maybe alluding to secret subtext? The angelic music is a spiritual nod to the loveliness of the mother and child, but also to the union of this little family, huddled together, camped like refugees under a blackening sky.

When we look at Mary we see her sleep is troubled. Joseph has an ass looming over his shoulder, incredibly close. Perhaps this indicates that Joseph doesn't understand what's going on, just like the trusty old donkey behind him.

In the darkness of what could be night falling or could be bad weather coming, the angel is a pillar of light. Once again Caravaggio is thumbing his nose at rival Annibale Carracci, who we met earlier at Santa Maria del Popolo (remember the horse's backside aimed at Carracci's alterpiece painting?). Here we have the ass looking at the angel from behind a tree, and the angel is a figure that Caravaggio has taken from one of Carracci's works, a painting on the ceiling at Palazzo Farnese, *The Judgement of Hercules*. In Carracci's painting, Hercules is choosing between two females, Vice and Virtue. Caravaggio has taken the nearly naked Vice and turned her into his angel. Carracci's Vice is not attractive: heavy and thick and more Renaissance-like when compared to Caravaggio's modern angel, so perfectly proportioned, who's weight shifts to his left hip as the breeze catches the front of his hair.

What Caravaggio was doing here is creating a comparison from the heavier, old school work of Annibale Carracci to the light, fresh, modern viewpoint of his own work. He gave his angel pigeon wings, which is such a novel piece of realism — everyone can relate to pigeons, who can relate to angel wings? He wanted everyone to compare their work and find his angel to be more beautiful than Carracci's Vice.

It gets even better. Do you recognize the face of Joseph here? It's Caravaggio's homeless drinking buddy from *The Crucifixion Of St Peter* at Santa Maria Del Popolo. And the Virgin Mary? None other than our friend Anna Bianchini, the child prostitute, this time looking so beautiful and tender. (I bet that alone caused an outcry at the time!)

GETTING THERE

Address: Via Del Corso 305.

WHAT'S NEARBY

Once again we are in the heart of Rome and in any direction you will find hundreds of things to go see. **Via del Corso** is one of the main shopping streets in Rome. You can follow it all the way to **Piazza del Popolo**. If you are heading in that direction you are a 5-10 minute walk away from **Santa Maria Sopra Minerva** and the **Pantheon** to your left, then **Piazza Navona**, **Campo de Fiori**, **Piazza Farnese**. (If you are looking for more Caravaggios you will find **San Luigi dei Francesi** just around the corner from **Piazza Navona**).

On the right hand side of Via del Corso you will find the **Trevi Fountain** and the **Spanish Steps**. Watch out for pickpockets!

In the opposite direction you are only a short walk from **Piazza Venezia**, **Palazzo Valentini**, **Trajan's Forum**, the **Roman Forum** and the **Colosseum**.

If you are hungry you are basically in the **Monti** district, so some of the best eateries in Rome are to be found along the little side streets in this area.

Also in walking distance you can find **Largo Argentina**, **Crypta Balbi** and the **Jewish Ghetto**.

7. Odescalchi Balbi Collection

THE CONVERSION OF ST PAUL, 1600

I have never seen this exciting piece, though I would love to. The Odescalchi Balbi collection is a private collection and is very seldom open to the public. You can research before your trip to see if there will be any public access while you are in Rome.

(There are several other Caravaggios in private collections in Rome, which I have not listed here as you can't go see them.)

8. The Capitoline Museums

JOHN THE BAPTIST, 1602

I have to confess I had this one all wrong. It wasn't until I read Andrew Graham-Dixon's book that I was able to look at this painting and see what I now have to presume was the artists intention for this work. At first glance the painting seems very homo-erotic. A naked John, played by Caravaggio's servant Cecco, has his legs oddly splayed as he leans back onto his fur while reaching up and around to embrace a ram. He looks out with a weird, sexually provocative expression. St John the Baptist's normal iconography doesn't appear to be present —he's not wearing a camel skin, no staff, no bowl and no lamb.

But here is what I learned from Andrew Graham-Dixon. Artists during Caravaggio's time would have seen Michelangelo's work as being the absolute peak of excellence. He had died seven years before Caravaggio was born and coincidentally, they shared the same name. Caravaggio would have studied the master's work, learned from it, and incorporated aspects of it into his own art.

This St John is a variation on Michelangelo's *ignudi* — the male nudes on the Sistine Chapel ceiling, telling the stories of the Book of Genesis. (By the second half of the sixteenth century the ignudi were deemed controversial and Daniele da Volterra was commissioned to paint fig leaves over their genitalia). Caravaggio's St John has been inspired by one of the four ignudi framing the *Sacrifice of Noah* on the Sistine Chapel ceiling. But there are differences. Michelangelo's ignudi have idealized, perfect bodies, where Caravaggio brings his realism. St John is a little thin, we can see his ribs and we can see dirt under his toenails. Michelangelo's perfect males rise up to heaven on the Sistine Chapel ceiling, while Caravaggio's real-boy is with us here on earth, where his toes have been in the dirt.

Graham-Dixon points out that St John is embracing the ram because it has been sent to him by God. And here are some more details that I had completely missed — in Michelangelo's work a sacrificial ram is being prepared for slaughter just a few feet from the *ignudo* that Caravaggio' St John is based on. (I now need to brave the crowds in the Sistine Chapel and try to find the ignudo and the ram.) In the upper right corner of *St John The Baptist* there are vine leaves, symbolizing the Eucharist. So our ignudo St John is forseeing the sacrifice of Christ and the salvation of mankind, and that is why he has the odd smile on his face. He sees the future.

Personally I think this painting really does straddle the sacred and the profane, but I think I understand it better now.

THE FORTUNE TELLER, 1594

Caravaggio was young when he painted this one, only 23 or 24 years old. Already the vagabond himself, he was well acquainted with the tricksters and con-men inhabiting the streets of Rome, and he immortalizes them in two paintings (this one and *The Cardsharps*). Both tell the story of the well-bred being conned by the hustlers.

In this one a gypsy girl is working a con on a well-to-do boy. We know she is a gypsy from her clothing: her turban and her woolen cape, clipped at her shoulder. His speaks to money, with his plumed hat, sword, his refined clothes — even the flash of satin lining in his coat. We can see he is mesmerized by this beautiful girl as she holds his hand in one of hers, strokes his palm and tells his fortune, while slipping his ring from his finger.

This was entirely topical at the time. Rome was in a time of social crisis, with beggars, rogues and thieves roaming the streets. Caravaggio was very much a man of the streets, violent and irascible, he hung out with prostitutes and drunks, so he would have seen this drama enacted many times. He probably felt some kind of kinship with these vagabonds, and we can see that in the forgiving way he paints his gypsy. She is not unkempt or ugly, instead he has made her beautiful, sweet and alluring.

The Cardsharps and *The Fortune Teller* marked a new moment in art. Paintings of vagabonds and rogues and tricksters started to pop up all over Europe, a genre created by Caravaggio.

WHAT'S NEARBY

Three main buildings make up the Capitoline Museum in Piazza del Campidoglio. Walk toward the river and you will see **Teatro Marcello** and the **Jewish Ghetto**, in the opposite direction you have the **Forum, Trajan's Market, Palazzo Valentini**, the **Colosseum** and **Domus Aurea**, and only five minutes further along the road you will be at **Basilica San Clemente.**

9. The Vatican Museums

If you are on a mission to see the Caravaggios in Rome, I can't leave out the Vatican Museums. This one is in the Pinocoteca.

THE ENTOMBMENT OF CHRIST, 1604 (ALSO KNOWN AS DEPOSITION FROM THE CROSS)

This is considered to be Caravaggio's greatest masterpiece. At 9.8 feet tall (300 cm) and 6.6 feet wide (203 cm) it is enormous. It is brilliant and beautiful and being a Caravaggio has a healthy dose of crazy behind it too!

It was commissioned by Girolamo Vittrice for his family chapel in Santa Maria in Vallicella (a few hundred meters west of Piazza Navona, by the river). The Vittrice family was part of the populist, pauperist wing of the Catholic church. This branch of the church stressed the importance of charitable works and wanted a return to simple worship rather than elaborate rituals, so Caravaggio's realism was a perfect fit.

The painting has traveled a bit — in 1797 it moved to Paris as part of the Treaty of Tolentino, before returning to Rome in 1817 to Pope Pius VII's Pinacoteca.

Again here, Caravaggio has taken a non-traditional route to tell the story of Christ's deposition from the cross/burial/entombment. This is not the moment he is laid in the tomb, but instead when he is laid on the anointing stone by Nicodemus and John.

There is so much going on here, you really need to breathe for a moment so that you can take it all in. There is so much drama and tension and tragedy in this painting. Caravaggio doesn't want to idealize the entombment, he wants the viewer to feel the weight of it, both the weight of Jesus' dead body and the crushing weight of grief they are all going through.

Firstly look at Jesus' body. It drops toward the stone, barely held onto by Nicodemus and John. You will see a parallel to Michelangelo's *Pieta* here — look at Jesus' limp arm, the veins, the way it falls. In *Pieta*, Michelangelo has the flesh of his arm bulging over Mary's hand, here we see it bulging over John's supporting hand, but as it does John inadvertently reopens the wound in Jesus' side. The weight of his dead body has John nearly dropping him while Nicodemus stoops and strains to bear the weight of him, locking his hand over his forearm as he grimaces and almost bear-hugs Jesus around the knees. Caravaggio shines his light on Christ's body, not his face, drawing our attention to the weight of it and the downward motion, while fading any scenery to black.

We have three women in the painting, starting with Mary of Cleophas in the upper right corner, hands raised in grief, then we drop down to Mary Magdalene, head bent into her hand, perhaps weeping, side by side with the Virgin Mary dressed as a nun, looking down at the body of her child. Caravaggio shines a second light on the three Marys, picking up the white in each of their outfits. This, paired with the positioning of their bodies, ending with the sheet dropping away over the edge of the stone and onto the plant emphasizes the feeling of weight falling, and gives more downward motion to the picture. It is quite, quite brilliant.

Personally I am taken with the level of emotion conveyed in this work. You can't help but ache with them.

And there is a crazy story that goes with it. The model for Mary of Cleophas and Mary Magdalene is Anna Bianchini's friend, Fillide Melandroni, child prostitute, courtesan and sometime girlfriend of Caravaggio. She moved to Rome from Siena with Anna and their mothers pimped them out when they were 13 and 14 years old. Fillide became one of the most sought after and well known prostitutes for the elite men of Rome. Caravaggio met her when one of his wealthy patrons, nobleman Vincenzo Giustiani commissioned him to paint her for him (*Portrait of a Courtesan*). She reportedly had a "violent nature" which may well have appealed to a dark and violent man like Caravaggio.

The plot thickens even more: Ranuccio Tomassoni was believed to be Fillide's pimp. In 1606 Caravaggio murdered him, supposedly due to a fight over Fillide, and it was this murder that led to Caravaggio spending the last four years of his life on the run and seeking papal forgiveness.

There was a lot of mystery surrounding the death of Caravaggio. He had no funeral or grave marker, but human remains found in a church in Porto Ercole are believed to be his. Scientists have established the bones belonged to a tall male, aged 38-40 (Caravaggio was 38) and are dated to around 1610. The bones indicate their owner had lead poisoning — high amounts of lead salts were found, which would explain his violent behavior.

WHAT'S NEARBY

You're at the Vatican. That's what's nearby!

Map of where to find Caravaggios in Rome (in geographical order)

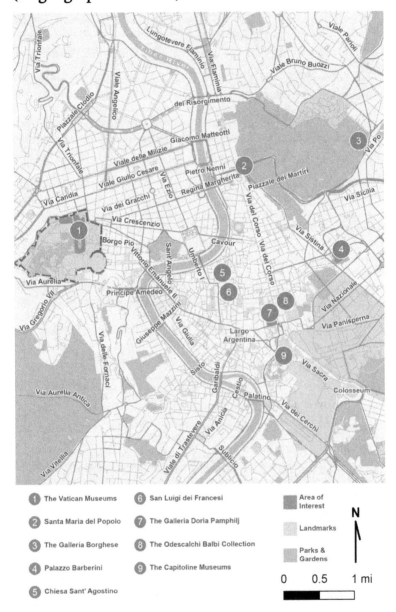

1. The Vatican Museums
2. Santa Maria del Popolo
3. The Galleria Borghese
4. Palazzo Barberini
5. Chiesa Sant' Agostino
6. San Luigi dei Francesi
7. The Galleria Doria Pamphilj
8. The Odescalchi Balbi Collection
9. The Capitoline Museums

Area of Interest

Landmarks

Parks & Gardens

0   0.5   1 mi

N

Museums in Rome

9.

Twelve Magnificent Museums in Rome

1. National Roman Museum at the baths of Diocletian

2. Palazzo Massimo al Terme

3. Palazzo Barberini

4. Villa Borghese

5. Palazzo Farnese

6. Villa Farnesina

7. Galleria Corsini

8. Palazzo Altemps

9. Galleria Doria Pamphilj

10. Palazzo Colonna

11. The Capitoline Museums

12. The National Etruscan Museum

I know I have said this before, but Rome is a living museum. Everywhere you go you are surrounded by art and history. It is overwhelming and amazing, and the magic doesn't wear off. Every time I arrive in Rome it takes my breath away.

So with art and history everywhere, why should you bother to visit museums? Because some of the greatest art in the world, some of the most magnificent statues and ancient treasures are here inside these incredible institutions, and readily available to you. Each of them is extraordinary and will enrich your Rome experience, and even though Rome is packed with tourists, you might walk into one of these museums and find yourself almost alone.

This is not a total list of museums in Rome, but these are my favorites.

1. The National Roman Museum at the Baths of Diocletian

The National Roman Museum is divided among four locations: the Baths of Diocletian, Crypt Balbi, Palazzo Altemps and the Palazzo Massimo (alle Terme). You can access all four on the same ticket within three days.

For me, this place was one of those *wow* experiences that totally took me by surprise. I sort of found this museum by accident. The Baths of Diocletian had been on my Rome list since forever but I felt no sense of urgency to get here. However, when I went to Crypta Balbi I learned that my ticket also was valid for Diocletian's Baths if I went within three days. I had intended to visit something off the Via dei Fori Imperiali (I don't actually remember where I was originally going), but when I got to the Forum area there were so many tourists everywhere I felt like I couldn't breathe. Now, I believe when Plan A doesn't pan out, Plan B is invariably better anyway (as discussed in my first book, *Glam Italia! How To Travel Italy*), and this was a definite Plan A/ Plan B situation. So I decided to head up to Diocletian's Baths instead and I'm so glad I did.

The ruins of the baths themselves are worth coming to see but, good Lord, *the statues*! I don't even know where to begin, and in all honesty if someone had tried to articulate to me just how much was here to look at I don't think I would have come even close to comprehending it. Suffice to say there is an enormous amount of sculpture here, especially from the first and second centuries: achingly beautiful works, in pristine condition. There is an indoor museum, which has a vast collection of spectacular sculptures and there is also a huge, colonnaded outdoor courtyard with sculptures in the center and many more lined up every couple of feet along all four porticoed walls. The area is substantial and I have no idea how many times I walked around it — I went round and round and round. There were a few artists scattered around drawing, and me. That's it. I essentially had the place to myself. Even though it was a really hot summer day in crowded Rome, I was here alone, walking through all this marble that not only was amazing to look at but that also cooled the air around me.

I sincerely hope that you will make the effort to visit the Baths of Diocletiàn. I had thought a 30 minute whip around would be sufficient, but I was here for more than two hours. I would have stayed longer. Give yourself a little extra time here.

WHAT'S NEARBY

From the Baths of Diocletian you are only a few minutes walk to **Palazzo Massimo alle Terme**. **Palazzo Barberini** is very close and also the church of **San Carlino alle Quattro Fontane**.

The National Museum at Baths of Diocletian is next to **Piazza della Repubblica**, so you can walk down Via Nazionale to the back of **Trajan's Market** (about 15 minutes). This walk takes you into the **Monti** district, which is full of wonderful little places to stop for lunch.

2. Palazzo Massimo alle Terme

This one is right across the street from the Baths of Diocletian.

Palazzo Massimo is housed in a wonderful neo-classical palace built in the 1880s. It was a Jesuit college until 1960 and in 1981 it became part of the National Roman Museum. It is considered to be Rome's main archaeological museum, and in all honesty if you haven't been here then you haven't yet seen the best of Rome's archaeological discoveries (which is really saying something!). It is also an art museum, but the art here just happens to be ancient.

As you walk through Palazzo Massimo you will recognize many of the artworks and sculptures from postcards and history books. Some of the most famous pieces of art from ancient Rome are in this museum. There are bronzes, marble sculptures, mosaics, elaborately decorated sarcophagi, jewelry and frescoes. This place is absolutely amazing!

Remember Emperor Augustus and the evil Livia from the *Ancient Rome* section of this book? She had a house on Palantine Hill (the House of Livia) in addition to her villa on the Via Flaminia. Here at Palazzo Massimo they have the frescoes from Livia's villa — the very best preserved Roman frescoes anywhere in the world. Not only the frescoes, but they have built replica rooms of those at the villa so that as you look at the frescoes you are seeing them in the context they were created and lived in. It is incredible. If this was the only thing you saw it would be worth the visit, but there are four floors of treasures here just waiting for you. I don't know what will blow your mind more — discovering this amazing museum or the fact that *there is no one here.* I can never wrap my mind around having these incredible museums almost to myself. This place is so big, even if a hundred people were here you would still feel like it was yours alone! Don't miss this place.

WHAT'S NEARBY

Palazzo Massimo alle Terme is just behind **Termini Station**. Depending on how your compass works it is neighbors with the **Baths of Diocletian**, across from **Piazza della Repubblica**.

3. Palazzo Barberini

I swear, the craziest stuff happens to me! I can be sitting in a corner, minding my own business and something insane will go down, something that defies belief (but which will make me a fabulous guest at a dinner party). You *just can't make this stuff up.*

So this is the bizarre tale of how I found myself at the Palazzo Barberini. It involves a painter, Gauguin, an art heist in London, a pensioner in Sicily and a red-haired, makeup artist & tour guide from New Zealand — me. (You can verify the various parts of this story on Google, except the part involving me.)

THE HEIST

Our story starts in London in 1970 with the heiress to the Marks and Spencer's fortune, Mathilda Marks. Mathilda owned some valuable art including a painting by Gauguin, *Fruits on a Table Or Still Life With a Small Dog*, and a painting by Bonnard, *Women With Two Armchairs*. On the day in question a group of thieves dressed as policemen arrived at Mathilda's home in London saying there was a problem with her alarm system. They asked her for a cup of tea and when she came back with the tray of tea and biscuits the two paintings had been cut out of their frames and the men were gone. For years this was a mystery in the art world. No one knew where the paintings went, there was no word of a private collector having secreted them away. There was just silence.

Fast forward to 1975 and we meet Nicolo, a worker at the Fiat factory in Turin. Nicolo liked lost and found sales and went to one at the local train station. Amongst the odds and ends that travelers had left behind on the trains over the years was a box with two dusty, rolled up canvases. The auctioneer told him they were worthless rubbish but he liked them so he bought them anyway for 45,000 lire (roughly twenty dollars). He took them home, put them in frames and hung them in his kitchen, where they enjoyed life for the next 40-plus years.

Eventually Nicolo retired and moved with his wife to the sunshine in Sicily. His two paintings found a new kitchen to hang in and life went on, until Nicolo's adult son happened to be looking though an art book and recognized the two works of art that he had grown up with! The story of the stolen art unfolded, experts verified the paintings, and then the governments tried to figure out who was the rightful owner. Mathilda was now deceased, and had left no heirs. Eventually it was decided that the paintings belonged to Nicolo.

Although the story became major world news, Nicolo remained anonymous (which was important due to the value of a Gauguin). Nicolo's Gauguin was valued at around 10 million euros.

AND HERE IS WHERE I ENTER THE STORY

Nicolo didn't want to sell his painting through a major auction house like Sotherby's or Christie's, and anonymity was essential, so his lawyer reached out to some private agents to quietly find a buyer. One of those agents knew one of my friends in Italy, and so I got a call: *Who do you know who might buy a Gauguin? Could you ask around your contacts and see what you can find?*

Could I??? My first thought was this could be the greatest dinner party story *of all time.* My second thought was if I were the one to find the buyer my name would be forever attached to Gauguin, even if I were the only one to attach it. And of course there was a commission if I did find the buyer, a commission with a staggering number of zeros! So I went to work on it, reaching out to my celebrity clientele, wealthy clients and international art dealers. The Gauguin was my life for months. I lived and breathed the Gauguin, my phone would ring in the middle of the night as representatives and agents for international collectors called from Singapore and Bahrain and other time zones across the globe.

I was about to head back to Italy so the agent asked me if I would like to have a private viewing of the Gauguin. I studied the painting and bought a dress that would be perfect to wear with it in a photo (the kind of photo that defines your life and quite possibly lives on after you do, a photo with a painting that would disappear into a private collection and possibly never be seen publicly again). He gave me a list of dates when he could come to Rome to meet with me, but on each of the dates he had available I had to be somewhere else with my Glam Italia tours. Just in case one of our schedules freed up, I carted my dress all over Italy for a month and then back to America. I never got my private viewing.

I came really, *reallllllly* close to securing the buyer. So close I could smell it. But while the numbers were being crunched another buyer flew in on a private jet and bought it. I was disappointed to get so close, but thrilled to have been a part of this wild story, if only peripherally!

When I returned to Italy in September, the government had negotiated for the painting to be hung at the Palazzo Barberini in an exhibition of recovered stolen art. I raced over to the Barberini, my fabulous dress no longer needed, as the painting was now hanging in the museum for all the world to see.

That was my first visit to the Palazzo Barberini.

THE PALAZZO

The Palazzo itself is incredibly lovely. Commissioned in 1623 by Maffeo Barberini (Pope Urban VIII) and completed in 1625, it is a beautiful example of Baroque architecture. It is also a twist in the intertwining stories of Bernini and Borromini. Borromini worked on this project with his uncle Carlo Maderno, the original architect, but upon Maderno's death was passed over in lieu of his arch rival Bernini who took over the work. Borromini stayed on to complete his section, and for a brief time the two rivals worked together on the Palazzo. Even if you're not an art lover, just come here for a stroll around.

For art lovers this one is a secret treasure. No matter how crowded Rome is with tourists it would appear that none of them know about this museum, because you tend to not see them here. You can breathe and you can enjoy some of the most important works of art in the world. Most notably Raphael's *La Fornarina* — the daughter of baker in the Trastevere who became the love of his life. You will also find three Caravaggios here: *Narcissus, Judith Beheading Holofernes* and *St John The Baptist* (read more about these paintings in the *Caravaggio* section of this book).

There are more than 1400 works here including paintings from great artists Filippo Lippi, Andrea del Sarto, El Greco, Tintoretto, Titian and Guido Reni.

THE ANCIENT TEMPLE UNDERNEATH THE PALAZZO

Rome is the gift that keeps on giving! In 1936 workers discovered a *mithraeum* underneath the palazzo. This is a second century BC temple to the god Mithrus, and contains incredibly well-preserved frescoes, astrological symbols and ten small panels depicting Mithrus himself.

GETTING THERE

If you will be there on the 2nd or 4th Saturday of the month you can book ahead to have a tour of the temple, which is otherwise closed to visitors. Tickets are available at www.coopculture.it

Address: Via delle Quattro Fontane 13.

WHAT'S NEARBY

The Barberini is just down the street from Borromini's **San Carlo Alle Quattro Fontane** and Bernini's **Sant'Andrea Al Quirinale**. You are also in walking distance to the **Baths of Diocletian, Santa Maria degli Angeli e dei Martiri, Santa Maria in Maggiore** and not too far from **Palazzo Massimo Alle Terme Museum of Roman**

Art.

4. Villa Borghese

Villa Borghese refers to not only the villa itself but also the entire park-like grounds, but I want to tell you about the Borghese Gallery, home to perhaps the most exceptional art collection in all of Rome.

This villa was never intended to be a home. It was built specifically to hold Scipione Borghese's personal art collection. Bear this in mind and you will notice a really beautiful harmony as art and architecture meet in a way that was designed to bring out the best in each.

Here you will find works by a long list of important artists including Caravaggio, Bernini and Raphael. Part of what makes this gallery so special is that it is not just a collection of great pieces, it is a reflection of Scipione's passions.

To understand the Villa Borghese you have to understand Scipione. His uncle became pope Paul V in 1605, who gave the previously named *Scipione Caffarelli* the name *Borghese* and made him a cardinal. In a superb example of papal nepotism Paul V gave Scipione incredible power as head of the Vatican government and as the pope's secretary.

Scipione amassed a fortune for the Borghese family through papal taxes and fees, and by using papal money to buy real estate. He realized that the best way to acquire and maintain staggering wealth was by owning vast amounts of rental properties. Having an Uncle Pope enabled him to use the power of the church to force people to sell their land (at below market value), other times just taking it. He bought entire towns and massive, massive land holdings. The family fortune was set to outlast Uncle Paul V's tenure as God's right hand man on Earth. (Papal corruption is astounding!)

These guys didn't have to actually believe in the Catholic church, nor did they follow its rules. When you consider the Catholic church's views on homosexuality, I find it interesting that Cardinal Scipione Borghese was rumored to be gay. Not only did he accumulate art with homo-erotic overtones (some of the Caravaggios), but he also moved his boyfriend Stefano Pignatelli to Rome. Stefano wielded all kinds of power and influence over Scipione, and Scipione "loved him to the point of insanity" which makes all of this even more intriguing. Pope Paul V made Scipione's boyfriend Stefano a cardinal in 1621. Seriously.

Scipione was a great patron of the arts, sponsoring several artists during his lifetime, including Caravaggio. Depending on how you interpret history, Scipione was also an art thief of sorts — in 1607 the pope gifted him 107 confiscated artworks. Pope and cardinal had quite the racket going.

When Caravaggio died, Scipione swooped in and "acquired" the paintings he had with him. Poor Caravaggio's body was lost, but his artwork was preserved.

If you enjoy art then a visit to Villa Borghese won't disappoint. The collection is incredible. If you enjoy a little intrigue with your art then read up on Scipione before you visit. He was brilliant and terrible and fascinating and genius, and knowing his story will make your experience even more enjoyable!

GETTING THERE

You *must* book your tickets ahead of time — there are no walk-ins here.

WHAT'S NEARBY

Villa Borghese is above **Piazza del Popolo**. You can walk up here from **Piazza Navona** and the **Pantheon**, pop into **Santa Maria del Popolo** to see the Caravaggios, then visit the art and the grounds at **Villa Borghese**. If you time it right you can catch sunset from up at the **Terrazza Pincio**.

5. Palazzo Farnese

We talked about Palazzo Farnese in a previous chapter. It is one of the most important renaissance palaces in Rome and is currently home to the French Embassy.

In its day this palazzo was home to cardinals and Pope Alexander Borgia. Pope Alexander's mistress (or at least one of them) was Giulia Farnese. The pope made Giulia's brother a cardinal and he moved into this palace, before becoming a pope himself — Pope Paul III. (When you consider all the non-Catholic things these characters were getting up to behind the scenes, it's enough to make your head spin!) With the money and clout that comes with the papacy, Paul III roped in some of the greatest artist and architects of the time, including the great Michelangelo, to work on his palace.

GETTING THERE

There is staggering artwork inside Palazzo Farnese, primarily the frescoes, but the only way to see the art here is to go on a tour. Because it is an embassy you can't go freestyling through, and the tours (offered in French, Italian and English) are limited. As far as I know (you will want to check this) the English tours are on Wednesdays. You have to book well in advance.

WHAT'S NEARBY

Piazza Farnese leads into **Campo de Fiori**, from which you can walk across the street to **Piazza Navona**. It is also directly across the river from **Villa Farnesina** and the beautiful **Trastevere** district.

6. Villa Farnesina

If you love Raphael (as I do) then this place is an absolute wonder.

In the early sixteenth century this beautiful villa was built by a wealthy Sienese banker by the name of Agostino Chigi. Chigi was a great patron of the arts. He had his villa designed by Baldassarre Peruzzi and decorated by artists including Sebastiano del Piombo, Peruzzi himself, Giovanni Antonio Bazzi (who was hilariously known as *Il Sodoma*) and the master himself, Raphael, whose frescoes here are achingly beautiful.

Alessandro Farnese acquired the villa after Chigi's death, and then on his own death it went to his nephew Odoardo, after which it became abandoned. It was occasionally loaned to Cardinals and royals, then became the home to Neopolitan ambassadors. In 1927 it became the property of the state.

RAPHAEL'S STORY

Two interesting facts about Raphael and the Villa Farnesina: the Villa originally had a set of stables on the property designed by him. After years of neglect they were demolished in 1808. I find it hard to believe that anything Raphael created was allowed to fall into ruin! Secondly, it was while working on this job that Raphael met the love of his life, Margherita Lute, the baker's daughter. Apparently she was washing her feet in the fountain, just down from his home in Trastevere, and he saw her and fell in love.

Raphael was quite the ladies man. In 1514 against his will he was engaged to Maria Bibbiena, niece of his patron Cardinal Medici Bibbiena. He kept stalling however and although their engagement lasted six years they never married. During the engagement he had no end of lovers, until he met and fell for Margherita. Apparently while painting the Villa Farnesina he was so distracted by his love for her that they had to move her in to live with him. He couldn't focus or function without her. Which of course adds to the beauty of the frescoes here — they are about love and marriage.

Raphael used Margherita as a model in several paintings including *La Fornarina* (The Baker's Daughter), which hangs in the Barberini. It is thought that Agostino Chigi organized for the two to secretly marry. In some of his paintings of her a ruby ring can be seen on her left hand. It had been painted over (perhaps by one of his students) to hide it from his fiancee and the cardinal and was later discovered. Margherita was lower class and would not have had a jewel of that value. In the painting of *La Fornarina* she has a blue ribbon around her arm with Raphael's name on it written in gold.

When Raphael died in 1520 he was buried in the Pantheon next to his fiance Maria Bibbiena. He had left Margherita enough money to live a comfortable life, but months after he died she retreated into a monastery in Trastevere.

There is some incredible art work at Villa Farnesina. My favorites though are the Raphaels. The beauty in the *Loggia of Galatea* and the *Loggia of Cupid and Psyche* becomes even more exquisite when you know the love story he was living while creating them.

GETTING THERE

Villa Farnesina is facing the river at the edge of Trastevere. It is open from 9am til 2pm Monday to Saturday. You need to book at least 15 days in advance.

Address: Via della Lungara 230.

7. Galleria Corsini

Next door to Villa Farnesina there is another incredible art museum, the Palazzo Corsini. The art here comes from the Corsini family's private collection. There are several Guido Reni works including *Salome with the Head of John the Baptist*, Caravaggio's *St John The Baptist* and Annibale Carracci's *St Francis*. You can also see works by Rubens, Poussin and Van Dyck. The collection is extensive.

You can pretty much guarantee there will be almost no one there to get between you and the paintings. The palazzo is wonderful and Galleria Corsini is a really lovely respite from the hustle and bustle of the city.

CRISTINA'S STORY

Of course there is a story to go with this one too. This story is about a troublemaking royal who lived in the palace during the seventeenth century. I always start telling the story of Queen Cristina of Sweden by prefacing it with *I swear I didn't make this up* and ending it with *you have to Google her in case I left out too much of the crazy.* I'm a firm believer that every building becomes more interesting when you know a bit about someone who lived there, so here is a look at Queen Cristina of Sweden, a sexually ambiguous (and enthusiastic) queen who abdicated the throne, dressed as a man, took part in a murder, converted to catholicism, was a patron of the arts and doyenne of Rome's underground scene, and lived a life of scandal.

Princess Cristina of Sweden had an interesting start to her life. She wasn't Italian. Her mother, Queen Maria of Sweden was totally nuts. She wanted to give the king a male heir, and when Cristina was born the midwives initially thought she was a boy (perhaps she was a hermaphrodite; she was definitely hairy and had a big nose). Once the mistake was discovered no one told the queen for days, and when she finally was told she attacked the baby!

King Gustavus didn't care that the baby was a girl. He had his sister Catherine take care of Cristina, and he took active interest in raising her to assume the crown, spending time teaching her manly(or at least more masculine) things. Maria had nothing to do with her. They say your environment molds you, and Cristina developed a love for guy stuff and an active disinterest in feminine things and the idea of marriage. She was super-educated for anyone at that time, let alone a girl, and had a passion for arts and languages, speaking Hebrew and Arabic. Not a pretty girl, and far from what we imagine a Swede to look like, she had dark wiry hair, a big nose and one shoulder sat higher than the other. And she was wild! She could be charming when it suited her, but she didn't much bother with social niceties or norms. At a time when it really wasn't done, Cristina charted her own course and made her own rules.

When the king died, crazy Queen Maria had his body embalmed and kept him in a room in the palace with candles and black velvet curtains. She refused to allow him to be buried *for two years*! She tormented Cristina to the point that the Chancellor had Maria exiled from Stockholm.

Meanwhile Cristina dressed like a man and chased girls. All countries in Europe were either Catholic or Protestant at the time and the pope saw that she was unstable and fragile, so sent his emissaries to work on converting her. This was a major coup for the Catholic church - flipping a Protestant royal. Sweden could cope with her dressing like a man and being a lesbian, but they couldn't let her keep the throne if she converted to Catholicism, so she was forced to abdicate four years into her reign. Queen Cristina is the only queen in Swedish history to abdicate.

After abdicating she lived in Holland but as her money started running out Pope Alexander VII scored a major PR win by inviting her to live in Rome as his guest. She arrived with the pomp and circumstance of a victorious Roman General. Bernini designed the coach she arrived in as well as a new facade for the gate through which she arrived into Rome, and the two became lifelong friends. The pope paraded her around, showing the world that he had converted a Protestant queen.

Cristina lived the party life in Rome and then, when in need of a job, decided she was qualified to become Queen of Naples which at that time was under French rule. She pitched the Frenchies on the idea and arrived in Paris to cement the deal, dressed as a man, causing a huge scandal and some fascination at her free-thinking wildness. When she discovered one of her trusted servants, Italian nobleman Gian Monaldeschi, had been secretly copying her letters and sending them to the pope, she ordered her guards to execute him. They chased him through the hallways of the palace and stabbed him to death. The murder of Monaldeschi wasn't well received and cost her the Naples gig. His family made sure that by the time she got back to Rome her already scandalous reputation was ruined. Over the next few years she made a couple more unsuccessful plays for thrones.

In Rome she was considered a barbarian, a designation she quite enjoyed and that fast tracked her to counter-culture revolutionary status — seventeenth century Rome had ever seen anything quite like her. She founded a theater and when the pope shut it down she started hosting plays in her palace. The pope forbade women to perform in theater, but Cristina gleefully ignored him. She championed the cause of the city's Jewish population. She championed freedom of thought and supported those who didn't align with the church's doctrine. Her bedroom was a revolving door of endless lovers, most of whom were female. She became a thorn in the establishment's side and for 20 years was the queen of Rome's underground arts and social scene.

RIARIO PALACE

The Riario Palace was Cristina's home from 1659-1689. An avid patron of the arts, under her guidance the first ever meetings of the Roman *Accademia dell'Arcadia* were held here at her home. (Along with endless parties!)

When she died in 1689 she had planned to have a quiet little funeral but the pope saw one last chance to use her as a marketing weapon. He had her embalmed and put on public display for four days so that mourners could come pay their respects to the queen who converted. He then gave her a funeral suitable for a pope and had her laid to rest in the Vatican graveyard reserved for popes! This wild, rule breaking, sexaholic, patron of the arts, who dressed like a man, is one of only three women in history to have the honor of being buried with the popes.

A monument to Queen Cristina and her (scandalous yet fabulous) contribution to the arts and culture of Rome was erected in St Peter's Basilica, where it remains to this day.

In 1736 Cardinal Neri Maria Corsini acquired the property, renovating and refurbishing the former Riario Palace into the current gorgeous Palazzo Corsini. Even though her palace was redesigned, I like to imagine Cristina cruising around the grounds here, dressed as a man, and bucking convention at every opportunity.

WHAT'S NEARBY

The Corsini Palace is at the edge of the **Trastevere**. If you walk along the river (with Trastevere behind you) it will take 20 minutes to get to **Castel Sant'Angelo** and another five minutes to walk to **St Peter's Square**.

From Palazzo Corsini you can cross the river at the **Sisto Bridge** and walk up to **Michelangelo's Unfinished Bridge**, the **Palazzo Farnese**, **Campo de Fiori** and **Piazza Navona**.

8. Palazzo Altemps (The Best Museum You Never Heard Of)

This is the fourth museum of the National Museums of Rome. (The other three are Crypta Balbi, Palazzo Massimo and the National Roman Museum at the Baths of Diocletian.) It is one of the greatest museums in Rome, especially if you love sculpture. This place is so spectacular that I recommend it goes on your must-see list.

I only discovered this place last year (2018), and I came here because it was on the same ticket as Crypta Balbi. Every time I go to Rome, I block off days on either side of each Glam Italia tour to explore more of the city. I call it *research*! However, even with my endless list of places to check out in Rome I had not so much as heard of Palazzo Altemps. (The fact that I can still stumble upon really amazing new things to see and do in Rome is in part what drove me to write this book — I come here several times a year. How is everyone else supposed to find them?)

If for no other reason, come here just to see the palazzo — it is beautiful beyond belief. From the porticos to the interiors, the frescoes are sensational. This place will take your breath away. The palazzo itself was built in the fifteenth century by the Riario family, and it was built on top of an ancient Roman foundation. In 1568 Cardinal Marco Sittico Altemps, nephew of Pope Pius IV bought it and made it his home.

SCULPTURES

But of course it's not just the palazzo, there is the art. Palazzo Altemps holds one of the world's most important collections of ancient Greek and Roman sculpture. Some of these pieces are so beautiful they bring me to tears. Here you will find a statue called the Ludovisi Gaul (*Gaul killing himself and his wife*). It is one of a pair of Roman copies of Greek bronzes dating back to around 230 BC. In this sculpture, a Gaul holds his dying wife in one arm while looking backwards at the approaching enemy, as he plunges a knife into his own breast. The Gauls had just been defeated in battle at Pergamon, and he chose death rather than allow Attalus' soldiers to capture him and his wife. It is angry and violent and haunting and desperate. Where most statues are static, with the subject immobile, the fierce movement in this one is *palpable*. The other statue of the pair is *Dying Gaul*, which resides at the Capitoline Museum. If you will visit both Palazzo Altemps and the Capitoline Museum then I recommend seeking out each of the pair.

The museum also holds a pretty major collection of Egyptian art. There is a lot to see here in a relatively small space compared to the huge museums, but nothing seems cramped. Here you'll find beautiful statues and sculptures with centuries old frescoes behind them and plenty of room to wander around and observe things from every angle. Even more amazing is that you may well be here alone! *No one knows about this place.* It is one of the best kept secrets in Rome. Instead of lining up in the heat outside the Colosseum with multiple thousands of people, you can be walking around in here, cool and comfortable, with almost no one around, taking in some of the most remarkable artwork in the world.

GETTING THERE

Address: Piazza di Sant' Apollinare 46.

Closed on Mondays.

WHAT'S NEARBY

Palazzo Altemps is right outside **Piazza Navona**. Walk from here to the **Pantheon** (around five minutes) or in the opposite direction to **Campo de Fiori**, **Palazzo Farnese** and cross the river into the **Trastevere**. From Piazza Navona you can also walk about two minutes to **San Luigi dei Francesi** to see the Caravaggios, or head down the street to our next amazing find, the **Galleria Doria Pamphilj**.

9. Galleria Doria Pamphilj

Remember our friend Pope Innocent X? This palazzo is part of his family history.

The Galleria Doria Pamphilj art collection is the largest privately owned collection in Rome. The palace and the gallery are still owned by the Doria-Pamphilj-Landi family, members of which still live here. (Pamphilj became Doria Pamphilj after a series of well executed marriages among rich and powerful families: the Pamphilj, the Doria, the Landi and the Aldobrandini. By 1763 the name had become Doria-Pamphilj-Landi.)

The art collection has been being amassed since the sixteenth century. When Innocent X died he bequeathed his art and furnishings from his palace in Piazza Navona to his nephew Camillo Pamphilj, and they gradually made their way over to this palace.

There are too many treasures to try and catalog for you here. The masters alone are astounding, but of the artists we have talked about in this book you will find some stunningly beautiful works by Annibale Carracci, Raphael and Guido Reni. A couple of the Caravaggios that we discussed in the *Caravaggio* chapter reside in this museum: *Rest on the Flight into Egypt* and *Penitent Magdalene*.

I want to draw your attention to one Velazquez portrait of Innocent X. It was commissioned by his sister-in-law/mistress/girlfriend Olimpia (remember her?). He isn't prettied up at all, yet this portrait is incredibly compelling. Some say it honestly captures the pope as a vindictive despot. Art critics and painters have said it is the best portrait ever created. I don't know that I would go that far, but I will say it is absolutely genius. Since 1927 it has been held in a specially designed room, with a sculptured bust by Bernini. Make sure you take a moment to visit this.

The palace itself is one of the largest in Rome that is still privately owned. There is a Hall of Mirrors that will remind you of Versailles. The apartments will remind you of Versailles too — over the top opulent and frankly just incredible. The art collection is held in the state rooms, four galleries that surround the courtyard, and the chapel which also holds the mummified corpse of the family saint. Can you imagine a) having a family saint and b) keeping its corpse in your family chapel?? (The closest thing to that in my life is our old cat who is buried in our back yard.)

A MODERN SCANDAL

The 1000-roomed palace was passed down through the family until it reached the three-quarter English Princess Orietta Pogson Doria Pamphilj. She married an Englishman, Commander Frank Pogson, and the pair did much restoration to the palace and the collection. On her death in 2000, both the palace and the art collection went to Princess Orietta's adopted English children, Jonathan Doria Pamphilj and Gesine Pogson Doria Pamphilj. These two adult children still live in the palazzo (but are not on speaking terms. They live in different wings of the palace so they don't run into one another).

Of the two, Prince Jonathan is by far the more interesting. In the 90s, prior to inheriting the palazzo and art collection, he was running a beach bar in Venezuela. He now lives in a ten-roomed apartment in the palace with his Brazilian partner Elson and their two children. He and Elson met at the opening of a Brazilian restaurant in Rome and married/became civil partners in Switzerland in 2006. They were one of the first gay couples in Italy to use surrogates, and their children were the first Brazilian passport holders to have two dads on their birth certificates.

In 2009 Princess Gesine went to court to challenge Jonathan's children's right to inherit the estate (which is especially shitty considering the fact that she and Jonathan were both adopted from an orphanage in England). The judge threw her case out. Gesine is married with four children.

GETTING THERE

I recommend allowing a decent amount of time to explore this palace and its collection. This is not one that you can whip through when you find yourself with a spare hour in Rome. If you take the audio tour of the palace the voice you are hearing is Prince Jonathan's. I've never met him but I would love to.

Address: Via del Corso 305.

Galleria Doria Pamphilj is open most days but is closed every third Wednesday of the month. Check the website for details.

WHAT'S NEARBY

Galleria Doria Pamphilj is very close to the **Pantheon** and **Santa Maria Sopra Minerva**, is only a few minutes walk from **Largo Argentina** and the **Jewish Ghetto**. **Trajan's Column**, the **Roman Forum** and **Palazzo Valentini** are less than five minutes walk from here.

10. Palazzo Colonna (One Of The Best Tours In Rome)

This gigantic palace is owned by the Colonna family. The Colonnas trace their ancestry back 31 generations to 1078. They are one of the oldest families in Rome.

Around 1200 the family moved to Rome and started building homes on the Quirinal. They built groups of homes which slowly became joined together into a fortress. The palace spans an entire city block.

It was a family fortress for 200 years across 1300-1500. Oddone Colonna became Pope Martin V in 1417 and named the palace the Pontifical Seat. He lived here from 1420 until his death in 1431. In 1527 during the sack of Rome more than 3000 Romans took refuge inside the palace walls. Which gives you an idea of the size of this place.

Once again this is a palace that will make you think of Versailles, even though it predates the French palace by centuries. It is so vast and so opulent, and *so decorated*. Every single room is a work of art. Part of this giant palace was built on the ruins of the Temple of Serapis. The construction of the palace took place over 500 years, so you notice an overlapping of architectural styles. The interiors reflect the different periods, which makes them even more interesting. It would be quite overwhelming, except that the only way to see this place is with a guide who, as well as explaining the history and the art, is giving you the family dirt!

Rather than give you a huge list of painters whose work is here I will just mention a few. Our friends Annibale Carracci and Guido Reni have work here, as do Tintoretto, del Sarto, Veronese, Ghirlandaio and Bronzino. Trust me when I tell you, the list of artists who contributed to this palace over the centuries is, like the palace itself, enormous.

GALLERIA COLONNA

There are several things in the palace I want to draw your attention to. The first is the Galleria Colonna. I know I keep using descriptors like vast and huge and enormous, but none of them adequately capture the size and volume of this gallery. It was built to impress, and at 76 meters long it really does. The volume of art within this gallery is staggering. Every inch is gilded, decorated, painted and adorned with statues. If I were left alone to look at everything here it would take weeks, and this is just one long room!

You may recognize the Galleria Colonna from the movie *Roman Holiday*. This is where the final scene in the film was shot. Audrey Hepburn comes out to speak to the journalists and we see a heartbroken Gregory Peck standing between the columns with his hands in his pockets and the gallery stretching out forever behind him. I worked with Greg when I was a makeup artist in Los Angeles. He was one of my all-time favorite clients — I adored him. We had memorable talks about art, and he always had the very best stories. I would dearly love to be able to stroll around this gallery with him and listen to him telling me the stories behind the various artworks.

FAMILY CHAPEL

The family chapel at Palazzo Colonna is pretty fantastic. While in there, pay attention to the figure of Jesus suspended over the altar. This was only discovered recently, having been packed away in a box for who even knows how many centuries. He dates back to Florence in the late fifteenth century, but the artist is unknown. It could be Michelangelo — look at it closely and see if you can see a resemblance to his work. My first thought when seeing it was of Michelangelo's Christ, in the church of San Spirito in Florence.

THE BEAN EATER

The final thing I want to bring to your attention is a painting by Annibale Carracci called *The Bean Eater*. At first glance I thought it was an Impressionist painting (laugh all you want). All the Carraccis we have seen so far have been Baroque beauties, resplendent in pretty pastel shades, the subject matter quite ethereal. This one however is from the *Arte Povera* (Poor Art) movement, capturing a simple Roman man with his hand on a chunk of bread, looking at us while he eats a bowl of beans. Now, I am no expert on Carracci, but I would never in a million years have thought this was his work! It is such a departure from his normal colors, style and subject. I wonder if somehow this plays into his battles with Caravaggio?

GETTING THERE

You have tour options at Palazzo Colonna. The first is to take a tour of the main palace, which in my opinion is *one of the best tours in Rome*. The second option is to add in the private apartments of Beirut-born Princess Isabelle, who married into the family in 1908. This is a lesser tour but a fascinating window into the lives of this excessively wealthy family. You can also tour the gardens. If you are unsure which to book have a look at the Colonna Palace website — it has several videos that will give you a good idea of what is on view.

Address: Piazza SS Apostoli 66, entrance at Via della Pilota 17.

Open to the public on Saturdays from 9am to 1pm and by private tour during the week

WHAT'S NEARBY

Palazzo Colonna is one city block from **Trajan's Column** and a block and a half from **Palazzo Valentini**. The **Roman Forum** and **Trajan's Market** are maybe five minutes walk.

It is also approximately two blocks from **Palazzo Doria Pamphij**. **Crypta Balbi** and **Largo Argentina** are just down the street.

11. The Capitoline Museums

The Capitoline Museums are the oldest public museums in the world, dating back to 1471. These may be the best known and most visited museums in Rome. Here, there are pieces by masters including Caravaggio, Rubens, Titian and Tintoretto. The museum is known for its spectacular collection of sculptures.

Sometimes I think the best way to approach the biggest museums is to seek out just a handful of items so that it doesn't feel so overwhelming. Here are some to look for.

SPINARIO

The *Spinario* is a bronze of a boy removing a thorn from the sole of his foot. He is completely perfect, from head to toe. He was designed for 360 degree viewing rather than just to be seen front on. He was sculpted in the Hellenistic style, which dates from 323 BC to 31 BC. Very few Roman bronzes remain, so this work is rare as well as beautiful.

LUPA CAPITOLINA

The *Lupa Capitolina* is a life-sized bronze of the she-wolf suckling Remus and Romulus. There is considerable debate as to its age. She was initially thought to date back to 500 BC but is now thought to possibly be from the 1200s. I'm sticking with 500 BC because that is more interesting. It would make her Etruscan. Pope Sixtis IV donated *Lupa* to the people of Rome, and in 1471 the twins were added.

GALANTA MORENTE

Galanta Morente (The Dying Gaul) is my favorite piece in the museum. It is the partner piece to *Gaul Killing Himself and His Wife* at Palazzo Altemps, and is an early Roman copy of a bronze that dates back to 230-220 BC. As with the sculpture at Palazzo Altemps, this depicts the defeat of the Gauls at Pergamon. As ferocious and desperate as the movement was in the *Gaul Killing Himself and his Wife*, the movement here in this sculpture is of pure defeat. Gaul is caught in the moments before death. His once powerful body is losing its strength as he collapses onto his right arm and bleeds from a stab wound in his side. You can practically see the life force draining out of him. What I find so remarkable about this sculpture is the pure humanity in it — his face isn't screaming or tortured as death comes for him, instead it is as if he realizes that this is it, and is taking his final breaths as he succumbs to death. There is so much beauty in the piece and it evokes so much empathy — I *feel* for him. The pain in his face contrasts the beauty of his body. As you walk around this sculpture, you see how magnificent and strong he was, right up until this minute. From behind you can see his right shoulder and arm straining to hold his collapsing body. Beside him there is a broken sword and a horn. He may have been the herald or trumpeter, leading the way into battle. We know he was a Gaul because of the torque around his neck and his mustache, both sported by Gaul's at that time. If you visit the Capitoline I really hope you will seek out this sculpture.

CAPITOLINE VENUS

The *Capitoline Venus* is lovely in form and I find her interesting because she is covering her pubic area as if ashamed, yet exposing breasts that may as well be the prototype for the boob-jobs of Hollywood and Scottsdale. Too me they look odd against the otherwise perfection of her body — they're too perky, too unreal, as if stuck on to her body. Regardless of her boobs, she is quite magnificent. Visit her and let me know what you think.

COLOSSUS OF CONSTANTINE

The last thing I want to tell you about is actually one of the first things you will see as you enter the courtyard — a series of pieces from a giant statue of another old friend of ours, Constantine. (Remember I told you how he sent his 80-year-old mom Helena to Palestine to pilfer some Jesus memorabilia? This is him, Constantine, the emperor who ushered in Christianity and began the decline of the empire by moving the capital from Rome to Constantinople, now Istanbul.) The pieces here in the courtyard are his head, elbow, knee, hand with the finger pointing upward, shin and two giant feet. Before you move on, notice his fingernails. (How on earth did they groom their fingernails so perfectly back then?) These pieces are from a statue that would have stood about 40 feet tall. It originally stood in the large space at the end of the Basilica of Maxentius and Constantine in the Forum. It was so huge it would have completely dominated the space. Apparently Michelangelo found the pieces and brought them up the Capitoline Hill.

One of the things I find fascinating about the head is that it is so different from all the sculptures we see of the emperors before him. The others were so refined. They combined a relatable humanity with idealism. You could identify with them being human, yet they were idealized like Greek sculptures, God-like. Our boy Constantine doesn't look even slightly God-like. He looks more like an Easter Island head than a god. His features are brutish and heavy, there is a giant cleft in his chin, the hairdo is freaky and makes his forehead look really short, but my favorite feature is his eyes. (What on earth??) He has bug eyes, oversized and made rounder by his semicircle eyebrows. (He must have been a treat to look at when he was angry and shouting! I wonder if people hid under tables in fear of his eyes exploding right out of his head?) Traditionally, most emperors are either looking at you or regally looking out, but Constantine's eyes make him look like a maniac. He isn't looking at us, he is looking beyond us. In its time this statue would have been painted, and I want to know what color they painted those eyes.

GETTING THERE

Address: Piazza del Campidoglio 1.

WHAT'S NEARBY

The Capitoline Museums are in Micheangelo's **Campidoglio Piazza**, above the **Roman Forum**. From here the Forum, **Colosseum**, **Trajan's Column and Market**, and **Palazzo Valentini** are immediately below you. From Trajan's Column walk up and over into the **Monti** district. From Palazzo Valentini you can walk back to **Palazzo Colonna** and **Galleria Doria Pamphilj** within minutes.

From the Capitoline you can also walk to **Teatro Marcello** and onto either the **Jewish Ghetto** or the **Forum Boarium** and **San Nicola in Carcere** in 15 minutes or less.

12. The National Etruscan Museum

Want to see some really, really old stuff? Things that make ancient Rome look modern? Then this is the place for you.

THE ETRUSCANS' STORY

The Etruscans were running the show here prior to the Romans. Their civilization dates back to somewhere around 850 BC give or take, and they lost power to the Romans around 350 BC. Their civilization was around for another couple of hundred years after that. During the Social Wars of Sulla and Marius in 90-88 BC, the last of the remaining Etruscan families joined forces with Marius and either assimilated or disappeared from there, with Sulla wiping out the last traces of them.

Etruscan civilization concentrated around Tuscany, Umbria and upper Lazio, although over the centuries they did spread out. The Etruscans were prolific builders, prolific wine-makers and (random fact) apparently held massive orgies of up to 1000 participants.

The word Tuscan is derived from Etruscan. One of the things I love when I'm in Tuscany or northern Lazio is looking at walls that were originally built by the Etruscans. I get a huge kick out of showing Etruscan building and artifacts to my Glam Italia travelers. Scattered throughout you can still see Etruscan tombs and sarcophagi, remnants of building skills, artwork, jewelry, their culture. (It blows my mind that we can still see this civilization 2500+ years on, when with all the technology we have now we still can't make buildings that last more than a few decades.) Orgies notwithstanding, I find the Etruscan civilization so interesting. If you come across any little museums holding Etruscan artifacts you should go in and have a look. In Lazio (the region Rome is in) you can find lots of Etruscan history around Viterbo and Sutri and Tarquinia. Orvieto has Etruscan treasures, as does much of Tuscany.

At the recovered stolen art exhibition that I saw at the Barberini (remember my Gaugin story?), a considerable amount of Etruscan treasures had been smuggled to Switzerland, including huge sarcophagi. These things had originally been dug up in the hills and in people's backyards. It made me wonder how much is still out there in the world in some bozo's private collection…

But let's look at the three parts of the National Etruscan Museum.

Villa Giulia

The villa itself is quite lovely. It was originally built for Pope Julius III in 1551-1555. Julius III was a connoisseur of the arts and had some fantastic people working on the building. Giacomo Barozzi da Vignola began the design, then the *nyphaeum* and garden structures were overseen by Vasari (Dan Brown fans may know Vasari from the Vasari corridor in Florence) and even Michelangelo worked on the project.

MUSEUM

The museum is on two floors of the villa and holds a wealth of Etruscan treasures, including jewelry, weapons, bronze urns, terracotta items and funerary artifacts. The show stealer is *Sarcophagus of the Two Spouses*, thought to be one of the great masterpieces of Etruscan art, from the sixth century BC. There was a similar pair of pieces at the Barberini exhibition, one of a man, the other his wife, each stretched out along the top of their respective sarcophagi. I haven't been to the National Etruscan for a while so don't know if those two pieces made it here, but I think they do belong with this collection.

VILLA PONIATOWSKI

Part of the Villa Giulia complex includes the Villa Poniatowski. I haven't been inside this one myself, but it's on my list. I have been told it holds Etruscan goodies from Umbria, Latium, and Vetus. I read somewhere that it has artifacts that date back to the 10th century BC! How amazing would that be?? If you do get inside Villa Poniatowski, please let me know!

GETTING THERE

Villa Poniatowski is only open on Saturdays from 3pm to 6pm, and on Thursdays from 10am until 1pm. Check the times and days before going in case they have changed.

Address: Via di Villa Giulia 9.

WHAT'S NEARBY

Villa Giulia is a little further out than most of the other places in this book. It's not far from the far end of **Villa Borghese's** grounds, but I wouldn't plan on walking it. I reccoment you take a bus, tram or taxi from **Piazza del Popolo**.

Ghosts of Rome

10.

The Ghosts of Rome

When you think about it, a city as old as Rome with a history as turbulent and violent as Rome's, it stands to reason there must be some tormented souls still floating around.

Before writing this book, I never really considered the possibility of ghosts. I personally have never sought out the ghosts of Rome (I prefer to devote my evenings in the eternal city to drinking prosecco and flirting with handsome Italian men). If Julius Caesar's ghost popped up and flirted with me I would be thrilled but I would be completely oblivious to any of the others. Though I wish I had thought of this earlier. When my son was 12 and we spent a week in Rome, we walked from Trastevere to Piazza Navona every evening to watch the jazz group he befriended. It would have been so much fun to be on ghost watch while there! I have had several Glam Italia travelers who have talked about ghostly experiences and who would have *loved* looking for the ghosts of Rome had it occurred to me.

If this sounds like your kind of thing, it could be fun to go on a ghost walk through Rome during a full moon or on the dates mentioned in the stories below. Even if you don't see any ghosts, Rome is fantastic at night. See the monuments lit up after the sun goes down, or join in the social scene that seems to happen every night, there is fun to be had!

On the off chance that you do manage to spot one, here is a list of the most well-known souls to look out for.

1. The Ghost of Beatrice Cenci (1577-99)

Beatrice may be Rome's most famous and most beloved ghost. A young girl wronged and ultimately put to death by none other than the Pope Clement VIII (apparently Clemecy wasn't one of old

Clement's virtues.) On the night between September 10th and 11th Beatrice is said to appear, walking along the bridge of angels leading to Castel Sant'Angelo.

Beatrice has been immortalized in an exquisitely beautiful painting by Guido Reni, in a tragedy by Shelley and in novels by Dumas and Stendhal.

In 1999 on the 500th anniversary of her execution, a commemorative plaque was hung by Rome's council in Via di Monserrato at the site of the former Corte Savella prison where Beatrice was held, saying:

From Here
Where Corte Savella Prison Stood
On September 11, 1599
Beatrice Cenci
Left, Heading To The Scaffold,
An Exemplary Victim Of An Unfair Justice

Beatrice was the daughter of Francesco Cenci, an aristocrat who was an immoral and violent brute of a man. She lived in the family mansion in Rome with her older brother Giacomo, her father's second wife Lucrezia and her young half-brother Bernardo. The family also owned a castle in Petrella Salto, not far from Rome. Francesco was frequently in trouble with the papal justice, and all of Rome knew of his savage treatment of servants and his vicious abuse of his wife and children. He was accused of raping multiple young women and of killing one who turned down his advances. His daughter Antonia appealed to the pope to either marry her off or put her in a nunnery — anything to get away from her sadistic father.

Francesco decided to leave town and moved some servants, his wife and poor, beautiful Beatrice to the castle in the country where he kept both under lock and key. It is thought that Beatrice spent months locked in the tower, victim to her father's violent sexual abuse. Some accounts say that Giacomo and Bernardo were there too, others just have Lucrezia and Beatrice.

Something had to be done about this untenable situation. One night Lucrezia put a sleeping potion in Francesco's drink and a hitman with an accomplice came in to do away with him. Something went wrong and he woke, so they hit him in the head with a hammer and chisel before throwing him off a balcony into the trash pile below. They made it look as though the balcony had given way.

The murder was discovered, confessions were tortured out of some of the players, but Beatrice was steadfast in her denial. She and Lucrezia were put in the Corte Savella prison and young Giacomo and Bernardo were put in the Tor di Nona prison, all four of them sentenced to death.

The people of Rome rose up, incensed at the injustice of it. But old Clement with his direct line to God decided that even if a father was raping a daughter it was fundamentally wrong for the daughter to kill her father. So at dawn on September 11th 1599, the four family members were taken to the Sant'Angelo bridge, where public executions were held. The piazza was full of people, including Caravaggio.

Poor Giacomo was tortured with hot pincers along the way. Lucrezia fainted and had her head chopped off with a sword. Beatrice was next, and walked forward with her head held high, her dignity and her beauty intact. Giacomo was wacked in the head with a mallet (which hopefully killed him) and had his limbs chopped off and hung on the four corners of the scaffold for a day. Bernardo had to watch it all and then was taken back to prison. He was stripped of all of his property which was then sold at a very low price to none other than the pope's nephew.

Personally I wish Beatrice had gone all poltergeist on Clement. I like to think I would have haunted him up one side and down the other. But instead the ghost of Beatrice, who became a symbol of the resistance against the aristocracy, on the night before her beheading, walks across the bridge with her severed head in her hands.

HAUNTS

Ponte Sant'Angelo, September 10th.

2. The Ghost of Olimpia Pamphilj

I am fascinated with Olimpia and have mentioned her earlier in this book. She was born to a humble family in Viterbo, which is roughly 50 km outside of Rome. However she had three major things going for her: she was beautiful, she was ambitious, and she was as cunning as a fox.

Olimpia married a rich man, who died, leaving her wealth and status. At the age of 20, she married one of the wealthiest men in Italy, Pamphilio Pamphilj. Not only was he 30 years older than her but was also the brother of a cardinal who, before long, became Pope not-so Innocent X. With a name like Innocent X you just know there has to be all manner of naughtiness going on, and there was.

Olimpia became not-so Innocent X's advisor and lover. Everyone, from ambassadors to politicians to artists to tradesmen, knew that she was the gatekeeper to the pope, so they plied her with gifts to get access to him. She was the Queen of Palazzo Pamphilj in Piazza Navona, and was instrumental in the creation of Piazza Navona as we know it now. The people of Rome loathed her but she didn't care — she had everything she wanted, oodles of money and power. On October 7th 1645, Innocent X made Olimpia the Princess of San Martino, making San Martino al Cimino her own little principality. Everything was coming up roses for Olimpia.

Innocent X's health began to decline, and he was given last rites on December 28th 1656. In early January 1657, as not-so Innocent X lay dying, Olimpia packed up two cases of gold coins and whatever else she could grab, had it all put into her black carriage and, knowing that without the pope she would have nothing, took off. Her carriage raced across the Sisto bridge toward Villa Pamphilj. She never saw Piazza Navona again.

Innocent X's successor, Alexander VII, had her exiled to her little town of San Martino al Cimino and demanded she return the gold coins, but she refused. Two years later Olimpia died of the plague.

Each year on the night of January 6th (the night of Innocent X's death), the ghost of Olimpia, dressed in black and clutching the stolen gold, races out of Piazza Navona and over the Sisto bridge in her black carriage drawn by black horses, her shrill laughter hanging in the air.

HAUNTS

Piazza Navona; Sisto Bridge. January 6th.

3. The Ghost Of Costanza Conti de Cupis

Piazza Navona has another famous ghost, Constanza Conti de Cupis. Shortly after Costanza married the nephew of Cardinal Giandomenico de Cupis the newlyweds moved into the family home, Palazzo de Cupis on Via Santa Maria dell'Anima. The Palazzo backs onto Piazza Navona.

Costanza was not only known for her beauty, but also for her beautiful hands. Her hands were so lovely that a local artist cast a mold of them and then made a model of one of her hands, which he proudly displayed in the window of his shop. One day a passerby stopped to look at the hand and made the prophecy that the woman who owned the hand would lose it soon. When she heard the ominous news Costanza was terrified she would be in an accident and so chose to stay sequestered in her home. To keep herself occupied she sewed. One day while sewing she pricked her finger with a needle. The finger bled and then became infected, her hand swelled and grew covered in sores as the infection made its way up her arm. Nothing could be done to help her, so her hand had to be amputated, but it was too late, the infection had spread throughout her body and she died.

If you are in Piazza Navona when there is a full moon look up at Palazzo de Cupis and see if you can spot the white outline of Costanza's hand in one of the windows.

HAUNTS

Palazzo de Cupis, during a full moon.

4. The Ghosts of Count Cagliostro and Lorenza

Just along from the Piazza Navona, past the Campo de Fiori, lies Piazza Farnese, behind which on the Vicolo delle Grotte the ghost of Giuseppe Balsamo, the Count of Cagliostro roams. Balsamo was an eighteenth century medicine man and freemason. When he was 17 years old he met his future wife here, a prostitute by the name of Lorenza Feliciani who worked out of a brothel on the vicolo. The two traveled throughout Europe together for years, during which time he put Lorenza to work in the old trade. When they eventually returned to Rome he was arrested for a long list of crimes including using witchcraft and magic. Balsamo discovered it was his wife who had reported him to the authorities. He avoided the death penalty but was sentenced to jail and confined to a cell in the Rocca di San Leo where he died four years later.

On nights when there is a full moon the Count of Cagliostro returns to the Vicolo delle Grotte and searches for his wife, calling her by name.

The ghost of Lorenza also appears, apparently especially in the Fall months. The figure of a woman with a black veil concealing her face walks silently through the streets of the Trastevere in the direction of Ponte Garibaldi, staying close to the walls. She crosses the bridge and walks to the Piazza di Spagna where the Count of Cagliostro was arrested. When a voice in the night calls out "Lorenza!" she laughs and disappears into the shadows.

HAUNTS

Giuseppe Balsamo — Vicolo delle Grotte, during a full moon.

Lorenza Feliciani — Trastevere in the direction of Ponte Garibaldi to Piazza di Spagna, Fall.

5. The Ghosts at Via Del Governo Vecchio 57

Honestly the Piazza Navona area is a ghostly hot spot!

Find your way to Via del Governo Vecchio, a narrow, cobblestoned old Roman street, wide enough for only one car and suitably eerie at night. Stop at number 57 and look up to the third floor windows. This apartment has been haunted by every kind of ghost. In 1861 it would seem a poltergeist was in residence. Neighbors would sometimes see objects floating past the windows, other times see them flying across the room, crashing into walls and breaking.

There would be loud banging and crashing and all manner of scary noises. Even the local police testified to hearing them! In the end it got so bad the family had to leave their home.

HAUNTS

Via del Governo Vecchio 57.

6. The Ghost of Mastro Titta

At the first sign of dawn by the Castel Sant'Angelo the ghost of Mastro Titta wanders, wrapped in a scarlet cloak. His real name is Giovanni Battista Bugatti and he was the papal executioner. Over the course of his prolific career he executed 514 souls. Bugatti lived on the Via delle Conciliazone, the road that dead ends into St Peter's Square. He can be seen walking to the Castel Sant'Angelo, the Piazza del Popolo and the Bocca della Verita', the three places he performed the public executions.

It is said that sometimes he stops to greet people he meets on the street to offer them a pinch of snuff or tobacco, as he did for the condemned prior to their execution. So if a stranger in a scarlet cloak stops to offer you a pinch of snuff early in the morning in Rome, say no!

Mastro Titta's scarlet cloak and snuff box now reside in the Museo Criminologico in Rome.

HAUNTS

Castel Sant'Angelo, the Piazza del Popolo and the Bocca della Verita'.

7. The Ghost Of Luca de Marchettis

This one is basically in my backyard — Monteverde is adjacent to my home base in Rome, the Trastevere. I have never walked down this street at night, but maybe one of these Roman nights I will.

Luca de Marchettis was a nobleman and a complete perv. He had a thing for seducing young girls and then killing them. Not wanting to continue with his penchant for underage sex and murder he tried to extinguish his blood lust with an exorcism, but ended up committing suicide by jumping off the balcony of his home on Via San Calepodio.

His villa stands empty and is a little creepy, covered in ivy — perfect for a ghost story.

The neighbors tell stories of lights going on and off in the night, even though no one lives there. They hear steps pacing inside the house, and walking to and from the house. Maybe Luca is out stalking more girls to kill? Or maybe he is pacing back and forth trying to deal with his guilt. Neighbors have seen his ghost walking away from the villa and later coming back. Occasionally a thud is heard, as if he has jumped from the balcony yet again.

Maybe you will witness the ghost of Luca di Marchetti ... (be sure to message me if you do!)

HAUNTS

Via San Calepodio, Monteverde.

8. The Ghost of Empress Messalina

Rome has plenty of ancient ghosts too. If I took men on Glam Italia tours I would love to parade them around the Coppian Hill at night just to see if they could attract Messalina's ghost...

Valeria Messalina was the infamous, uber promiscuous wife of Emperor Claudius. She was so promiscuous that she supposedly once challenged Rome's most famous prostitute to a sex-off contest to see who could have sex with more men in one night. Messalina won with a grand total of 25. It has also been said that the empress was a regular at a local brothel, where she worked under the name "She Wolf".

Claudius turned a blind eye to her antics until she married a Roman senator and plotted for him to overthrow Claudius and replace him as emperor. At this point she had finally gone too far (the sex-a-thon wasn't too much???) so Claudius sent a courier to order Messalina to commit suicide. One of the greatest historians of the time, Tacitus, wrote that she understood her fate and put her hand to the dagger but in her terror applied it ineffectually to her throat and breast. A blow from the tribune drove the blade through her.

So, there was that.

Claudius' woman picker was apparently faulty, because his next wife Agrippina ended up poisoning him with mushrooms.

Although you don't hear of Claudius' ghost rambling around, Messalina is said to be busy haunting the Coppian Hill near the Colosseum, looking for new lovers. Rumor has it that she sneaks up on handsome young men and pinches their bottoms.

HAUNTS

Coppian Hill near the Colosseum.

9. The Ghosts of the Colosseum

When you think about how many slaves, gladiators, random people and wild and exotic animals met their death inside the Colosseum during its prime, and how many homeless people lived, fought and died there during the dark ages, of all places in Rome surely the Flavian Amphitheater has to be riddled with ghosts!

Colosseum ghost stories are rampant, telling of screams, animal growls, ghostly figures on the stairs and along the walkways, and eerie cold patches of air on otherwise boiling hot Roman days (or nights).

If you take a tour of the tunnels below the Colosseum, pay extra attention. Gladiators and slaves, those preparing to kill or be killed, the savage and the terrified, must have crowded those same tunnels on game days at the Flavian. If you are there on a hot day you will notice how incredibly chilly these tunnels are. Sure, you can say it's the stone keeping it cool, but you won't feel the chill everywhere, just there. Also be aware walking through and around the Gate of Death, and don't be surprised if you suddenly get covered in goosebumps. Plenty of people report feeling the frigid cold and an awareness of a very unsettling atmosphere. Some of the creepy things in the tunnels have included ghost sightings, hearing whispers and even being pushed. I haven't been down there in years, but will pay attention next time I go into the tunnels...

Ghost sightings at the Colosseum include a soldier with a red shirt showing from under his armor and a shield in his hand, guarding the building. There are many, many reports of ghostly apparitions moving through the hallways, going up and down stairs and even sitting in the seats. People have heard crowds cheering, night security guards have heard the sounds of people crying in the vaults below.

I have no idea how many times I have been to the Colosseum, both during the day and at night, but I have never once seen a single ghost.

HAUNTS

Colosseum.

10. The Ghost of Nero in the Walnut Tree

I've added this one in because since doing the tour of Domus Aurea I have become fascinated with Nero. The archaeologist who took me through the golden palace told me that everything we know about Nero is wrong. I think she means a sizable chunk of it is debatable, and that he was made out to be worse than he actually was, but she was so passionate and so emphatic that now I want to learn more about him. And it just so happens that he is one of the ghosts of Rome.

An area outside the Porto Popolo once known as the Porto Flaminia was the place where prostitutes, atheists and prisoners who failed to repent before being executed were buried. Once Christianity got kicking these heathens and heretics were banned from being buried on sacred ground, so off to the graveyard of the wicked they went. There's nothing quite like proximity to a graveyard to get a good ghost story cooking.

The story of Nero's ghost is tied up with the creation of the church of Santa Maria del Popolo and the newly elected Pope Paschal II's crusade to save the people of Rome.

After committing suicide Nero was buried in his family tomb, the tomb of the Domitii Ahenobarbi, which was at the foot of the Pincian Hill. A landslide buried the tomb and on its ruins a giant walnut tree grew, a tree so huge it was said to be "so tall and sublime that no other plant exceeded it in any way". Before long the tree became the haunt for demons who would harass and frighten the locals, as well as travelers arriving to Rome through the Porta Flaminia (by the prostitutes' graveyard). Stories of travelers being possessed, beaten, strangled, murdered and totally terrified abounded. The Porta Flaminina and the Via Flaminia were an important access route into Rome, and before long the entire population was scared. Nero's ghost was said to have come back in the form of crows who would sit in the walnut tree and feast with witches and demons.

Pope Paschal II fasted and prayed for three days, at the end of which he had a dream that the Virgin Mary gave him blow by blow instructions on how to free the city from the scourge of the demons.

In 1099, on the Thursday after the Third Sunday of Lent, Paschall II lead a procession with the entire clergy and population of Rome along the Via Flaminia until they reached the demon infested area of Nero's walnut tree. He performed the rite of exorcism and then struck the walnut tree at its root, causing the evil spirits to burst out, screaming madly. The tree was removed and at that point the remains of Nero were discovered. Paschal II had them thrown into the Tiber river. On the site where the walnut tree had stood, Pope Paschal II then laid the first stone of the altar of what would become the church of Santa Maria del Popolo.

If you look inside the church you will see all manner of macabre and creepy skulls and skeletons decorating the tombs. The exorcism and the subsequent erection of the church seem to have rid the city of Nero's troublesome ghost. But if you are in the area of Santa Maria del Popolo at night it wouldn't hurt to keep an eye out for him, or for a murder of crows…

HAUNTS

Via Flaminia; church of Santa Maria del Popolo.

11. The Museum of the Souls of Purgatory

There are no actual ghosts here but if you are interested in ghosts you might enjoy seeing this little museum (*little*, as in there are only about 12 items).

The story of this place begins with a French religious mission, the Order of the Sacred Heart, a group who prayed and held masses for those trapped in purgatory. Along the Tiber river not far from the Vatican, they had a little church, Our Lady of the Rosary, and a Friar by the name of Victor Jouet. In 1897 a fire broke out in the church, and when it had been put out Jouet found the image of a sad, suffering face imprinted on one of the walls. Convinced it was a soul stuck in purgatory, crying out for help, this was the physical evidence he needed to prove that purgatory existed and that there were souls there that needed to be freed. Jouet decided to build a new church on the site, the Church of the Sacred Heart of Sufferage. Pope Pius X gave him permission to travel around Europe collecting other records of souls stuck in purgatory. Much of what he collected perished in another fire, but he had given the church 12 important pieces already and these remain in the museum to this day.

One of the relics comes from Mother Isabella, the Abbess of a monastery in Todi. One night she was visited by the deceased former Abbott, Father Panzini. In order to prove to her that he was suffering in purgatory and in need of prayers and masses to release him, Panzini placed his flaming left hand on her desk, and then used his burning finger to make the mark of the cross. He also placed his hand on her arm, burning through the fabric of her tunic and scorching her skin. The cut out section of her tunic and the section of the burnt desk are in this museum.

Another relic here is a book with a hand print burnt into it. This story dates back to 1815 in Metz when Margherite Demmerle' was visited by a soul identifying herself as her mother-in-law, who had died 30 years before in childbirth. She asked Margherite to make a pilgrimage to Our Lady of Mariental and requested that two masses be said for her (the mother-in-law). Margherite asked her for a sign so the soul placed her hand on Margherite's book leaving a hand print on the page. After the masses had been said, her mother-in-law appeared to Margherite again, telling her that she had been freed from purgatory. The book with the hand print is on display at the museum.

GETTING THERE

Address: Lungotevere Prati 12.

WHAT'S NEARBY

Walking distance to the **Castel Sant'Angelo, St Peter's Square** and **St Peter's Basilica.**

Markets in Rome

11.

Eight Fantastic Markets in Rome

1. Campo de Fiori

2. San Cosimato Market

3. Campagna Amica Market

4. Porta Portese Market

5. Fontanella Borghese Market

6. Borghetto Flaminia Market

7. Mercato Monti

8. Lungo Il Tevere Market

Rome has great markets: food markets, antique markets, flea markets, art markets, fashion markets and markets to search for consigned designer handbags. I absolutely love wandering through outdoor markets. Not only do they afford you some fabulous shopping but they also give you a window into local culture.

I always stay in vacation rental apartments when I'm in Europe, partly for the freedom they afford me and partly because it gives me a chance to feel like I'm living there and participating in local life. One of my favorite things to do as a "local" is shop at the local markets.

In Rome I tend to shop at the same food markets over and over and as a result get to know some of the characters working there. I long ago gave up planning what I would be buying at the market. Now I just ask them what I should make. They argue back and forth with each other, hum and ha, scratch chins, think about it for a bit, and then they tell me what I'm having. It's Rome at its most hilarious and fabulous and delicious! There always seems to be a story behind the produce: *this asparagus just arrived from Puglia last night,* or *we only have this for one more week and then it goes out of season…* and so the tale unfolds. Then they tell me how I must prepare it (the way it has been prepared for centuries). Their recipes are incredibly simple, and I have to tell you, every single time I've tried them the food is amazing! I try to drop by the next day and tell them all about it. They always want to know every detail and genuinely seem delighted.

Much of my travel happens on a budget, so having some meals at home can save lots of money. There is a special kind of magic when you're sitting in a beautiful apartment that is hundreds of years old, maybe it has a fresco or two, maybe it has fantastic architecture and ocher walls, with light and life streaming through giant windows, while you enjoy a glass of local wine and a meal prepared the way it has been done for the past few hundred years. That's when I feel at one with a city.

If you are staying in a hotel, or won't be preparing any meals while in Rome, don't skip the markets. They're still fun to visit. Buy a piece of fruit or a bottle of olive oil, or just wander through the stalls and have a look around.

ITALIAN FOOD MARKET RULES

1. Everything is grown and made locally.

   The fruit and vegetables haven't ripened in a truck driving across country. There is no Monsanto and no GMOs — this is fresh, real, ripe food that was picked yesterday and should be consumed today or tomorrow.

   Be prepared for a flavor explosion! None of these fruits and vegetables are factory farmed and they don't require additives. In America, you often load up with additives to coax out some flavor, but here in Rome when you bite into something as simple as a tomato you can taste the hot Lazio sun under which it ripened and the fertile, volcanic soil where it grew.

   The fish you are buying is from local waters. The cheeses are generally from the region you are in, as are the meats. Food here is seasonal. If it's out of season you won't find it.

2. DON'T TOUCH!

Some market stalls may have signs saying *Non Toccare!* Most won't. It's implied. Unlike at home, you cannot pick up and squeeze fruit and you cannot handle the vegetables.

You ask for three apples and the vendor will choose the three best apples for you.

1. Campo de Fiori

Campo de Fiori (Field of Flowers) was originally a flower market and has been operating for 400 years. In 1869 the fish and vegetable market in nearby Piazza Navona was moved to Campo de Fiori and has remained there ever since.

Until recently, this was a market for locals to buy their meat and cheese and produce. You still see some of them there, but now it is more of a tourist market. You can still buy fresh flowers here, as well as fruit and vegetables, cheese and prosciutto. There are also T-shirt stalls, stalls selling linen dresses, leather bags and belts, plenty of stalls selling bags of pasta and seasonings to take home in your suitcase. There are numerous stalls selling souvenirs and an entertaining guy selling gadgets that turn carrots and zucchini into shapes and noodles and heaven only knows what else. (A word to the wise: don't try to haggle with him — he is wickedly clever and will get the best of you! One of my Glam Italia travelers wouldn't believe me about haggling. She became more and more demanding, thinking she was bringing him down on price. He was faster at math then she was, and she ended up walking away thinking she got one over on him, not realizing she had just paid nearly double the asking price! To this day he remembers it and me, and always laughs and calls out when he sees me, asking if I have any more customers for him!)

This really isn't a market to haggle at and you can come across as being very rude.

The piazza where Campo de Fiori Market is held each day has an interesting history. The streets around the piazza are named for the tradespeople who used to occupy them: the street of the key makers (Via dei Chiavari), the street of the tailors (Via dei Giubbonari), the street of the crossbow makers (Via dei Balestrari) and the street of the hat makers (Via dei Cappellari). This was always a place for local commerce.

It was also a place for public executions. On February 17th 1600, philosopher Giordano Bruno was burnt alive here for heresy. All of his books were put on the Index of Forbidden Books at the Holy Office. In 1889 a statue of him was erected in the piazza, apparently on the exact place of his death. His figure faces the Vatican defiantly, a martyr to free thinking. Personally, I find it hard to believe that Jesus would have been into burning people alive — by all accounts he was a pretty compassionate fellow. Nevertheless there were many public burnings here in his name, including Marco Antonio de Dominis, a scientist and theologian who made his firey exit in 1624.

GETTING THERE

The Campo de Fiori Market runs every day from early morning until around 2pm when the market packs up, street sweepers clear away the detritus and the statue of Bruno watches over the piazza as it turns into a social hub. Ringed with bars and restaurants, Campo de Fiori stays busy late into the night.

WHAT'S NEARBY

Campo de Fiori is right in the heart of Rome. Coming from the river you can see **Michaelangelo's Unfinished Bridge** then walk through **Piazza Farnese** with its giant bathtubs and the beautiful **Palazzo Farnese**. On the other side of Campo de Fiori, cross the road and walk into **Piazza Navona**. You are within walking distance of the **Pantheon**, the **Trevi Fountain** and the **Spanish Steps**.

Beneath your feet **Pompey's Theater** stretches from Campo de Fiori to **Largo di Torre Argentina**.

Caravaggio fans are close to the church of **San Luigi dei Francesi** and the breathtaking frescoes of *The Calling of St Matthew*, *The Inspiration of St Matthew* and *The Martyrdom of St Matthew*.

2. San Cosimato Market

This one really is a market for local Romans and it is a two minute walk from my apartment in Rome. (I always stay in the same apartment in the Trastevere, a stone's throw from Piazza San Cosimato and its morning market.) Whether you are picking up items for an antipasti tray later in the day or choosing tonight's dinner, this is the place to go.

San Cosimato Market is one of the newer markets in Rome, only dating back to the early 20th century. These are family-run stalls and many of the vendors are family members of the original traders. You won't find Made In China souvenirs here, but you will find incredible ingredients and vendors only too happy to tell you how to prepare them.

From Monday to Saturday (6:00am to 1:30pm) the piazza becomes a marketplace, with some freestanding stalls and a row of built-in stalls. This is the place to buy fruit and vegetables, fresh fish, all kinds of meat from steak to prosciutto. You can find the best local cheese here as well as cheese from further afield, and fresh handmade pasta that will ruin boxed pasta for you forever.

Everything closes at 1:30pm and the piazza becomes a social hangout. Mothers bring their children to play in the little park, old men chat and watch the world go by, teens flirt with and preen for each other. This is a great place to observe Roman life without the tourists.

On summer nights you may find a giant movie screen set up in the piazza and rows of wooden chairs filled with the locals, and more spilling out of the windows in the buildings above. I have wandered down here on balmy summer evenings and watched Kate Hudson movies with dubbed Italian voices, surrounded by old couples holding hands, little kids enthralled with the screen, teens flirting, thirty-somethings, forty-somethings, nuns and priests... the whole community. It's wonderful.

WHAT'S NEARBY

Piazza San Cosimato is in the middle of the Trastevere, just below the **Piazza Santa Maria**. You can visit the **Church of Santa Maria in Trastevere** with its stunning mosaics, you can explore and fall in love with the cobblestoned streets of the Trastevere. If you want to see some underground churches you are close to **San Crisogono** on Viale Trastevere and also to the church of **Santa Cecilia**.

From the Trastevere you can cross the **Sisto Bridge** and wander up to **Michaelangelo's Unfinished Bridge**, **Piazza Farnese**, **Campo de Fiori**, and **Piazza Navona**. You are also less than a 10 minute walk from the art at **Palazzo Farnesina**, after which another 20 minutes walking along the Tiber river will take you to **Castel Sant'Angelo** and **Vatican City**.

In the other direction you can cross the **Garibaldi Bridge** and walk into the **Jewish Ghetto**. You are close to **Teatro Marcello, San Nicolain Carcere, Palazzo Valentini**, the **Roman Forum** and the **Colosseum**.

The Trastevere is very central. From here, you can walk to almost everything you want to see.

3. Campagna Amica Market

This place is a foodie's paradise.

The Campagna Amica Market is an indoor food market that happens on Saturdays and Sundays. If you are a foodie and if you are lucky enough to be in Rome on a weekend you should definitely check it out.

The market sells the very best seasonal fruit and vegetables available in Rome. Honey straight from the hive (don't leave here without trying Italian honey!) the freshest olives, salamis and other fresh meat, fish, cheese, bread, baked goods, pasta — even flowers and herbs. It's all here and it is amazing.

All of the food, wine and oil sold here is produced by local farmers from the region around Rome, and is *Zero Kilometer* food. (Zero Kilometer is food that is produced, sold and consumed locally — food that has traveled zero kilometers.) These are non-industrial products and do not go through the global trade chain. Everything goes directly from the farm to the market with no middle man, so the price stays low, the food stays fresh and the quality isn't diminished by waiting in storage in supermarkets. Zero Kilometer has additional eco benefits as there is no long haul transportation so the environment doesn't suffer from indirect pollution.

Campagna Amica is a marketing project organized by Coldiretti, a farmers trade union. They created a brand under which products can be easily identified by consumers, but also so that quality, authenticity, traceability and safety can be maintained. They promote environmentally friendly agriculture and offer the best farm-to-table experience.

Chances are you will see few if any tourists here. Maybe a handful of fellow travelers, but mostly you'll see local Romans who travel clear across the city to shop at this market. There are tables outside where you can sit and enjoy lunch — the food is so good you will want to at least have a snack!

Getting There

Check the hours online, but typically the Campagna Amica market is open Saturdays and Sundays from 10:30am to 7pm.

The market is located at Via di S. Teodoro 74, which is close to the Circus Maximus.

What's Nearby

The market is not far from the **Bocca della Verita**, the **Aventine Hill**, and **Teatro Marcello**. It is a quick cab ride to the **Pyramid of Cestius** and **Ostiense**.

4. Porta Portese Market

This one is Rome's largest and most well-known flea market. It is massive. Plan on getting wonderfully lost in the maze of stalls selling everything including old records, antiques, old rugs, and vintage Fendi. You can find amazing fabrics here, picture frames, old mirrors — you name it. It is a great place to buy really authentic souvenirs that weren't made in China and that won't fall to pieces by the time you get home. This is the best of flea market shopping. Even if you don't want to buy anything, it is fun to look around, especially in the cooler months. (I always think flea markets have an extra layer of intrigue under a slightly cloudy sky.)

The Porta Portese Market reaches about a mile in length and spills into the side streets. (Did I mention that its huge??) It is vibrant, colorful, noisy and full of Romans!

GETTING THERE

The market is open every Sunday from 5am to 2pm, and the earlier you get there the better!

Located in the Trastevere at Via Portuense and Ippolito Nievo.

WHAT'S NEARBY

The Porta Portese Market is close to the Church of Santa Cecilia, but as it is a Sunday the church will be in use, so check before heading over there. It is also in walking distance to everything in the Trastevere.

Across the river you are close to the Campagna Amica market, the Jewish Ghetto and Teatro Marcello. It is pretty much exactly opposite Via

Mamorata, the street that runs up the heart of one of the very best foodie neighborhoods in Rome, the Testaccio. Wander up Via Mamorata, have lunch and then continue up to the Pyramid of Cestius and the Cemetery for Non Catholic Foreigners. It is about a 30 minute walk, but very much worthwhile. From there it's a quick cab ride to Ostiense, or to anywhere from the Colosseum to the Trastevere.

5. Fontanella Borghese Market

Years ago I read an article that described this market as "one of Rome's most elegant living rooms, tucked between the Tiber and the Via del Corso." They had me at *elegant living room...*

This is a Monday through Saturday market that has been around since 1947 and is a must-see for art and literature lovers. The 20 *edicola* (small box shops) remind me of the bookstalls along the left bank in Paris. Here you can find books, posters, etchings, old cameras and maps, lots of unique objects and antiquey items that make amazing souvenirs.

The vendors here call themselves 'dealers in minor antiques' and obtain strictly controlled licenses to sell here, which ensures there are only a small number of stalls and that they sell quality merchandise. The vendors here are super knowledgeable and are happy to tell you the stories behind the pieces they have, as well as all kinds of fascinating details about the time period something is from.

This is not a flea market or a place to hone your bargaining skills. This is an *experience*.

The piazza itself is interesting too. One side holds the University of Rome's School of Architecture and the other is the facade of the Palazzo Borghese, former home of Napoleon's sister Paolina.

GETTING THERE

The market is open Monday to Saturday, from 9am to 7pm.

Address: Largo Fontanella Borghese.

WHAT'S NEARBY

The Fontanella Borghese market is in walking distance from the **Piazza di Spagna** neighborhood with all its high end shops and eateries. You can take in the **Spanish Steps**, **Trevi Fountain** and **Pantheon**, all of which are an easy walk from each other.

Caravaggio fans, you are not far from **Basilica Sant'Agostino** and **San Luigi dei Francesi**. It's only a 10 minute walk to **Piazza del Popolo** and the church of **Santa Maria del Popolo**, which is in turn just minutes from the **Villa Borghese**. So you can check out multiple Caravaggios within close proximity. Check all of their opening times first.

You are also just a lovely neighborhood stroll away from the Tiber river and the **Ponte Sant'Angelo** with its ethereal angle statues leading you to **Castel Sant'Angelo**.

6. Borghetto Flaminia Market

This flea market is also held every Sunday and is not far from Piazza del Popolo. It's not a cheapie flea market — you will pay an entrance fee and the merchandise isn't bargain bin fare. Wardrobe stylists and fashionophiles love this market because the glamorous local ladies tend to unload their wares here. From Gucci handbags to Fendi coats, Pucci dresses to Dolce and Gabbana sunglasses, you never know what you will find. Those who love vintage designer items will be endlessly happy! This market also has antiques and other cool stuff, but the designer goods are the most exciting!

As with any market you can come here and not find anything, or you can find an absolute treasure trove. You can bring back enough vintage Louis Vuitton bags to sell and pay for your entire trip, or you can find just one. Or none.

If you do find designer bags go over every inch of the bag, examine the stitching, the hardware, the inside and the outside. Be aware that buying and selling counterfeit designer bags is illegal in Italy. I have never heard of anyone accidentally buying a counterfeit at the Borgehtto Flaminio Market, but it pays to be vigilant anyway.

GETTING THERE

The Borghetto Flaminio market is at Piazza della Marina, 32.

WHAT'S NEARBY

The market is not far from **Villa Borghese**. From Piazza del Popolo it's a nice walk down to **Piazza di Spagna**, **Trevi Fountain**, the **Pantheon** etc.

7. Mercato Monti

I feel like this one is one of those glorious insider secrets that you dream about discovering.

This is a market for designers who haven't quite broken through yet. From handbags to sunglasses, shoes and clothes, the merchandise is wonderful! It's not cheap but it's not expensive either. Don't come here looking for bargains or planning to haggle. Come here planning to get something pretty incredible that no one has back home. I know all my wardrobe stylist friends from my makeup artist life would die to get their hands on the fashion and accessories here.

This market is fantastic.

GETTING THERE

The Mercato Monti happens Saturdays and Sundays in the basement level of the Grand Hotel Palatino at Via Leonina 46 in the trendy Monti Rione. You can enter from the hotel lobby or from the street at the basement level on the other side of the hotel.

Mercato Monti has its own Facebook page so you can keep up with what's going on and find out which designers are featured each month.

WHAT'S NEARBY

The market is in the heart of the Monti district, one of the best areas to eat in! You won't see many tourists, but instead eateries will be full of local Italians — always a good sign!

You are not far from the church of **Santa Maria in Maggiore** and from there if you are up for a walk you can meander on up to the **Baths of Diocletian** and the church of **Santa Maria degli Angeli e dei Martiri**. In the other direction the Monti backs onto **Trajan's Market**, the **Colosseum** and the **Forum**.

I really hope you will wander around the Monti while you are there. It is a gorgeous slice of old Rome with something magnificent around every corner!

8. Lungo Il Tevere Market

Lungo Il Tevere is a social hub with a little bit of everything on offer to further electrify those balmy Roman nights in mid-summer. Although technically not a market I'm including it here because you need to go!

There are vendors selling clothing and accessories, there are restaurants (including a Tex Mex!), fun bars where you can enjoy cocktails beside the river in gardens strung with lights. Also long stretches where local artists can display their work. Music plays, there are fussball tables set up — it really is tremendous!

Whether you want an aperativo, a full meal or just want to have a look around, this spot really is an adventure! You will see Romans of all ages enjoying a summer evening out. Last summer (2018) there was a black and white photo display stretching along the waterfront showing movies shot in Rome and identifying the different shooting locations. It was a small thing but all the ladies on my Glam Italia tour got a huge kick out of it and it was fun to check out all the places we had been in the context of the films. Every year there is something different.

This place is very safe, well-lit and comfortably full of people. There is no human crush and you will have plenty of room to wander around but also to people-watch — Romans are so effortlessly glamorous!

In case you are thinking there will be drunks rolling around everywhere, there won't be. Italians are very social and prefer to be out chatting to friends than to sit in front of the TV at night. They will have a drink or two but you won't see them drunk or aggressive.

I asked one of my drivers, Pasquale, about this and he said being drunk or aggressive implies that you are not much of a man because you can't hold your wine! Who would want to look like less of a man? Love it!

GETTING THERE

Roman Summer — June to August. You will see the tents set up along the Trastevere side of the riverbank, from Ponte Sisto to Ponte Sublicio.

WHAT'S NEARBY

You are along the Trastevere, so there will be amazing restaurants immediately behind you inside the neighborhood. The **Piazza Santa Maria Trastevere** is fun at night, with performers, fire dancers and magicians in front of the fountain. **Piazza San Calisto,** just 100 feet away, has bars full of locals. The entire area is fun every night of the week.

On the other side of the river is the **Jewish Ghetto**, which is just magic at night! It is amazing to wander through, but it is also a lovely place to sit at an outdoor table with some Jewish artichokes and a glass of wine.

Food & Wine in Rome

12.

What to Eat in Rome

Food and wine are an important part of any Italian experience. More than just sustenance, they are a huge part of the culture and the local identity, as well as the social fabric of the place. Meals are eaten at a table, not consumed walking down the street. Italians eat with family or friends, phones are put away, humans interact with humans, make eye contact, talk, laugh and enjoy sensational food. Each time I arrive in Italy I am always amazed watching locals at restaurants and eateries just engaging with one another. When I return to America after a month in Italy I am totally stunned watching people in restaurants *not* interacting with one another!

In my first book *Glam Italia! How To Travel Italy* I described how there isn't just one Italian cuisine. There are many. Every region has its own food and wine, and within each region there is more food and wine specific to the various smaller areas. I talk about all the different parts of Italy in that book, and created a guide to each region and which food and wine I think you need to try depending on where you are. (If you have the book on the Kindle App on your smartphone, you may find that guide handy to quickly look up what to order in the town or region you are in.) I also covered how to choose a restaurant and how to avoid tourist traps, so make sure you get up to speed on that before you head to Italy.

ITALIAN FOOD

Where I live in America, cuisine isn't so specific geographically. For example, although Cajun food belongs to Louisiana you can find it everywhere. Boston clam chowder is available nationwide, as is Tex Mex. Here in the US, Italian food is often heavy, cheesy, fatty and dripping in a sugar-enhanced tomato sauce. I don't care for American-Italian food in general, which saves me countless calories. But Italian food in Italy is completely different!

In addition to being regional, Italian food is also seasonal and local. Most of the time the produce, cheese, meat and fish that you are eating will have come from within a few miles of where you are standing. Produce that is out of season is seldom available and Italian recipes are designed to blend the flavors of the season perfectly.

My first piece of advice to anyone traveling to Italy is: don't mess with the menu. In America you frequently see people requesting changes to the menu — swap out artichokes for green beans, fat-free ranch on the side, this instead of that, hold this, add something else, you know what I mean. In Italy this is the height of rudeness. The recipes aren't designed to be swapped out or changed. (And they do not have ranch dressing, let alone fat-free ranch! In Italy, salad dressing is olive oil, sometimes with balsamic vinegar.) I always make a point of explaining this to my Glam Italia travelers, and generally this hasn't been a problem. Even people who have wanted to swap out menu items have ended up happy with the meal in its intended form. Trust that the chef has his eye on the ball when it comes to designing his meals. Then sit back and enjoy!

So, rather than trying to find something familiar on the menu, try the local cuisine. You won't see lasagna everywhere. Spaghetti and meatballs is American, not Italian. Outside of tourist traps (places you do not want to eat) you won't find Caesar Salad (it's actually Mexican, not Italian). You won't see garlic bread on the menu and they won't have Fettuccine Alfredo. Pizza in Italy is nothing like pizza in America. Forget the Italian food you know and try the local, regional Italian food. It is honestly fantastic.

Rome, like all the other regions in Italy, has its own cuisine, which changes according to the season. It is known for organ meats, dense pastas and thin crust pizzas.

Here are my recommendations for typically Roman cuisine to try while you're in Rome. I had a hard time narrowing it down — there are too many wonderful things you need to try!

Street Food

The concept of street food in Rome can be a little confusing. You don't see locals walking down the street, eating, the way you do in the US — other than maybe with a gelato and even then they tend to be more stationary when eating. So street food in Rome is more like a little something you stop to eat on the way home.

You can often see students and young people sitting on an outdoor staircase eating street food, or maybe leaning against a wall. Occasionally I see someone sitting on a city bench eating. I suspect people also buy street food to take home to eat. And even though it is a street food, you'll see people sitting inside little eateries eating suppli.

Although there are some American fast food places in Rome, you seldom see Romans eating fast food, and I can honestly say I have never seen a Roman walking down the street eating McDonalds! (That doesn't mean it doesn't happen, but these eyeballs have never clocked it!)

1. SUPPLI

Suppli (soo-plee) is the ultimate Roman street food. Much like the Sicilian *arancini* they are a rice ball with *ragu* and melted *mozzarella* inside. *Suppli* often but not always uses a *risotto* instead of plain rice. Once the ball is made, it is rolled in egg then breadcrumbs and then fried. They are really fantastic and will leaving you wanting more!

2. TRAPIZZINO

Trapizzino is a relatively new Roman street food. In 2008/2009 chef Stefano Callegari created these triangles of pizza base, sliced and filled with classic Roman foods such as meatballs, chicken cacciatore or tongue with green sauce. They are served in a paper cone, making them convenient to eat outdoors, are inexpensive and combine the best of Roman flavors. The original store is in the Testaccio district, which is foodie heaven and one of the best areas to go eat anyway.

Trapizzino, Via Giovanni Branca 88, Testaccio

3. PORCHETTA

Still on the street food/ light food subject, you have to try the *porchetta panino*. This is slow roasted pig, sliced hot and served in a fresh baked bread roll or *panino*. *Porchetta* doesn't need any additives — don't add mayonnaise or mustard or any other accoutrement, just eat it the way it is supposed to be eaten, sliced hot and sandwiched inside fresh bread.

I love getting *porchetta panini* at local markets, where I think it is at its best, but sometimes I stumble upon a lunch place with amazing *porchetta* sandwiches. Remember calories don't count in Italy. You will be walking so much that you will come home looking svelte anyway.

4. Pizza

It's a tough call, but my favorite pizza in Italy is served in Tuscany and in Rome. I know my friends from Napoli would be horrified to hear that, especially as Naples is the home of pizza. (Pizza in Naples is incredible, but it has a slightly chewier base. Tuscan and Roman pizzas have a thin, almost crisp base, which I prefer.)

Even if you just arrived in Rome from Tuscany or from Naples you still must try Roman pizza. It is light, fresh and incredibly delicious. And it is the complete opposite of American pizza. Roman pizza is not dripping in fatty cheese, doesn't have a sugary tomato sauce, and won't have different toppings. (Pepperoni is not an Italian food and you won't find it on pizza here. *Pepperoni* in Italian means large bell peppers.) Expect simple, well-paired toppings, and often fresh raw vegetables on top.

Whenever I'm in Rome I eat at **Carlo Mente** in Trastevere at least once, and always order the same thing. In fact, the waitresses don't even ask me what I want, they just raise an eyebrow at me and I nod back at them. They bring me this pizza that resembles a light margherita pizza with fresh *arugula* (rocket) on top. It is so perfect that I have zero interest trying anything else!

Carlo Mente, Via della Lungaretta 101, Trastevere

5. CARCIOFI

You will see this everywhere — *carciofi* is Italian for artichoke. There are two types you must try while in the Eternal City. The first is Roman style, *carciofi alla Romana*, which are simmered in olive oil, white wine, garlic and herbs. They are so tender and delicious you won't be able to remember Rome without them!

The other type of artichokes are Jewish artichokes or *carciofi alla giudia*. The best place to eat these is in one of my favorite haunts, the **Jewish Ghetto**. Any restaurant you try there will serve these fantastic, fried artichokes. They have the texture of potato chips, and are the perfect food to snack on with a glass of wine at one of the tables outside. The main street of the Ghetto is gorgeous, with incredible ruins, old buildings, ambience — the perfect Roman eating experience!

My three fave spots to have carciofi are **La Reginella**, **Ba'Ghetto** or **Nonna Betta**.

6. FIORI DI ZUCCA

Another Roman food experience is eating the delicious fried zucchini flower. Stuffed with *mozzarella* and anchovies (although you can have them without anchovies if you're not a fan), battered and deep fried, you have to at least try them while in Rome.

Before you turn up your nose at the thought of anchovies, know that anchovies in Italy are not the same as anchovies in America. At home I would scale a high fence and run up a hill to get away from what I consider to be a vile and over salty insult from the sea. However, anchovies are prepared differently in Italy and in my experience they run from palatable to delicious. If you're not sure, try one *fiori di zucca* with anchovy — you don't have to eat it if you don't like it. Or encourage the person you are traveling with to order one and try a bite!

A LITTLE STORY ABOUT ANCHOVIES

On my first trip to Sicily, in a restaurant we were served a dish of tiny fish fillets dredged in local oil and lemons, as part of the antipasti. They were so good I ate the lot and then had to order more. I didn't understand the Italian name of the fish and kept asking the waiter to tell me again, eventually having him write it down for me. I googled it and discovered I had been gobbling fresh anchovies!

Admittedly I have never had anchovies as delicious as the way they serve them in Sicily, anywhere other than Sicily. Sometimes I am a little hesitant to order them on something larger, like a pizza, but I am always game to try at least one anchovy-stuffed *fiori di zucca*.

Pasta

There are many amazing pasta dishes specific to Rome, but these three cannot be missed.

7. BUCATINI AL AMATRICIANA

Bucatini is a roman pasta. It is a long, fat spaghetti-tube noodle with a hole running through the middle. As far as pastas go it is a thick, hearty pasta rather than a thin linguini style noodle. *Amitriciana* is a roman pasta sauce made with *guanciale* (cured pork cheek), tomatoes and local *pecorino* from Amatrice. Sometimes it also has onion.

I was having lunch with a friend in the little eatery next door to Palazzo Valentini, killing time before going on the Palazzo tour (which I highly recommend. See the *Underground Rome* chapter for details). While we were sitting there an extraordinarily glamorous Roman woman sauntered in and sat one table over from us. She was madly chic, had a figure to die for, and quite a commanding presence, one of those women who stops traffic. I couldn't take my eyes off her. I wanted to *be* her.

I had ordered an ordinary non-fattening salad, and was expecting her to order water and a piece of lettuce. Instead she ordered a glass of red wine and a huge bowl of *Bucatini al Amatriciana*. And she ate every last bite of it. I caught her eye and we got chatting part way through her meal (which was a good thing or she might have confused me with a stalker!) She told me that this place had the best *Amatriciana* in all of Rome, and that she came and ordered it for lunch once a week. She told me that it is impossible not to eat the entire bowl as the *Bucatini al Amatriciana* there is so incredibly good.

I keep meaning to go back there and order it myself (mostly so that I can be like her), but I live in fear of my pants exploding right off me if I ate that much. Knowing my luck the incredibly handsome fellow who works next door at Palazzo Valentini (he looks like the mad king on *Reign*) would choose that moment to walk through the door!

Wear your stretchy pants and put *Bucatini al Amitriciana* on your list for Rome!

Terre e Domus, Foro Traiano 82, Roma (Next door to Palazzo Valentini)

8. CARBONARA

If you have already read *Glam Italia! How To Travel Italy* then you already know my Carbonara story when I was eating in Piazza San Cosimato with one of my Glam Italia tour groups. But Rome is full of Carbonara stories, so I'm going to tell you another one.

This one also takes place in the Trastevere, but on the south side of Viale Trastevere. It was my final night in Rome, after spending six weeks in Italy with back to back tours. I always plan a few days alone in Rome at the end of the tours and am tearful when it is time to leave. Rome is quite safe to wander around at night, so I was out strolling, soaking up as much of the city as I possibly could before flying home the next morning. I was deep in the south side of the Trastevere when I stumbled upon an ivy covered restaurant/trattoria called **La Cornucopia a Trastevere**. I had seen it before but hadn't written the name down and had never found my way back to it, so decided that this night it must be the Roman gods of dining telling me I had to eat here.

I was the only non-Italian in the entire place, and every table was full (which are two signs of a great culinary find!). The owner/manager (not sure which he was) and all the waiters were gorgeous, flirty Italian men, and not only did they quickly separate the unused end of another large table to make me one of my own, but in a flash they had a little vase of flowers, a candle and a complementary glass of wine there for me too. I swear even if you are on your own you are never alone in Italy! They all came by throughout the evening to chat and keep me company, and the glam thirty-somethings as well as the older patrons in the restaurant took time to lean over or come up to my table and chat for a moment. I doubt I was of any interest to them and their glamorous lives, it was just part of their friendly and welcoming nature.

I was chatting to my waiter, who was a delightful boy in his early twenties and who was having fun practicing his English on me. I told him it was my last night in Italy and how sad I was to be leaving. I also told him I had absolutely no idea what I wanted to eat. In the sweet, naive manner of a boy who hasn't yet learned guile or the art of deception he very earnestly told me that the only thing I should consider was the Carbonara. He followed that by proudly stating it was the very best Carbonara in all of Rome. Quite a claim, but who was I to doubt him?

So the Carbonara arrived, and it was sensational. The kind of incredible that makes you slow the world down and eat at a borderline geriatric speed. My God it was good!

Whatever you think you know about Carbonara, forget it. And then order Carbonara at a non-tourist restaurant in Rome. I would never in a million years order Carbonara at home (where it is heavy, creamy, gluggy. Just looking at it you feel your arteries harden and know it is an express trip to your thighs with a tummy ache to follow). In Rome, Cabonara is divine.

Every chef in Rome has his or her own spin on it, from which pasta to use to which cheese, but one thing is universal — they never, ever use cream. You may find it made with *pancetta* or with *guanciale* or with one of a thousand related options (I have never had it made the same way at any two restaurants). It could have *Pecorino Romano* or *Parmigiano Reggiano* or a combination of the two. It will typically have black pepper. The star of the show is the egg. Some places use just the yolk, others the whole egg, but all of them create a thickened sauce that never tastes eggy, and that binds perfectly to the pasta they are using.

Carbonara is a signature pasta dish of Rome and you absolutely must try it. But *not at a tourist restaurant.* If you are not sure how to choose a restaurant in Rome (or anywhere in Italy) there is an entire chapter on it in *Glam Italia! How To Travel Italy.*

And in case you were concerned — let me assure you there are no calories in Roman Carbonara and the carbs don't count, so you can eat it without guilt!

La Cornucopia a Trastevere, Piazza in Piscinula 18/15 Trastevere, fronte Isola Tiberina.

9. CACIO E PEPE

This is another traditional Roman pasta dish, and as far as I am concerned it is the perfect comfort food. After a long day of sightseeing, or when I just want to sit quietly with a bowl of pasta and a glass of wine, or any time I don't want to think about what to order or have make any complicated decisions (sometimes tour guiding can leave your brain completely fried), this is my go-to dish. It is ridiculously simple yet completely delicious, and it leaves you full and content.

Cacio is the local slang for *Pecorino Romano*, which is a salty, aged version of sheep's milk cheese, and *pepe* is pepper. *Cacio e Pepe* is made with a thick, spaghetti-like pasta, normally *tonnarelli* or *bucatini.* It is hearty and satisfying and when I have been on sensory overload all day in this bustling city, both my brain and my belly appreciate its simplicity.

Meat

Okay, in the interest of complete honesty — I don't eat red meat, so I can't tell you about these from personal experience, but they are revered as being quintessentially Roman dishes and I have meat-eating friends who have raved about them.

10. SALTIMBOCCA

Translated this means *"jump in mouth"*, so if I did eat read meat I would be compelled to at least try this. Slices of veal get either topped with or wrapped in *prosciutto crudo* and fresh sage and then marinated in white wine. It is most often served in a white wine sauce. *Saltimbocca* has been described to me as succulent and delicious.

11. TRIPPA ALLA ROMANA

My sister-in-law, who is also one of my all around favorite people in the world, absolutely *loves* tripe, or *trippa* as it is known here. Just the thought of it makes me gag, but *Trippa alla Romana* is a classic Roman dish, and those who like tripe love it!

The tripe (cow's stomach) is sliced and then simmered in a sauce made of slow cooked tomatoes with fresh mint and *pecorino*. You'll find it in the *Secondo* section of the menu, and also sometimes as a *panino*. If you are in the Testaccio neighborhood (the serious foodie neighborhood) there is an old style panino place in the Testaccio Market called **Mordi e Vai** that makes *Trippa alla Romana panini*, and always has long lines of locals waiting to get them.

Mordi e Vai, Testaccio Market

Fish

Now we're talking! I eat seafood almost every day. In Rome I have ordered so many fish dishes, I don't even know where to begin. Half the time I don't know which fish I'm eating, but I have never been disappointed. If I see Branzino on a menu I will invariably order it — sea bass is fantastic in Italy!

12. BACCALA'

This is a Roman-Jewish salted cod that is fried in egg batter. It's really, really good. You might see it as a street food or you might see it in a restaurant. The closest thing we have to it is the battered fish in fish and chips.

Baccala' (cod preserved in salt) was originally from the Basque. Before it is ready to eat, *Baccala'* is rehydrated by being soaked in fresh, clean water for 48 hours, with the water being changed every 8 hours. Did I mention it's really good?

STOCCAFISSO

Cod as we know it, fresh or frozen, is *merluzzo*. *Stoccafisso* (stockfish) is air-cured, while *Baccala'* is salt-cured. Although I've seen *Stoccafisso* on a million menus, I had no idea what air-cured actually meant. Apparently *Stoccafisso* is a Norwegian thing. Norway has a unique climate with dry air, low precipitation and cold temperatures, making it the perfect place for air-curing cod. I had never stopped to think about where cod would be air-cured (I had actually never devoted a single thought to the art of air-curing fish) but it is cured in open tents, as it has been for centuries, and when the fish is preserved this way it can last for years! Who even knew that years-old air-dried fish could be a thing?? *Stoccafisso* gets pounded with a wooden mallet to break down the fibers and is then soaked for 72 hours before it is ready to eat. Norwegian *Stoccafisso* is considered to be the very best in the world, so if you see it on a menu give it a whirl.

Cheese

There are so many different cheeses in Italy! Every region has its own cheese, and within every region there are sub-regions with *still more* cheese. They get super specific too, because the hills and the grass the sheep/cows/goats/buffalo are grazing on are going to impact the flavor. Although cheeses from all over are wonderful and can make for a fabulous cheese board it stands to reason that local cheese blends exquisitely with local produce, meats, or fish.

I make an effort to try at least a couple of cheeses from whatever region of Italy I am in. I don't for a minute pretend to be wildly conversant in cheese, and am learning as I go. In a restaurant or market, I tend to just ask which cheeses are local. Luckily for me Italian cheeses don't seem to be as pungent and stinky as the Frenchies.

13. PECORINO ROMANO

Pecorino is a sharp, hard cheese made from sheep's milk. *Pecarinos* are everywhere in Rome, largely because the Lazio climate, landscape and the flora are perfect for sheep, and as such Lazio produces more *pecorino* than any other cheese. There are loads of variations of *pecorino* but the one that is in all the famous dishes (*Carbonara, Cacio e Peppe, Amitriciana*) is *Pecorino Romano*.

Pecorino Romano has more flavor than *Parmigiano*, which is another reason it is used extensively in Rome. One of my friends serves slices of it drizzled with honey or paired with figs or slices of pear. It never tastes quite as fabulous when I try to impress people with this at home — maybe you need honey from Lazio? Regardless, buy some at a Roman market and try it with a glass of crisp white wine at the end of the day.

14. MARZOLINA

This is a goat cheese from the Frosinone area south of Rome. It is made from the first lactation in March, (hence the name). Once made, it is dry-salted, put in molds and then it sits out on wooden slats for a few days, being turned every day. The cheese then spends months in demijohns filled with oil, which is changed around four times per year. After eight months soaking in the oil, the cheese turns white and becomes hard. *Marzolina* can be sweet and rich, and if seasoned during its oil soak it can also be spicy.

Baked Goods

15. MARITOZZI

For all the large scale eating they do in Italy, breakfast is a rather simple affair. An espresso or cappuccino and a *cornetto*, which is an Italian version of a croissant. In Rome, the *cornetto* is big, but there is also a breakfast bun called a *Maritozzo* if you want something more substantial. It is a fresh sweet bun, sliced open on an angle and filled with a barely sweetened whipped cream. I can't eat this every day, but once in a while I will give it a whirl. They look impressive, and if you are in Rome and are wandering down the street for a morning coffee you should try *Maritozzi* at least once (even if you mostly just eat the bun and only have a little of the cream).

16. PASTICCERIA BOCCIONE JEWISH BAKERY

This is one of my absolute favorite things to do in Rome! Until you know where it is, it is hard to find, even though it is right on the main street of the Jewish Ghetto. Boccione is a teeny tiny bakery with no sign on the door or on the wall outside. If you're not looking you will miss it!

Pasticceria Boccione (or Forno Bocciano) has been around forever and is famous for having fabulously surly staff and only a handful of baked goods that never change. Although I have to say as much as I prepare my travelers that they are likely to be scowled at, it has never happened. I've actually found the servers at Boccione to be quite friendly.

There are two items that you can not leave this bakery without trying:

PIZZA DOLCE

Pizza dolce (sweet Jewish pizza) is a dense, brick-like bar of sweet dough absolutely bursting with almonds and pine nuts, chunks of candied fruit and raisins. They bake these throughout the day, so you can still get a warm one in the afternoon, but buy extra to take back to your hotel or apartment for breakfast the next day. The tops are slightly burnt and crisp, the insides soft — honestly *this* is my favorite thing to have for breakfast in Rome. I have started more mornings in Rome than I can even count with coffee made in a moka and a Jewish pizza. They are completely guilt free too, because every day in Rome you will walk off more calories than you will find in one of these.

CROSTATA

Crostata (pie/tart) is the other thing you really need to try here at Boccione. It is famous all over Rome, so sells out quite quickly each day. It also has a great story behind it. This is the double-crusted crostata. These are stuffed to bursting with a mixture of ricotta and wild cherry (*ricotta e visciole*) which is the big favorite, or ricotta and chocolate (*ricotta e cioccolato*), or almond paste and wild cherry (*mandorla e visciole*). The tops of these tarts are always blackened, so don't be put off — it is how they are meant to be. They are sold whole for 24 euro or in slices. The staff here can't be bothered monkeying around, so if you ask for a slice you will normally get 1/4 of the tart. Keep that in mind if there are a couple of you wanting just a slice. One is plenty to split between two people.

If you are not sure which to try, go for the *crostata ricotta e visciole*. City-wide that is the one the *forno del ghetto* is best known for.

Pasticceria Boccione (or Forno Bocciano), Via del Portico d'Ottavia 1, Jewish Ghetto

THE JEWISH GHETTO

Throughout history Jews always did well in Rome. They were liked and respected, and as a group lived across the river in the area known as the Trastevere, from a time before Christ until 1555. On July 14th of that year, Pope Paul IV sent down a papal bull, the *Cum nimis absurdum* (which in my opinion was completely absurd, so well named). The first words of the decree were, "since it is absurd and utterly inconvenient that the Jews, who through their own fault were condemned by God to eternal slavery..." Essentially the bull revoked the rights of the Jewish community, placed religious and economic restrictions on Jews living in the Papal States and subjected Jews to restrictions on their personal freedom as well as other degradations. The bull established the Roman Ghetto, and ordered that the Jewish people of Rome (which at that time numbered around 2000) live there. So they were moved across the river from the Trastevere into the Ghetto, where conditions were horrific. The river would overflow and flood regularly creating a swampy mess, housing was wretched, in fact life was pretty wretched. The Ghetto was gated and those who were let out to work by day were locked back in by evening. They weren't allowed to own property or to practice medicine among Christians, yet when a doctor was needed at night the gates would be opened to let him out. Jewish men were required to wear a yellow hat and women to wear a yellow kerchief on their heads. (We must have been raised with a different bible in New Zealand, because try as I might I can't find the part where Jesus, King of the Jews, required, recommended or even asked for persecution of Jewish people. Call me crazy, but it seems to counteract everything he stood for.)

It wasn't until 1882 that the requirement for Jews to live in the Ghetto was abolished.

Today the Jewish Ghetto is one of the most chic and pricey residential areas in Rome, so don't be put off by its awful past. It is incredibly beautiful, is home to some incredible ruins (see the *Ancient Rome* chapter) and has wonderful places to stop and eat at reasonable prices. It is fantastic spending evenings there dining al fresco, or swinging by the best bakery in Rome (assuming you can find it).

Back to the Crostata…

The ricotta and cherry *crostata* came about because the absurd decree stated that Jews were forbidden to sell or trade in any dairy products. How do you hide ricotta? Bake it into a tart, disguise it with cherries and then cover it with a crust. Burn the top a little and no one's going to look.

13.

Where to go Wine–tasting in Rome

There are of course plenty of places to go wine-tasting in Rome. You see signs for it everywhere. On my Glam Italia tours we have already been wine-tasting in various wineries around the country so I haven't done a lot of wine-tasting in Rome, but I can tell you about three really fantastic wine-tasting places and the tremendous experiences I have had at them.

17. RIMESSA ROSCIOLI

This place sits a block back from the river between the Sisto and Garibaldi bridges on the east side (not the Trastevere side). You might expect Rimessa to be full of tourists, but it isn't. Instead you will find it full of Romans of all ages, with a few scattered tables of travelers. Rimessa is a combination of a wine-tasting venue (a very cool place to stop for a glass of wine and some snacks) and a restaurant.

First, the food is fantastic.

Second, the ambience is fun and lively and interesting, with the bubbling chatter of Romans enjoying an aperitivo or a meal in perfect balance with the music playing. (Have you ever noticed how often music is too loud or the noise of the people is too loud, and you can barely hold a conversation? This place has the balance just right.) You can comfortably chat with your friends here without straining to hear them.

Third, the wines are impressive. Rimessa has an extensive array of wine from all over the country, even obscure wine from far away places. They have more than 400 wines with at least 70 available by the glass.

When I've been there, the sommelier/waiter handling our table has been great too. He didn't just show up for a night at work, he was *really into it*. Not only was he friendly and personable, but he asked so many questions about what types of wine we liked and what food we liked and made his wine-tasting choices for each of us based on that equation, rather than giving us all samples of the same wine. He turned what could have been an hour of wine-tasting into an entire evening out. We had fun, we were in the kind of place you want to keep coming back to (and I do), and we all ended up carrying or shipping bottles home, but even more than that he crafted *an experience* for us.

When I travel I'm looking for an *experience*, and Rimessa creates a fabulous experience. At no time do you feel like they are just trying to sell wine. Their goal seems to be a wonderful night out for their clientele, and if you want to buy wine at the end of it then they can take care of that too.

Rimessa Roscioli also offers cooking classes, private group tastings and a variety of other options.

As with any restaurant or wine bar there is always the chance it will be closed or have moved, so check ahead and see that it is still open.

Rimessa Roscioli, Via del Conservatorio 58. Telephone: +39 06 68803914
Email: winetasting@rimessoroscioli.com

18. VINO ROMA

This is an entirely different experience. Vino Roma wine-tastings are about teaching you about Italian wine and food pairing. You will come away from it feeling quite educated and confident in which wines to order when you are out and about, and which wines specifically work with the food you are ordering.

"Not only will you feel a lot more confident choosing your wine, you will see how much more enjoyable it is to drink Italian wine when you know your Primativo from your Refosco!" From the Vino Roma website

They had me at *Primativo*!

They also offer food walking tours, and will give you lists of wine bars and eateries with recommendations for wine and food to order.

Vino Roma's wine-tasting area is fresh and modern, but make sure they take you down to the wine cellar – it's 1000 years old!

You need to book ahead for this one, so check out their website at www.vinoroma.com

Vino Roma, Via in Selci 84/G (the G is important – it is about 7 doors down from the regular #84)

19. BEPPE E I SUOI FORMAGGI

Seriously though, what could be more fun than a place called *Beppe And His Cheeses*? This place has a cheese room, a wine room and a wine cellar for tastings.

Beppe Giovale is a cheese producer from Piedmont, and the cheeses here are mostly his own. You can buy them as well as several of his other products to take home. You can also sit here and eat them. (Yes, they are sensational.)

Beppe's partner Francesco runs the wine side of the business, featuring mostly wine from Piedmont. The tastings are wonderful.

Once you know where Beppe's is you will end up popping in for wine and cheese whenever you are in the neighborhood, which just happens to be close to everywhere you want to go! Beppe's is located in the Jewish Ghetto.

Beppe e I Suoi Formaggi, Via Santa Maria del Pianto 9A/11, Jewish Ghetto

Local Wines

My first rule with ordering wine when I'm in Italy is to ask the waiter or sommelier what he recommends. He knows which wines pair best with what you're eating. If you are in a non-tourist eatery, you will usually find that the house white or house red are really good,.

Lazio, the region that Rome is in is a predominantly white wine region — 95% of the wine produced in Lazio is white wine.

If you want to buy a bottle of wine to take back to your apartment or just want to order something local, here are a couple to look for. If you're in a restaurant, ask for a recommendation.

20. FRASCATI

Frascati is a local white wine from the town of Frascati. This is a very uncomplicated wine. It is low alcohol, fresh, crisp and light, making it ideal on hot Roman days.

Frascati dates back to Ancient Rome and probably even before that. Romans referred to it as the 'golden wine' and in Ancient Rome it was much sweeter than it is now. *Frascati* can be dry or slightly sweet, and with the varieties of grapes that are allowed to be used it can have some different flavors too. Often citrusy, or with notes of apple or nuts, I put it in the same space as New Zealand Sauvignon Blancs, French Sancerres, Pinot Grigios — lovely, light, summery wines.

21. CASTELLI ROMANI

Castelli Romani is the DOC appellation for wines that come from the hills south east of Rome. The hillside vineyards of the fourteen Castelli Romani villages occupy a fresher, cooler climate than the plains below, and because of this they create a crisper, fresher wine.

There are some high quality, fine wines from this area but its proximity to Rome and the colossal demand from the city has made it largely a quantity over quality wine area. The altitude, proximity to the sea (about 12 miles/20 km) and the rich, fertile, volcanic soil all come together to allow for high yields.

Castelli Romani white wines are predominantly dry and still, although there are some sparkling spumante wines and some sweet wines from here too. *Frascati* is part of the *Castelli Romani* group. The whites are made mostly from Trebbiano and Malvasia grapes, which make the classic central Italian white blends.

Castelli Romani reds also use grapes typical of central Italy: the Montepulciano and Sangiovese grapes.

If in doubt when ordering wine in Rome, you can't go wrong with a Castelli Romani wine. Because it comes from only about 15 miles away you know it is going to pair nicely with whatever local food you are ordering to eat. But still ask the waiter for recommendations…

FOOD TOURS

There are tons of food tours available in Rome. I haven't done any myself so can't recommend specific ones to try, but if I were to choose a food tour I would find one that goes to the Testaccio. There are plenty that do, because this neighborhood is absolute foodie mecca. When I have researched food and wine tours for my Glam Italia travelers I have found lunchtime tours, aperativo tours, dinner tours — really they do run the gamut and you can easily fit them into or around your schedule. The Testaccio food market is well known, and if you wander the area in the evenings you will see restaurants bursting with locals, which is exactly what you want.

Beyond advising you to go to one of the big foodie areas (Testaccio, the Monti and Trastevere, or a combination thereof) I have one other major recommendation when choosing a food or wine walking tour: book with a small owner-operated tour or, if the tour is part of a bigger company, only book a tour that takes just a few people. If you search Trip Advisor you will find small tours with wonderful reviews. They will take you to smaller neighborhood eateries, giving you a more personal experience. Another benefit to being on a small walking tour is that the guide is reliant upon you giving him or her a fabulous review (and you *must* take the time to give them one). When you are an owner-operated business or part of a small business you really do have to go the extra mile and give a bit more to your clientele. The guides talk to you in a different way and give you an entirely different experience. In my opinion it is the absolute best way to do any tour.

Busloads of tourists or larger group tours are not going to show you the personality of Rome. Also, big tours have set menus at set restaurants who have no need to turn out anything special for you. Last year I did a big business tour out to Tivoli. The guide was good (well, he knew the answers to questions) but his canned schtick was like watching a bad seventies sitcom. He would even wait for the laugh. I felt at all times that I didn't matter, my hard earned money didn't matter, and that even if the tour was shitty he would still be paid and tomorrow there would be another busload to tell the same lame jokes to. I remember thinking that he wasn't even really paying attention, he was just running the same lines as he does every day in each place we stopped. Honestly it made me want to throw up. A small group/owner-operator enterprise can only survive in business if they are doing an amazing job. So read the reviews and go with someone who caps the group at ten or twelve people.

Best Instagram Spots in Rome

14.

The Best Instagram Spots in Rome

Maybe you are a 'gram maven or maybe you just want to take some really amazing photos for yourself. Either way this is the city to take photos in! Rome is dramatic, romantic and dazzling, depending on the time of day you are shooting.

Assuming you don't have a lot of time in Rome, but still want some amazing photos, here are the best places to take photos that are quintessentially Rome. (I have built this book around things to do that don't involve the Colosseum, Trevi Fountain, Spanish Steps or the Vatican, but the big four do make their way into this chapter.)

1. The Colosseum

This has to be the single most identifiable place in Rome, but also one of the most crowded, depending on when you are there.

If you want full body shots of yourself with the Colosseum, standing in front of it, walking across the front of the structure or standing on one of the stone blocks with the building behind you, you can get glorious shots between sunrise and 8am and then again in the late afternoon and early evening. If you go early in the morning you can catch the sun rising through the archways.

From shortly after 8am until early evening the front area is completely packed with tourists so you can't get a clear shot of anything apart from your head.

Look to see where the sun is — you want the sun shining on the subject of your photo, you don't want to be shooting into the sun. The Colosseum is spherical, so you can walk around it until you find that sweet spot. Roman skies in the summertime are sensationally blue. If you move to the shaded side of the Colosseum you can get incredible shots looking up into the structure with the intensely blue sky immediately above.

Another great place to get fantastic shots of the Colosseum for the 'gram without the cast of thousands getting in the way is just across the street. Across Via dei Fiori Imperiali you will see the Metro station. With your back to the Colosseum, facing the Metro, look to the right and you will see a staircase that takes you up the hill a short way. You may have to wait in line to get your turn, but you can sit, stand, jump, or eat pizza on the wall and get amazing shots of the Colosseum behind you.

2. The Trevi Fountain

The Trevi Fountain (along with the Spanish Steps) is one of the most iconic images of Rome.

If you are unfamiliar with the Trevi Fountain, it is the largest baroque fountain in Rome, and perhaps the most beautiful and most famous baroque fountain in the world. It stands 86 feet high and 161 feet wide, and is made from travertine and carrara marble. At its center stands a giant statue of Oceanus, looking fierce and majestic, commanding his horses while covering himself with a cloth. Below him two tritons wrangle horses that are bearing his chariot. One horse is rearing up and is held by a young triton while the other horse is calm and is held by an older triton who is announcing their arrival by blowing into a shell. All of this, with the backdrop of the Palazzo Poli, makes it a sensational site to visit.

Trevi got its name because it was the junction where three streets met (*tre* = 3, *via* = street) and marks the end point of the Virgo Acqueduct, created 19 BC by my favorite guy, Agrippa! Above the statue of Abundance to the left of Oceanus you will see a relief of Agrippa commanding his generals to build the acqueduct.

Part of the reason the Trevi Fountain is so wildly popular is that is has appeared in many movies set in Rome, including *Roman Holiday*, *La Dolce Vita* and *Three Coins In The Fountain*.

Have three coins in your pocket (this is a major pickpocket area, so you don't want to be opening your bag or wallet searching for coins) and using your right hand toss each one over your left shoulder into the fountain. The first means you will come back to Rome, the second means you will find new romance, and the third means you will get married soon!

During the day those thousands of people who were waiting outside the Colosseum all seem to make their way here too, so it is invariably packed with humans — some of whom are pickpockets. It is near impossible to get a really killer photo here during the day. Your two best bets again are at sunrise and in the evening.

If you get here at 7am, chances are the only other people you see will be fellow instagrammers. This is the best time to get great photos of just you, your outfit and the fountain. By around 8am it will start filling up and you will have tourists in your shot. Hundreds of them.

3. The Spanish Steps

The Spanish Steps are another iconic site in Rome and during the day it gets super crowded.

They were built to connect the Trinita' dei Monti church at the top with the Spanish Square and Embassy below. The baroque design of the staircase is really beautiful, mixing curves with straight sections and creating lovely terraces to sit on. It can be a fabulous place to just sit and watch Rome happening below you (albeit with hundreds of other people around you!).

At the bottom of the steps, on the right hand side, is the house where Keats lived and died. This is now a museum.

At the foot of the stairs is an early baroque fountain called the Fontana Barcaccia (Fountain of the Old Boat). This is attributed to Pietro Bernini, father of our friend Gian Lorenzo Bernini. Legend has it that during a massive flood in the sixteenth century a fishing boat from the Tiber river was carried to this exact spot.

To get the best Instagram pics of the Spanish Steps you need to be here at sunrise. This is your best chance of getting the place to yourself and getting those wonderful, sweeping photos.

You always find people hanging out on the steps in the evenings, especially in the summer months, so are unlikely to get that great shot without a ton of photobombers behind you!

The steps face west, so if you go to the top in the evening you can get beautiful sunset photos. There will be lots of people around but you can still take a great shot.

4. St Peter's Square

This is the piazza in front of St Peter's Basilica. From Michelangelo's curving colonnades, to the statues of the Apostles, to the obelisk in the middle, to St Peter's itself, there is a lot to photograph here! It is all white, so is a great place to photograph a pop of color (don't wear white!).

Every day St Peter's Square will be packed to bursting, so to get the piazza empty or close to it, you need to come very early in the morning or late in the evening. It is *gorgeous* at night!

Another fabulous time to photograph here is in the late afternoon leading up to sunset. The light gets hazy and then washes everything in apricot. One of my Glam Italia travelers got a sensational photo standing on Via della Conciliazione with St Peter's behind her, late in the afternoon. There were lots of people around but it didn't matter — the haze and the beautiful light made the photo extraordinary.

5. The Roman Forum

The secret to getting amazing photos at the Forum is to get up high. From the end opposite the Colosseum, head up the stairs next to the Wedding Cake building (Vittorio Emanuele II) and you will find the best lookout spot. Throughout the day you can take great photos up here with almost no one around. You get beautiful, clear shots of the Forum buildings and if you want to be in them yourself you are about 25 metres higher than the crowds.

As you walk around up here you will spot many incredible places to take photos, so make sure to explore a bit before going back down.

6. Via dei Coronari

This beautiful pedestrian street stretches from Piazza Navona to the bridge of angels by Castel Sant'Angelo. Every way you turn you see fabulous Roman street scenes, and because it is a pedestrian street you can get out in the middle to take photos without getting run over! One of the really famous Instagram spots is the little alleyway next to Gelateria del Teatro. It has a perfect (ancient) staircase running up one side and the Cucina Teatro on the other. It is utterly gorgeous.

7. Via Margutta

This is another sensational Roman street to photograph. Approximately two blocks from Piazza del Popolo, Via Margutta runs parallel to Via del Babuino on the Villa Borghese (park) side. There are countless wonderful things to photograph here, from building entrances, to ivy clad buildings and views along the street itself.

8. The Monti District

This is one of my favorite areas in which to wander aimlessly. There are numerous cafes and eateries — it's one of the big foodie areas, and it is incredibly charming. Stroll up and down the side streets and you will find no end of lovely places to photograph. I don't even know how many times I have walked along Via della Madonna and taken the exact same photos over and over, it feels like I do it every time I'm in Rome!

9. Giardini degli Aranci

The terrace here is one of the most gorgeous places to take photos at any time of day. The view is so crisp and clear early in the morning, and if you want Instagram sunsets I personally think it is the best place to be (see the next chapter on Roman sunsets). I also spend sunsets up on the Janiculum Hill and it is stunning, but it's hard to get a great photo there. Up here the angle is just right, the view is perfect, and you can pretty easily make photo magic.

10. The Trastevere

I am completely biased because this is my neighborhood in Rome, but honestly it is just stunning. Spend some time exploring the Trastevere *on both sides* of Viale Trastevere. There are countless exquisite little piazzas, ivy covered buildings, and perfectly peeling ochre walls. Trastevere is a banquet for your eyes and for your camera lens. The neighborhood is charming. Around every corner, down every side street and alley way there is something to look at and photograph. There is also quite a bit of graffiti here so you can mix up old world charm with some more gritty imagery.

Whatever time of day or night you are here, you will be impressed.

TAG!

#HowToTravelItaly
If you are posting Rome pics on Instagram please tag me so I can see them!

Looking at photos of Rome is one of my favorite things, and since my first book came out readers from all around the world have been tagging me in their photos when they are in Italy, or when they're in airports and on planes and trains reading my book. I can't even tell you how thrilling it is — it always makes my day. I have two Instagram accounts, @Corinnatravels and @HowToTravelItaly. I hope to see you on the 'gram!

Sunsets in Rome

15.

The Best Places to
Watch the Sunset in Rome

1. The Orange Gardens

2. The Terrazza del Pinco and the Terrazza Viale del Belvedere

3. The Garibaldi Bridge

4. The Janiculum Hill

5. St Peter's Dome

6. The Terrace of Castel Sant' Angelo

7. The Aqueduct Park

"Maybe what glitters in the air above this city are souls, so many of them rising from this same earth that they become visible, get shuffled around in the wind, get blown thirty miles west, and settle across the shining plains of the Tyrrhenian Sea."

~Anthony Doerr, *Four Seasons In Rome*

There is a quality of light that settles over certain cities when daylight is transitioning to nightfall. A quality of light so deliriously soft and sensuous that for centuries and no doubt millennia it has lured artists and lovers to its most luscious viewing points to breathe it in, document it and revel in it. One of the more famous is Venice, a city with sunsets that bathe everything in a soft focus, old movie light, creating colors too beautiful to describe, in hues you don't see anywhere else. A lesser known (or perhaps lesser realized) treat is sunset in the city of Rome.

At street level it is hard to see how gorgeous Roman sunsets are. There is too much going on, too many people, too many breathtaking sights and too much history — Rome can be a glorious sensory overload that overwhelms its more delicate moments so that you can miss them if you're not seeking them out.

Summer sunsets in the Eternal City wash everything in an apricot glow. If you take yourself to any of the vantage points below you will see monuments change color for a moment or an hour, see the soft haze rising heavenward, and feel 3000 years of history wafting through the air. I challenge you to try it just once! Sunsets in Rome are magical and here are my favorite places to experience them.

1. The Orange Gardens

The terrace of the Giardino degli Aranci is one of the most beguiling places to watch the sun set over Rome.

Treat yourself to a leisurely afternoon walk up the Aventine Hill, one of Rome's loveliest and quietest neighborhoods. Pass ruins and rose gardens to the Piazza dei Cavalieri di Malta. Look through the famous keyhole in the green door to see St Peters perfectly framed (you have to do it) and then keep going a little further uphill to the entrance to the orange garden, also known as Parco Savello.

The entrance is easy to find because it is right next to a fountain that looks like the Bocca della Verita, shooting water into a giant bathtub, which was once a travertine-covered thermal bath. You may spot a nice old man selling chestnuts — he always seems to be there.

Prepare to be wowed as you follow the wide pathway between the towering umbrella pines, with orange groves on either side, to the terrace and one of the most exquisite views of Rome. In front of you lies Trastevere and the dome of St Peters, to your right the *centro storico* (historic center). The views are incredible and can be enjoyed at any time of day, but I love them best at sunset.

There will be other travelers up here as well as some locals. Sit on the ledge of the wall high over Lungotevere Aventino for the perfect instagram photo — you will never catch me doing it because I am terrified of heights, but I can enjoy your pictures instead!

I recommend getting up here early to secure your perfect spot. Although seldom crowded it can get busy with those in the know seeking the ideal photo. This is a really lovely place to have a picnic, and/or enjoy the view with a glass of wine and some antipasti. If

Rome is getting too busy for you it is also a nice place to escape the hustle and bustle and get some quiet time with a good book.

If you are looking for another incredible Instagram photo op, or can't get up here for sunset, try to be here just as the sun is rising. You will be glad you did.

GETTING THERE

Giardini degli Aranci/Parco Savello, Via di Santa Sabina. Open 7am til sunset, year round.

WHAT'S NEARBY

Perched up on the Aventine you can wander up here after looking through the **Knights of Malta's keyhole** (plan your time well — there can be long lines to look through the keyhole!) From **Teatro Marcello** walk along to the **Forum Boarium** and the **Mouth of Truth**, then take the stairs up from **Lungotevere Aventino**.

Another option is to walk up from **Circus Maximus** or from **Testaccio**. You are not far from the **Pyramid of Cestius** and the **Cemetery For Non-Catholic Foreigners**. At the bottom of the hill catch a cab to **Ostiense**, or after sunset walk down into Testaccio to eat.

2. The Terrazza del Pincio & the Terrazza Viale del Belvedere

Up above the Piazza del Popolo is the Villa Borghese, home to great artworks, a beautiful park and two of the most stunning views of Rome, both of which are ideal places from which to take in the sunset.

The park has a famous hanging terrace that runs from above the Piazza to the Spanish Steps. This is the Terrazza del Pincio. From here you can look out over the circular Piazza del Popolo, which looks much prettier from up high, and Flaminio Obelisk, one of 13 ancient obelisks in Rome. Look a little further and you can see all the way to St Peter's.

As much as it is known to have some of the best panoramic views of the city, there are surprisingly few people up here, making it perfect for taking photos!

Continue south along the path to the second viewing point, Terrazza Viale del Belvedere. As if it is even possible, the view just gets better! To your right you will see St Peter's and to the left you can see all the way to the Wedding Cake, the Vittorio Emanuelle II monument that shares a wall with the Forum. Look carefully and you might see the top of the Colosseum.

Remember that apricot light I was telling you about? It literally drenches all the buildings across the city. It is completely gorgeous.

What's Nearby

Starting at **Piazza del Popolo** you can whip into the church to see the Caravaggios, spend the late afternoon in the **Villa Borghese art gallery** before taking in the sunset. From there follow the path and come down the **Spanish Steps,** wander along to the **Trevi Fountain** for a night time viewing and then meander over to the **Pantheon** or **Piazza Navona** for an aperitivo.

3. The Garibaldi Bridge

From sunset until sunrise there are some sensational views of St Peter's dome from the Trastevere end of the Garibaldi Bridge. Look toward the Sisto Bridge (the one with the circular hole in the middle), then look up and slightly to the left and you will see the dome. It will be bathed in peachy, apricot light as the sun goes down and once night falls it is all lit up. The Sisto reflects its mirror image on the river and with the dome above it becomes one of the most stunning photos you will take in Rome.

I cross the Garibaldi Bridge at some point most nights in Rome and every time this view sucks the oxygen right out of me. It never ever stops being spectacular. Every single time I stop and take exactly the same photo, just in case it might be even more perfect this time. At this point I no doubt have somewhere between 100 and 1,000,000 of them and God only knows how many I will have by the end of this summer!

One night when coming back across the bridge in the wee hours I came across a group of nuns on the other end of the bridge taking selfies. I had never thought of nuns carrying cell phones let alone being versed in the art of the selfie. I stopped and took group photos for them, by which time I couldn't stop laughing as they did star jumps and squealed and made funny faces and posed. I guess I haven't spent enough time around nuns because it never occurred to me that the sisters of the cloth would have a wild side, let alone get crazy on a bridge in Rome at 2am. I earned some major brownie points when I persuaded them to come to the other end of the bridge and see the best view of all. After which I spent another ten minutes taking even more group photos for them on each of their phones.

4. The Janiculum Hill

Above all else, Italians have a love of beauty. I think this is why at the end of the day the Monteverde and Trastevere locals come out for a stroll on the Janiculum Hill to watch the sunset. This is my favorite place to be as the evening begins. Apart from the incredible views across the city there is the added bonus of there being almost no tourists taking up the space. Sometimes I see students from the American Academy or the Spanish Academy, both of which are nearby, but generally they aren't around during the summer. So that leaves neighbors walking their dogs, lovers on dates, parents walking their babies, local folk young and old. Italians are so friendly and easy going that I inevitably find myself chatting away with a local who points out some new sight I hadn't noticed before, or explains some fascinating piece of local history, or tells me about some amazing place I must visit while in Rome.

Maybe that's just how Rome works. You get away from the tourist crowds and the city opens itself up to you. A random stranger, be it a mother walking her baby, an old couple taking a stroll, or the fellow from the baker's shop, tells you where to see some secret underground church, where to get the best *suppli'*, where to find the very best gelato in Rome (Gelateria del Teatro, in case you were wondering).

My first venture up to the Janiculum happened that way. A neighbor walking his dog stopped to tell me that the best views of Rome were at the top of the death defying, enormous staircase at the end of the street (Viale Glorioso). I didn't entirely understand what he was saying (I missed the bit where he told me there was an easier route at the end of Via Geofreddi Mameli), but with every muscle in my legs on fire I climbed the devil's stairs and experienced the magnificence of watching the Roman sunset from the Janiculum Hill. It also marked the last time I used that route to get there — now I take the much easier route at the end of Via Mameli.

Once you have climbed the stairs, follow the road up and you will come across your first viewing point. To your right the city is spread out before you, to your left is the Fontana dell' Aqua Paola. This fountain was built in the 1600s to celebrate the reopening of an old Roman aqueduct.

Have a quick look around, but keep walking to the Garibaldi Monument just a few minutes further along the road. From here you get the best views of the city. The Janiculum Hill is not one of the seven hills of Rome, but it could be number eight. Its position across the river (Trastevere) separated it from what was Rome, but gives the advantage of having the city stretch out in front of it, uninterrupted. From here, you can see everything you have visited during the day: trace your way from the Colosseum along the Via dei Fori Imperiali to the Wedding Cake building of the Monument to Vittorio Emanuele II. Follow your gaze left from there and you will see a mushroom-like building, this is the Pantheon. I love asking the people around me to help me figure out the different sites, and Romans being so proud of their fantastic city are always happy to point out the various buildings and landmarks.

You can't see the Vatican from this viewpoint. That's because it's behind you, to your left. Cross the road and you'll see the dome of St Peter's bathed in orange as the sun sets. It is absolutely glorious.

Next, backtrack and find gorgeous little bars and restaurants as you walk back down the hill to the stairs and back into the Trastevere.

Once is never enough on the Janiculum. The views, the quality of light, the color of the sunset, the haze of souls floating above the city... this spot is above reproach. You will want to come back for more.

If I'm in Rome chances are you will find me up here at the end of the day. And I am easy to spot — I'm the only one up there with red hair...

What's Nearby

Time your afternoon to visit the underground church at **Santa Cecilia** then wander across **Viale Trastevere** into the heart of the Trastevere. Wander along the little cobblestoned streets, stop for a coffee or a wine or something to eat (a coffee will cost you one euro here) and check out the local shops. **Piazza di Santa Maria in Trastevere** sits in the middle of the neighborhood and although lovely by itself, is also home to the incredible **Basilica Santa Maria in Trastevere**, an absolute must see.

From there stroll down to the darling **Piazza Cosimato**, have a look around and then walk all of two minutes to the easy staircase up to the **Janiculum/Gianocolo**.

After the sun has set, wander back through the Trastevere. It is magical at night (and very safe). On the corner of Viale Trastevere and Lungotevere (the road that goes alongside the river) you will find the **Garibaldi Bridge**. Walk out a few feet and you will see the dome of St Peter's lit up at night and the Sisto Bridge below it reflected in the water. I take all of my tour groups to see this, and every time I take the same photos over and over — I can't help myself.

Cross to the other side of the river and head into the **Jewish Ghetto**, even if you came through here during daylight, because it is quintessentially Rome by night. Order a glass of wine and some Jewish artichokes at **La Reginella**, **Ba'Ghetto** or **Nonna Betta** for the perfect ending to a lovely evening!

5. St Peter's Dome

One of the most glorious sights in the world comes at sunset from the top of the dome of St Peter. The dome was designed by none other than Michelangelo himself and is the highest dome in the world. Technically you are much closer to God up here. And let me tell you the view is staggering. You look out over the colonnades of St Peter's Square and along the Via della Conciliazione, making up the shape of St Peter's key, ending at the Castel Sant'Angelo. Look further and you can see all the way to Tivoli (it's out there somewhere) and on to forever.

If you have thighs of steel, by all means walk the 550 steps up to the top. If not, you can pay for an elevator to take you up the first 320 steps and then do the remainder on foot. Be advised it gets pretty tight, the space is small, but once you are up there the view makes the discomfort on the way up worth it. I am far too claustrophobic, so you won't find me up there. I would probably have a panic attack at the thought of coming back down, and either have to be airlifted off the top of the dome (which also wouldn't work as I am terrified of heights) or I would just have to spend the rest of my life up there (perhaps not such a terrible fate).

If you are strong of thigh and fearless of soul, take lots of pictures while you're up there and tag me on your Instagram so I can see!

GETTING THERE

You get to the dome from the portico entrance of St Peter's Basilica.

Check online ahead of time to find the hours as they change seasonally. The cost is 10 euros with the elevator, and you can't buy online ahead of time. Sometimes there are lines to go up the dome, but again it depends on the time of year. When you are going up in the late afternoon most of the cruise travelers and tour bus travelers have already left, so even in the high season you can find yourself there with no wait time.

WHAT'S NEARBY

The **Vatican** and **St Peter's**. You are also just down the street from **Castel Sant'Angelo** and the beautiful **bridge of angels**.

6. The Terrace of Castel Sant'Angelo

This one is more my speed. It's not so high and not at all claustrophobic. It's down the street from St Peter's, beside the Tiber river. We've already gone over its provenance — Hadrian's Mausoleum. Castel Sant'Angelo pops up throughout this book, a favorite haunt for the Ghosts of Rome, a landmark to keep you from being lost, a great place to visit for Dan Brown fans.

Ever since seeing his love-shack in Tivoli, Hadrian has been one of my favorite emperors, so I think it's fitting that one of the most dynamic places to enjoy sunset is from the Terrace of the Angel, atop the dynamic tomb of this dynamic man.

This is a wonderful place from which to enjoy a Roman sunset. In fact, it is one of the very best places to watch the sunset, due to its unique location. The panoramas across the city are sweeping and magnificent. You can see all the way to St John Lateran, and you can look back at the dome of St Peter's, which truly is one of the great landmarks of Rome. Below you, the beautiful bridge of angels straddles the Tiber. You are going to love these views.

7. The Acqueduct Park

If you are up for an adventure outside the city, love a mesmerizing view and enjoy Roman history, then I have an ideal sunset spot for you!

Eight kilometers from the city center is *Parco degli Acquedotti* (the Aqueduct Park), a 240 hectare space that is home to more than half of the 11 Roman acqueducts. Far, far from the madding crowd, you will find almost no tourists here, just a scattering of local Romans enjoying the view.

The aqueducts themselves are quite spectacular— an incredible feat of engineering, not only for the job they performed during the centuries of Roman rule, but also for the fact that here they are 2000 years later, still standing proud.

This is a wonderful place to bring a chilled bottle of Frascati and some cheese and olives to enjoy while you wait for Mother Nature to give you the show of a lifetime. The colors of the light as it meanders from afternoon to late afternoon, early evening sunset and into the night, over and around and through the archways of the aqueducts makes for an experience you will never forget. You can *feel* the centuries of history here. Take absolutely stunning photos of the sun moving through the aqueducts, and the silhouettes it makes as it heads for the horizon. Be sure to scope out your photo-taking spots before the sun makes its final moves.

GETTING THERE

One way to come out is to hire a driver and have him wait for you for a couple of hours while you take it all in. The other is to catch the Line A train from Termini station and get off at the Guilio Agricola station. From here it is a seven minute walk to Acqueduct Park (Parco Acquedotti).

Entry to the park is free.

Rome After Dark

16.

Rome After Dark

Rome is amazing at night. Spectacular. Magnificent. Glorious. Insert your own superlative.

The social fabric of the city is such that everyone comes out in the evenings for an after dinner walk, a glass of wine, the chance to catch up with friends. Rome is full of little cobblestoned streets with sidewalk tables outside restaurants, ivy climbing up the walls of centuries old piazzas, vespas buzzing around, and people everywhere. You can wander around with no agenda or head to somewhere in particular. Stop for a snack or stop for a meal or, like me, walk off some of the day's sins.

The city is remarkably safe, people are friendly and the evening atmosphere is fun. Even better, the streets that were crowded with tourists just a couple of hours earlier are now wide open for you to walk along. You can see everything without throngs of humans blocking your view, and rather than feeling like you are part of a tourist invasion on the city you can feel a little like a local.

Here are some things you need to do at night in Rome:

1. Walk the Monuments By Night

You've seen the monuments by day, now come walk them after the sun has gone down. You will get a whole new perspective on them! They are lit up beautifully, make for sensational photo ops, and without the tourists everywhere, take on a whole new magic. In the last few years they have started playing multimedia displays on them, changing from static images of how they looked in the glory days to videos of people dressed as the people of ancient Rome, wandering in and out of the columns and buildings. It's quite wonderful.

From Piazza Venezia take in the Forum, Trajan's Column and Trajan's Market by night. Walk up to the Colosseum on the Trajans' side of the street and come back down the Forum side.

The Colosseum is gorgeous at night. Soft light comes out of the archways, and more soft light beams up into the building itself. It will take your breath away.

As you walk back along the Forum there will be artists and musicians around, adding to the ambience, and from the many viewing points along the rail you can not only enjoy the Forum, but you will also see small groups taking night time tours. It's beautiful!

Once you get back to the Wedding Cake building (Vittorio Emanuelle II) follow the road to the left and walk down to Teatro Marcello, which, like all the other monuments, is lit up too. From there you can wander into the Jewish Ghetto and over onto Tiber island, before heading into the Trastevere.

The Trevi Fountain is an entirely different experience at night. The crowds are gone, the pickpockets have scored their loot for the day, and now you can really see the fountain. Being there during the day always makes me anxious as I not only have to make sure I don't get pickpocketed but am also responsible for keeping a constant eye on my travelers, keeping them safe. By night it is much more relaxing, and you can really take in just how majestic and beautiful this fountain is.

The Spanish Steps at night take on a very Dolce Vita vibe.

The Pantheon is more beautiful by night because yet again the crowds are gone. You are not alone though — the sidewalk tables are full of winers and diners enjoying their evening.

2. St Peter's By Night

I love taking my travelers to St Peter's during the day to give them an idea of the craziness of the crowds. But we come back at night to really see the piazza and the basilica (from the outside). Be advised (but not worried) that you will see homeless people and those making pilgrimages sleeping on the benches and in some of the doorways as you walk up to the piazza. During the day there are beggars everywhere, but by night it's a different crowd and the beggars are sleeping. (Honestly I find it a bit weird that the richest church of them all has so many homeless and pilgrims outside it at night. You would think they would provide food and warmth for the poor — but who am I to judge?)

Piazza San Pietro (St Peter's Square) has to be seen when the sun has gone down. By early morning it starts filling up with people again so you can't see the splendor of it empty. The way they light it up is gorgeous — I don't think anyone else sees beauty the way the Italians do, and maybe this is why St Peter's after sunset has a palpable beauty. You don't just see it, you feel it, and it is ethereal. You won't be there alone — there are always plenty of others taking it all in, and the look of wonder on their faces will be matched by your own. You will fall in love with St Peter's by night.

3. The Trastevere

I know I talk about this neighborhood a lot in my books and blog posts but it is my Roman home and perhaps the coolest neighborhood of them all. So I think it deserves a little attention!

At night the Trastevere is a place where Romans go out. Full of little cobblestoned streets and picturesque piazzas with ivy running up the walls, when you dream of Rome this is what it looks like! It is exquisitely beautiful. By night all the locals are out. Eating in the lovely little trattorias, stopping for a glass of wine with friends or hanging out in the cool local bars, this is the place to be. Everyone is out until late too, so the night is just buzzing with conversation and fun.

The main piazza, Piazza Santa Maria in Trastevere, with the light bouncing off the mosaics of the church is just heavenly and the piazza itself, with restaurant tables spilling onto the sidewalk, and renaissance ochre walls punctuated by open windows, in this sumptuous light looks like a Fellini film. You are going to love it.

All summer long there are street performers in the piazza each night (my favorite is a fire-dancer who has been there as long as I can remember). The street leading down to Viale Trastevere is full of market vendors and eateries and atmosphere. Nearby, Piazza San Cosimato (a market square every morning) becomes an open air movie theater at night during the summer — not every night, but enough nights for you to keep an eye out for it. Chairs are lined up, the local residents come out en masse and the homes with windows facing the screen have families all grouped together enjoying the show.

4. The Jewish Ghetto

I come here for dinner at least once every time I'm in Rome, and normally more often than that. You just can not beat sitting out under the stars here with a glass of wine, some great food and ambience that you could never dream up. You are quite literally surrounded by history dating back centuries before Christ, ruins of temples and Roman theaters, Renaissance rebuilds, cobblestones, the awful history of what happened to the Jews here coupled with their ultimate triumph — turning it into some of the most expensive real estate in Rome. It is chic yet casual, mostly populated by upwardly mobile Romans in the know and a sprinkling of travelers, not tourists. I don't think most tourists know about this place, it's more a place that travelers will amble into to soak up the experience.

If you're not sure where to eat, **La Reginella** always takes great care of me and I have never had a less than wonderful meal there. Anthony Bourdain loved **Nonna Betta**, and **Ba'Ghetto** is also always good.

5. Movies in the Piazza

I started doing this in Piazza San Cosimato in the Trastevere but it happens elsewhere too. Summer nights in Rome are gorgeous, and everyone wants to be out. Sometimes when I am walking over to the Jewish Ghetto at night I will stop to watch outdoor movies on Tiber Island. It's surreal being in the middle of this jaw-dropping history display with people who live with it every day, and have come out to watch a giant screen showing Italian movies and American ones with Italian voices. It is such a simple thing, yet magical.

6. Drinking Culture and *La Bella Figura*

One thing you will notice when walking around at night in Rome, and in fact all over Italy, is that Italian culture is incredibly social. Everyone is out and about interacting with other humans instead of watching the Kardashians or game shows or playing X-Box. Bars are full, sidewalk tables are full, everyone is out. You will see a glass of wine in hand and hear the bubbling buzz of conversation and it will go late into the night, even on a Tuesday (which blows me away!), but there are two things you won't see: drunk Romans and aggressive, violent Romans.

In most places in the world if bars are full there will be drunk people. Men plus booze tends to lead to some aggressive posturing, loud mouthing, pushing and shoving, and even fighting. You just don't see that here. To the point that you notice that you're not seeing it. My friend Pasquale who works with me on my Amalfi Coast tours explained it to me. He said if he saw a friend drunk he would be saying, *What's wrong with you? You're not man enough to hold your wine??* And he also said he would be humiliated for anyone to see him drunk, let alone someone he knows.

La bella figura (cutting a beautiful figure) is an essential philosophy in Italian life, and a concept that is hard for non-Italians to comprehend. It pertains to how one presents themselves to the world. You will notice that Italians are seldom sloppily dressed. You don't have to have money to have style, and from rich to poor, to everything in between, Italians ooze style. They tend to carry themselves well; from posture to demeanor there is a sense of making the best possible impression in all things. Just look around you, almost anywhere in Italy and you will see beauty in everything — landscapes to architecture, from art to the pairings of colors in a piazza. This appreciation of beauty is part of their identity, which is why you don't see women walking around in yoga pants and gym clothes, and you don't see men in graphic T-shirts with cargo shorts and chunky running shoes. In Italy, even the crazies have a sense of style.

I will never forget being down in Lecce and not being able to take my eyes off the town crazy — not because he was mentally ill and not because he was expensively dressed (he wasn't, he was clearly poor) but because, while saluting and marching up and down the street thinking he was a soldier, he still carried himself well and his oddball outfit was intentionally put together. He may not have had many of his mental faculties firing quite right and I'm sure he couldn't tell you what day or year it was, but he still retained a sense of *la bella figura*. One of the women on my tour was wearing camouflage, which excited him no end! He kept saluting her and standing to attention and calling out, "Hello Captain!" I wouldn't let anyone laugh because although he was funny it would have hurt his pride.

The philosophy doesn't end with visual beauty, *la bella figura* is also defined by behavior. Knowing how to interact with people and be gracious in any social or public setting. Good manners and an inner sense of decorum are a crucial component of *la bella figura*, and I think this is a big reason why you don't see Italians drunk all over the place.

Of course there are bad parts of any town and of course you need to be aware of your surroundings anywhere in the world at night. There will be exceptions to every rule and maybe one night I will spot some drunk Italians in Rome. The point I want to make is that you should go out and enjoy this city at night. Walk through the neighborhoods, enjoy the cafe culture, visit the monuments, visit the night market along Lungotevere in the summertime. Enjoy an icy cold glass of white wine — but don't get drunk!

Day Trips from Rome

17.

Ten Day Trips From Rome

One of the things I love about traveling in Italy is that you can move around the country so easily and effortlessly. The train system is brilliant, high speed trains move you from one end of the country to the next, and it is a very economical way to travel.

You can be based in Rome and take day trips to Venice or Florence or Naples or most major cities — it's very easy. I prefer to stay in one or two places and make day trips, rather than be constantly packing up and moving to another city. Taking day trips by train is a wonderful way to see the country. I always think it's like being inside a National Geographic TV show, the views from the train windows are so spectacular.

You *can* rent a car and drive, but I have driven all over Italy and you couldn't pay me to drive in Rome. The traffic is completely mad. So I mostly use the train. If you haven't used the train system in Italy before, I have an entire chapter in *Glam Italia! How To Travel Italy* that walks you through it step by step. Get the Kindle App on your smartphone, download the ebook, and use it to guide you through the train stations and get to where you were planning on going, on time and stress-free.

If I won the lottery, I would quite happily hole up in Rome forever, riding its trains to fabulous places. These are the first places I'd visit.

1. Florence

Florence is a spectacular city. If your travel itinerary doesn't allow you time to spend a few nights there you can still buzz up for a day on the train. The high speed train from Roma Termini station to Florence Santa Maria Novella station takes an hour and thirty minutes, and the scenery is gorgeous the entire way. I recommend taking an early morning train and arriving in Florence before the crowds. One of my favorite things to do is walk the heart of the city (Duomo, Piazza della Signoria and Ponte Vecchio) at 8am, ahead of the tour buses and cruise tourists. You have a magical morning hour where the city belongs to you and you can see all the statues and beautiful buildings unencumbered by thousands of tourists.

I normally take Italo trains to Florence, and their last train back to Rome leaves Florence shortly before 10pm. If you are taking a day trip to Florence, stop at Al Antico Vinaio before you head back to the train station and pick up one of their unbelievable paninos for the ride home. They are enormous, made with fresh Tuscan ingredients and only cost five euro each! I promise you, this will be the best sandwich you have every eaten in your whole life. Everyone I take there tells me they will only eat half now and take the other half home for the next day. Then they eat the entire thing — they are just so incredibly good!

2. Naples — Pompeii and Herculaneum

Not everyone has heard of Pompeii, and some people just give me a blank stare when I talk about it, so here is a quick refresher:

Pompeii was a beach town at the base of Mt Vesuvius. It had its own community but also hosted the summer homes of Rome's wealthy and elite. Mt Vesuvius was just another mountain covered in vineyards and farms, its soil incredibly fertile. No one knew it was a volcano, and in fact there wasn't even a word for volcano at the time — no one had ever seen one. The top of the mountain was the same as any other mountain or hill, it didn't have a crater with bubbling lava, it was just green and verdant. In 79AD Mount Vesuvius erupted. The town of Pompeii was covered in 20 feet of volcanic ash and pumice and completely disappeared, not to be discovered again until the 1700s. The city was frozen in time, and it provides an incredibly detailed snapshot of every aspect of life in 79 AD. Although only partially excavated, today Pompeii gives us our only real view into what ancient Roman life was really like.

I recommend doing a little of your own research to get some context before going to Pompeii. If you can, book a private guide when you get there (one with loads of great reviews), otherwise get an audio-tour. Pompeii is absolutely amazing, but it really helps to have some direction, so the guide/audio-guide is helpful. There is so much incredible detail to examine here, you will be glad you did!

Pompeii is a suburb of Naples and is very easy to get to. From Rome Termini station take the high speed train to Naples (about an hour and twenty minutes) then the little local train to the Pompeii Scavi stop.

When you have seen Pompeii, get back on the train and go three stops to Ercolano. From the train station it is a few minutes walk to Herculaneum, but it is well worth it. Pompeii was covered in ash and many of the buildings were crushed, so you can't really picture them in all their glory. Also much of the color is gone. The city had been full of artwork and the frescoes inside the homes were sensational.

At Herculaneum, you can see how tall their multi-storied buildings were, and the vibrant colored frescoes inside all the homes. When we talked about Emperor Augustus' home I told you the frescoes were Pompeii-style, now you will see what I mean. From the bold reds to the subject matter, this was its own art movement.

The reason the two sites are preserved so differently is that Pompeii was covered in ash, and the people died from heat blasts up to 500 degrees (at which point Celsius or Fahrenheit is irrelevant) or from the ash and pumice raining down on them. The people of Herculaneum died because the wind changed and blew all those noxious gases over the city. The city remained intact. Thinking boats would come to rescue them, the people went down to the beach. The men were on the beach and the women and children were sheltered in the caves below the city when the gases killed them all. The bones are still there, in situ.

A visit to Pompeii first will give you an idea of what happened, and an incredible window into life there. Follow that with a trip to Herculaneum — it will blow your mind. Every time I go to Pompeii and Herculaneum I *still*, after all these years, am completely floored by the contrast of these two towns. It really is an amazing experience. I always make plans with myself to come back in the winter and spend days exploring the two sites more, but each year rolls around and I somehow don't get back.

During the summer months Pompeii and Herculaneum get really, really hot. Make sure you have a water bottle (you can refill it inside Pompeii at the water fountains) because there is only one cafe inside Pompeii itself and you will need lots of water! There is no shelter from the sun, so wear a hat and sunscreen. (I live in Phoenix, a city that gets more than its fair share of really hot days, and I still find

Pompeii very hot in the summer.) Also make sure you are wearing sturdy footwear. There is a lot of walking here and it's all on ancient Roman roads, so flip flops and sandals are a *really* bad idea.

NAPLES

If you make a day trip to Pompeii, allow yourself some time in Naples on the way back. Make sure you try the coffee — it is the best coffee in the world! Not only do they have a special way of preparing it but the volcanic water of this region gives it a little something extra. I book my trains in and out of Naples to allow me time to get coffee when I arrive and before I leave — Naples coffee is so good there is no way I will miss getting a cup in each direction!

Naples is also the home of pizza. It is different from pizza anywhere else in the world, so you need to try some while you are here. In Naples it is normal to have one pizza per person, and they are quite big, so I tend to share one with someone. Don't expect American-style pizza toppings either. It is very simple and delicious! You will be glad you tried it.

3. Capri, Ischia or Procida

Another fabulous day trip you can make using Naples as a base is to one of the islands off its coast, such as Capri, Ischia or Procida (and there are others).

Your day starts the same way, by high speed train from Rome Termini station to Naples C.Le. I definitely recommend departing Rome early in the morning and arriving in Naples around 8am. The last ferry to leave Capri each day departs around 6pm, and believe me you will want every single minute possible on the island. Take a taxi from the train station to the ferry (if I remember correctly it is a set fee of 15 euros for the taxi) and then take a ferry or hydrofoil over to the island of your choice.

Most people first time around want to go to Capri. I am there multiple times per year, and although it is definitely the most touristy of the islands, if you walk not even five minutes out of Capri town you are in a whole different world! Whether you want to wander around the island, take a convertible taxi or a bus up to Anacapri and the Blue Grotto, or charter a private boat and go around the island, you can have a really wonderful day here.

Another island in the chain you may want to do a little research on is a teeny tiny island called Procida. It is a little fishing village with brightly colored houses all along the waterfront — one of the 10 most colorful places on earth. Walk around the front side of the island then head over to the far side for lunch and swimming. It's been a couple of years since I was last there, but I adore Procida. It is so pretty! When I have been there it hasn't been touristy at all — it's more a weekend getaway for people from Naples. Part of the movie *Il Postino* was shot here too.

Ischia is different again, less touristy than Capri, less colorful than Procida, perhaps best known for day spas and relaxation. You may recognize it from movies such as *The Talented Mr. Ripley.*

I definitely recommend researching Procida and Ischia before making a day trip, just to make sure they are your type of island. If in doubt head to Capri — you'll love it.

Once again, plan some time between arriving back in Naples and taking the train back to Rome so that you can grab a coffee and some pizza.

4. Tivoli — Hadrian's Villa and Villa d'Este

Before I came here the first time, I looked at the different ways to do an excursion to Hadrian's Villa and Villa d'Este. In the end I decided a bus tour was the best option (though I'm really not a tour bus person). Although you technically can get there independently by public transport, it is messy. Alternatively you would need to hire a guide and a driver and that is too costly for most people. So when I wanted to see this place, I booked a tour with Viator. This was the tour I mentioned earlier, and I have mixed feelings about the experience.

The cons were that:

- I'm not much of a big bus tour person. I like small groups with private guides who have to work for their money and put their heart and soul into it.

- I felt the guide phoned it in. He had his schtick and he stuck to it, using the exact same corny jokes at the exact same time as he must do every day, pausing for laughs, fake acting and making the experience feel like McDonalds — homogenized and lacking authenticity.

- It was clear to me that his prime focus was making sure that everyone ate at his friend's restaurant and bought leather goods from his other friend's shop. I get it that he makes kickbacks from them and it's part of how he earns his money, but it was annoying anyway.

The pros were that:

If you asked him absolutely *anything*, he knew the answer. He grew up in Tivoli and was a wealth of information. He seemed like a nice enough fellow and in his defense he probably spends all day every day with tourists — people who want to get off the bus, take the photos, and get back on the bus without much interest beyond that. People who probably want to be told where to eat rather than wander around and choose something themselves.

Without intending to, he made me fall in love with Emperor Hadrian. I'm somewhat mortified to tell you that prior to this day trip I knew nothing about Hadrian. Now he is one 0f my obsessions.

Hadrian was gay and the love of his life was a Greek boy named Antinous. The two of them had a love shack at Villa Adriana, they traveled everywhere together and when Antinous died unexpectedly Hadrian was beyond grief stricken. He had numerous statues made of his love and even had him deified. I think this love affair is so significant because when you look back through the emperors and the leaders of the republic all we see is fierceness. Great leaders, yes, but everything was about war and battles and conquering and expansion. Other than Antony and Cleopatra we don't see much in the way of passionate love. Or overwhelming love. Admittedly Antinous was very young, but from what I can tell he loved Hadrian, and back then they were marrying off girls younger than he, so the age thing probably wasn't an issue. I have been a makeup artist my entire adult life and as such have lived a life heavily populated with gay men. Makeup artists and gay men go together like peas and carrots. Many of the people who are closest to me, who I love the most in the world, are gay men. My life would be so bland without them — I don't even care to think about it! So I am convinced that had I been around at the time, Hadrian and I would have been *great* friends! *Best* friends! When Antinous died I would have kept Hadrian company listening to the ancient Roman equivalent of Broadway show tunes and putting on face masks (assuming of course he didn't have me beheaded — it would seem that he did more than his fair share of killing and persecuting, but I choose to ignore that).

This man was a great leader, and a brilliant emperor. He is one of Rome's five great emperors in fact. On top of that he was a lover of art and architecture. He built himself the most exquisite villa below the town of Tivoli outside of Rome. Now in ruins, some of it was pilfered, almost all of the travertine and marble was looted and taken up the hill to Villa d'Este but enough remains to help us understand how incredible this giant villa complex was. You can still see remnants of marble floors; walls and ceilings soar skyward, letting you see how huge they were.

One of the truly spectacular sights, which somehow is still intact, is a recreation of Canopus in Alexandria, a long pool lined with statues. Though the water is green, the entire area is really beautiful. Our guide pointed out olive trees on the property that are centuries old. There is so much to see here — I am definitely coming back.

Villa Adriana (Hadrian's Villa) is a UNESCO World Heritage site. The entire property covers around 297 acres. Hadrian didn't much care for the emperor's palace on the Palatine Hill so from 128 AD he moved here permanently and ran the Empire from Villa Adriana, with the entire court living out there as well.

I honestly feel that had I tried to see Hadrian's Villa without a guide explaining everything I would have missed too much so, canned jokes and restaurant kickbacks notwithstanding, I recommend coming here with a guided tour.

From Villa Adriana we got back on the bus and went up the hill to the town of Tivoli. After lunch we had about 90 minutes to spend wandering around Villa d'Este. This one has another story to tell about wayward and wealthy cardinals.

Villa d'Este is a sixteenth century villa built by Cardinal Ippolito d'Este, one of the wealthiest cardinals ever. During this time, when the church ruled everything and there was no free press to report the goings on, popes and cardinals were marrying and having mistresses and orgies and generally getting up to no good — D'Este had a wife and four sons, which I find endlessly entertaining. He took an enormous amount of land from the locals to build his spectacular villa, and robbed marble and travertine from Hadrian's place down the hill. At one point he had 12 lawsuits against him, but he didn't care, he was building his palace anyway.

The most famous features of Villa d'Este are the gardens and their fountains. D'Este diverted the Aniene river to provide water to the most spectacular series of fountains and water exhibits you will ever see. It happens on several levels, working their way down the hill to the bottom of the garden, and everything is powered by the water, including a huge fountain that plays Renaissance music several times per day. Make sure you find out what time the musical fountain is scheduled to play and time your visit to be in front of it when it does. It is quite incredible. As you are walking down to the musical fountain the walls are lined with statues with water flowing out of their mouths. Part way down you'll see two fountains the man of the cloth had made for the pleasure of his sons — a pair of female creatures with giant breasts from which water arcs out. (I wonder if he gave himself a round of Hail Marys to make up for that?)

The day trip to Tivoli to see Hadrian's Villa and Villa d'Este is tremendous, and well worth doing. And who knows — maybe you too will become fixated on Hadrian.

5. Orvieto

Just an hour from Rome by train, the Umbrian border town of Orvieto is an absolute treasure. From the train station you take a funicular up the hill to the medieval town.

Orvieto is famous for its cathedral, which is thought to be one of Italy's most beautiful. The stripes on its exterior will remind you of Siena, and the Luca Signorelli frescoes on the inside are thought to have been Michelangelo's inspiration for the ceiling of the Sistine Chapel. This is a fabulous town to wander around, duck down little side streets and alleyways, explore and photograph. The local food is wonderful and of course there is incredible Orvieto wine! Plan you day to include a nice long lunch with a bottle of local red.

There is much more too. This is Etruscan country and their history is everywhere. You can go below ground to one of the most unique undergrounds in all of Italy — the Etruscans dug a labyrinth of tunnels and rooms below the city of Orvieto 2500 years ago. When you are exploring down here you are getting in touch with some *really* ancient history.

Marlena di Blasi's book *The Lady in the Palazzo: An Umbrian Love Story* is set here in Orvieto. She and her husband Fernando live here now, after spending 1000 days in Venice, followed by three years in Tuscany. I love all of her books, and recommend that you read them before traveling to Italy, especially *The Lady in the Palazzo* before going to Orvieto. I get a kick out of recognizing the various streets and shops and eateries she talks about in the book — I think it's always fun to know a place from a book or a movie and then walk those same streets myself. I don't get to Orvieto as often as I would like but when I do go there I always keep an eye out for di Blasi. I have never seen her (and don't really know what I would do if I did see her. What do you do in that situation? Introduce yourself and say "I've read all your books and I want to be friends?" She might think I was a maniac and call the police). One day I am bound to run into her. I just hope I don't do anything embarrassing, like spill my wine or fall over!

6. Viterbo

Viterbo is a wonderful little medieval town about an hour from Rome by train. During the 13th century there was a 20 year spell when it was home to the pope. It is also the area my favorite villainess Olimpia Pamphilj came from. It is considered to be one of the best preserved medieval towns in all of Italy and is a great place to wander around and breathe in the history.

Viterbo has a population of around 60,000 so has loads of options for places to stop for a coffee, a meal or a glass of wine. The Pope's Palace and the hot springs are the big tourist sites, but in my opinion the very best way to enjoy Viterbo is to go there with no agenda and a big appetite.

7. Civita di Bagnoregio

This one takes a little planning to get to but you can combine it with a trip to Orvieto.

Civita di Bagnoregio, also known as *La Citta Che Muore* (The Dying Town) was founded by the Etruscans on a hilltop not far from Orvieto, 2500+ years ago. Over the millennia the town has been slowly eroding and falling down the hillside. In 2006 it was placed on the World Monuments Fund's watchlist of 100 most endangered sites, due to the dangers it faces both from erosion and unregulated tourism.

Civita is architecturally fantastic. Due to it being so remote and isolated much of the architecture that spans back centuries is unaltered. It was the birthplace of Saint Bonaventure, who died in 1274. Since then his family home *fell off the cliff* as the land eroded.

There are no cars in Civita. The only way into the town is over a walking bridge that crosses a giant chasm and looks like the Great Wall of China. It makes Civita an island in the sky with 365 degree views. The year round population has dwindled to only *five* people, as the old folks have died and the young ones moved away. In the summer the population swells to around 100. Tourists have bought some of the homes and modernized them a little but Civita still feels like a place that time forgot.

As you wander around you see buildings that are just a facade — the rest has fallen down the hill. The town is very picturesque and is a photographer's dream. Be sure to visit the little church in the heart of town, originally an Etruscan temple it was re-purposed as a Roman temple before finding its way to Jesus. Chunks of the temple columns line up outside like soldiers, guarding the church and the town's secrets.

The town stays alive and functioning with the help of restaurants and artisanal shops selling local goods. This is definitely not a tourist town, which in my opinion makes it even more wonderful. We stopped into one of the eateries for some local bruschetta (definitely recommended!) and the owner showed us a giant (now retired) olive press in the middle of the restaurant that for the past 1500 years, up until the 1960s, was operated by blindfolded donkeys walking round and round in circles all day, pressing the local olives. Not much of a life for the donkeys but a fascinating, touchable piece of local history.

Without a car, the best way to get to Civita di Bagnoregio is to take the train to Orvieto and then the bus to Civita. If you're visiting both Orvieto and Civita in one day I would advise getting an early start, going to Civita first, then spending all afternoon and evening in Orvieto.

8. Tarquinia

If you enjoy looking at Etruscan history you will love this one! It is a little trickier and more time consuming to reach (a two and a half hour train + bus combo), but well worth it. This place is sensational.

Tarquinia was one of the most important Etruscan towns and has a fascinating history. The necropolis is one of Italy's most important Etruscan sites. It is a burial ground that dates back to the ninth century BC, which puts it in the Iron Age! Six thousand tombs have been excavated here, 140 of which have vivid, incredible frescoes, 20 of which are open to the public. I am amazed to see artwork that old, and to see what they considered important back then. These are burial tombs, and the Etruscans chose to go into the next life surrounded by happiness and beauty. The frescoes depict women dancing and singing and rather than being somber or religiously pious these paintings are all about joy. When I consider that my house is only 20 years old and already needs to be repainted it is staggering that these frescoes are more than 2500 years old, have withstood not only time but the elements, wars and God only knows what else,and still the color holds true.

While here make sure you visit the Museo Archaeologico to see some pretty amazing Etruscan artifacts.

Because this place takes some getting to, I recommend doing some research prior to going, to determine what you want to see and when it opens.

9. Ostia Antica

This is a large archaeological site on the coast, about 15 miles from Rome. Its name comes from "os" which means mouth and "tia" from the Tiber river. This was Rome's sea port. Barges would come up the Tiber to Rome from here. Over the millennia silt has caused the oceanfront to move out two miles, so it looks a little different geographically now.

From the steep amphitheater to Neptune's Baths, to the Thermopolium (an ancient cafe with a bar and traces of the old menu still frescoed on the wall), a trip to Ostia Antica is almost like visiting Pompeii — without the volcano! The mosaics are sensational and are alone worth making the trip for, but there is much here to see. The preservation of the ancient buildings, mosaics and frescoes is amazing.

When you are planning your trip, look into going on a guided tour of the *Case Decorate* (decorated houses). There are guided tours on Sundays at 10:30am, but check dates and times before you go in case there are other options. You can't go inside the houses without a guided tour and you will definitely want to see them if you can.

If you have young boys with you they will love seeing the ancient public toilets at the Terme del Foro. Twenty well preserved toilets line up along a stone bench. Going to the bathroom was a social event back then and they would all sit there shooting the breeze while going about their business.

You get to Ostia Antica in a mere 25 minutes by train from Pirimide Station. Wear good walking shoes and plan on being there for several hours. It is pretty incredible and there really is a lot to see here.

10. Ponza

This one really is one of Rome's best kept secrets — an idyllic island in the Mediterranean where Romans go to chill. There is only one road on Ponza, almost no cars, and everybody just walks from the boat to their accommodation or their beach excursions. Unlike Capri, Ponza doesn't come with a hefty price tag. It's not a place to show off your latest Chanel bag or Gucci sun-frock, it's a place to slow down and enjoy the beautiful beaches, swim in the Med and fill your belly at any of the local eateries.

You can book boat excursions around the island with lunch on board and as much swimming and snorkeling as your heart desires. I have also found excursion companies that will bring you here for the day, take you out on a boat, and get you back to port with enough time to peruse the local shops and get a gelato before taking you back on the ferry, and then on to Rome.

When you see Ponza you will be amazed that such a gorgeous island can be here and no one seems to know about it. When I close my eyes at night the beautiful views of Ponza are the screensavers on the back of my eyelids. Don't miss it.

Tips for Travelers to Rome

Keeping yourself safe

Whenever you travel anywhere you have to be aware of your personal safety and the safety of your belongings. I have always found Rome to be a very safe city with relatively little violent crime. However, there is an issue with gypsies and pickpockets so you need to do a little planning to protect your valuables from them. (Don't stress about this. To put it into perspective, in the US if someone wants your valuables they might pull a gun or a knife on you. In Europe the gypsies will fleece you without you even knowing it.)

So let's talk about gypsies and pickpockets (they aren't always the same) and how to best protect yourself.

LEAVE YOUR VALUABLES AT HOME

The more loot you are flashing the more attention you are attracting. Diamonds, expensive watches, expensive jewelry — leave them at home.

SEPARATE YOUR MONEY

Don't keep all your proverbial eggs in one basket. If you are using a money belt keep most of your cash and cards in it. Only take out one card and the cash you'll need for that day. That way if you get robbed you haven't lost everything.

Don't keep your wallet in your pocket, and definitely not in your back pocket.

DON'T FLASH CASH

Some people like making a display of pulling out their cash and counting it off, but this is seriously unwise to do in any major tourist city. That big fat roll you like to peel bills off at home needs to stay at home. Be really subtle with your money while traveling.

DON'T GIVE MONEY TO BEGGARS

They really tug at your heartstrings, but they're supposed to. You will see some beggars looking as though they live in abject poverty, especially near the Vatican or the other big churches. It's a con. I see the same faces year after year. One is a woman who is normally lying in the gutter begging on the road leading to the Vatican. I've seen her whip out an iPhone when no one was around. (Last summer she had the iPhone X while I was tooling around with the 6S.)

These beggars are often gypsies and they work in groups. While you are digging into your pocket for money, her partner is watching which pocket you got that cash from. Next thing you know they have followed you down the street and your money is gone, along with your watch.

KEEP YOUR HANDBAG CLOSED

Seriously, these guys are skilled. Keep your bag closed at all times. If it has a zipper, keep it zipped up. If it has a snap closure, keep it snapped and wear the side that opens against your body.

WEAR A CROSS-BODY BAG

Women should wear a bag with a strap that goes over your shoulder and crosses your chest (aka a cross-body bag). Not a shoulder bag. A cross-body bag is much harder to steal and much easier to keep control of because you'll never have to put it down.

DON'T PUT YOUR BAG OR CAMERA DOWN AND TURN AWAY

This sounds so obvious but people do it all the time. Thieves know you're going to do it, so they watch for the moment to grab it. I feel as though I am constantly nagging my travelers to do up their handbags and to stop putting their camera or bag down. It is honestly the most difficult thing on my tours! As soon as I turn around someone else has put their camera or handbag down and looked away.

You have to be totally cognizant of all of your belongings at all times, especially when you are in a busy place, like queuing to enter the Colosseum or Vatican, the Spanish Steps or the Trevi Fountain.

Also be careful when walking down busy streets *near* the big tourist sites. These streets are great for pickpockets because there is a massive flow of tourists who have let their guard down now that they are away from the big sites.

NEVER HANG YOUR BAG ON YOUR CHAIR

Don't ever hang your bag on the back of your chair while eating out/having a coffee/doing anything. Always keep your bag on your body (see why a cross-body bag is ideal?). Thieves are so quick when taking off with your bag, you won't even know its missing until its long gone.

WATCH YOUR iPHONE

Apparently iPhones are a hot commodity for pickpockets. If it's not in your hand it needs to be somewhere a pickpocket can't get it, such as locked inside your handbag (not in your pocket). Don't put it down and turn away, and don't rest it on the table at a restaurant/coffee bar/anywhere.

LOCK DOORS AND WINDOWS WHEN YOU LEAVE

Just because you can leave windows open at home doesn't mean you can while away. Check they are all closed and locked before you leave your room, regardless of which floor you are staying on. The same goes for doors, they will have multiple locks on them for a reason. Use all the locks, every time. Make sure that the door to the street is pulled closed and locked too.

I once spent two nights in Prati — never again. Although the area is nice enough, the owner of the B&B told me they had massive problems with gypsies and that guests kept forgetting to lock the front door, or leaving it ajar, letting the gypsies in. Seriously — lock everything you can.

DON'T TALK TO STRANGERS

This sounds a little harsh, but bear with me. If someone approaches you looking for help/directions/with questions, just keep moving. Think about it. No Italian will confuse you with being a local. You don't look like them, dress like them, wear your hair like them or use the same body language and gestures as them. Italians will spot you as a foreigner immediately. Other travelers won't think you're a local either. So ask yourself why this person is approaching you. If you are lost, would you ask another tourist for directions, or are you going to ask a local?

Gypsies, pickpockets and scam artists look just like tourists. The one thing they need from you is for you to be distracted. The split second your guard drops they can access everything they want. When I was first traveling in Europe gypsies were easily identifiable — they were big Romany women wearing giant floor length skirts filled with hidden pockets. You could spot them a mile off and easily steer well clear of them. Nowadays the bad guys and gals look like everyone else. They will dress like American tourists, priests, housewives or school kids. They are pros and they know that most of us are nice people who will instinctively stop to help — that's just how we are wired.

MY PICKPOCKET STORY

The only time I have ever come up against pickpockets (touch wood never again) was while walking away from the Trevi Fountain (pickpocket central) down Via dei Sabini toward the Via del Corso. I hate going there during the day, especially with a tour group (which is the only reason I do it). But everyone wants to see the Trevi so I end up taking them. I am on edge the whole time I'm anywhere near there, because it's my job to keep my travelers and their belongings safe. We were walking along and my eyes were everywhere, like Kevin Costner in *The Bodyguard*, and thank God for that, because in the crowd moving down the busy street I was aware of someone getting a little too close. As I was turning toward the person I felt a hand on my bag. (I wear a cross-body bag and keep the opening against my body.) Everything happened really quickly. I registered that she was a pickpocket and was trying to steal from me. But instead of pushing her away for some stupid reason I grabbed her. (Seriously — don't ever do that. It was incredibly stupid.) Her crew scattered like a pack of rats, scurrying in every direction. They always operate in groups, so by the time you realize they've got your watch or your wallet it has been passed off three times and is long gone. She had an empty tote bag that she was using to hide her hand while trying to get inside my bag. Clever. She didn't get any of my belongings, but had my guard been down she probably would have.

I have played the entire event back over and over in my mind in the years since. I am still horrified at myself for grabbing this girl rather than pushing her away, and at how badly it could have gone (what if she'd had a knife?). But what sticks in my mind the most is that she was just a kid, maybe 14 or 15 years old, dressed like any other kid her age. If I hadn't been so on edge watching over my group she wouldn't have pinged my radar at all.

And that's how it goes with scammers and thieves. They look like anyone else. So keep in mind there is no reason for anyone to approach you while you are in Rome (or any other city in Europe). Don't let anyone inside your physical space. If you find yourself in the middle of a crowd on the sidewalk, step into a shop or stand back against the wall and let the crowd move on. And don't engage with strangers.

DON'T TAKE PHOTOS WITH GLADIATORS

Or at least be on high alert if you do take photos with gladiators. Some of the high tourist areas, especially the Colosseum and Forum, have gladiators wandering around outside, ready to pose for pictures. Of course you pay them for the opportunity, but beware, there has been considerable trouble with these characters and at times they have been banned from these areas.. Women have complained of being groped or inappropriately touched, and men, women, girls and boys have been pickpocketed by them.

You might think you would feel it if someone is picking your pocket, getting the goods out of your bag, or stealing your watch. You won't. They are pros at this and long before you even realize you've been robbed your stuff will have been handed off to several other players and are long gone. You won't find them in the gladiator's pocket.

Tickets

- Buy tickets to big attractions online before leaving home. For the Colosseum and Forum (same ticket) go directly through Coopculture. One time I bought them via Expedia only to find when I got to the front of the line at the ticket booth that they were no good. There were a bunch of people who had also bought their tickets on Expedia and we all had to buy new ones.

- Check to see which tickets will give you access to multiple museums. Some tickets are good across seven days for multiple places — for example, one ticket gets you into the Baths of Caracalla, the Mausoleum of Caecilia Metella and the Villa dei Quintili and is good for a week. One ticket will get you into Crypta Balbi, Palazzo Massimo, Palazzo Altemps and the Baths of Diocletian, and is valid for three days. Find out and plan your visits accordingly.

- If you don't buy Colosseum tickets in advance you can be in for a multi-hour wait to get in, but there is a way around it. If you are in line at the gates to the Forum on Via dei Fori Imperiali at 8:30am there will be almost no one around. They are all up the street waiting outside the Colosseum! Buy your ticket here and go into the Forum at opening time (8:30am). There will be no one there, so you can spend all the time you want exploring the Forum and Palatine Hill before heading to the Colosseum where you will be in the shorter line for people who already have tickets.

- If you already have tickets and there is a big crowd at the Colosseum, do the same thing. Walk down the street to the Forum and visit that first. Fewer people know about the gates on the Via dei Fori Imperiali, so it is generally a quicker way in.

- If you are planning to visit the Colosseum and Forum in the summer months make sure you go first thing in the morning. Be there for the 8:30am opening because it gets seriously hot there during the day. The combination of huge crowds and stifling heat is truly awful, so if you can get these two outdoor sites out of the way by lunchtime, before the big heat of the day descends, you will be glad you did!

- As of 2019 they are only selling online tickets for Colosseum access and tickets are timed, so you have to be in line a half hour before your scheduled time. The system is new and so far my guides are telling me it is far from perfect. It could become just the way they manage the process during tourist season, or it could be something they try and then discard. My advice is to buy your tickets online at Coopculture and read up on what the rules are. During the summer it is going to be very hot, so try to book your tickets for the 8:30am slot when the Colosseum opens.

- Check opening hours. Many or most places will close over lunchtime. By checking ahead you can maximize what you can achieve in one area of the city in one day. Almost every place will be closed one day per week, often Mondays. (The Colosseum is open every day.) Churches are often closed for several hours in the middle of the day and are usually closed to tourists during services.

Getting Around Rome

Most of the things to do in this book happen within a mile and a half to two mile radius of Largo Argentina, so unless you have bad knees or hips, or don't have much time, they are walkable. Look at the maps in this book and see how close they all are, and then group things together where feasible.

Taxis are generally not expensive and I have used them often in Rome without a problem. However I do sometimes read about travelers having issues with taxis while in Rome. My recommendation is to ask the driver how much it will cost to go to your destination *before getting in the car*. If they tell you 20 euros from the Colosseum to the Vatican just walk away — they are scamming you.

TAXI METERS

Taxi meters should be set to the following rates:
Monday—Saturday from 6am to 10pm the start rate for the meter should be set to 3 euros.
Sundays the meter should be set to 4.50 euros.
After 10pm the meter should be set to 6.50 euros.
The first piece of luggage is free but each subsequent piece is an additional 1 euro.
The first four passengers don't incur an additional fee but after that there is an additional 1 euro per person.

AIRPORT TRANSFERS

When you book your accommodation in Rome ask the hotel/airbnb/bed and breakfast or wherever you are staying to book you an airport transfer. At the time of writing this book (2019) the fare from airport to hotel was a flat fee of 50 euro (no matter where you're staying). Don't let anyone tell you it is more, or that that fee is just to the city walls or any other nonsense like that. If your hotel or host has organized the driver for you, you can be relatively certain that you won't get scammed.

Another way to do it if your host doesn't take care of it for you (most will) is to hire a driver. I always recommend finding people through Trip Advisor. As much as people like to bash Trip Advisor it is a fantastic resource. You will find that everywhere you go vendors want you to write them a good Trip Advisor review. I scan the first 50 reviews and see what people are saying. I look for consistent five star reviews, written across a decent span of time — if it's all in one month I would be a bit suspicious. If I am reading reviews that are consistently saying the same good things then I will book that company. I do also click on some of the reviewers to see what else they have been reviewing — have they reviewed a variety of things, or just this company?

A taxi from the airport to the center of town should cost 48 euros, but be careful. Only ever get a taxi from the taxi stand outside the terminal. Official taxis have SPQR on the door. Ask the price before getting in. There should be a uniformed person wrangling the taxi line.

Never accept a solicited ride. Taxi drivers are not allowed to come into the terminal and solicit fares. Anyone doing that (and you will see plenty of them) is up to no good.

There is an express train that goes from the terminal at the airport to Termini station in the center of Rome. It is called the Leonardo Express. Follow the train signs once you exit baggage claim. There is a ticket booth and there are also ticket machines. The fare is 14 euros. Make sure you validate your ticket at the validating machine (there's one at the beginning of each platform) before getting on the train.

Once you arrive at Termini you can get a taxi to wherever you are staying. Again, only get one from the taxi stand.

HIGH SPEED TRAIN

If heading to another city you can go directly to your next train. In December 2018 a new Frecciarossa high speed train service was scheduled to open at Rome Fiumicino airport with trains taking you directly to Florence, Venice and I think Genoa. I haven't used it yet and the website at the time of writing this hasn't got any information on it. I will check it out when I am in Rome this summer and will write about it on my CorinnaB's World blog, as well as in my newsletter. (Make sure you sign up for my newsletter for this and other handy info for planning travel to Italy. Just visit my blog www.Corinnabsworld.com to sign up!))

HOW TO HANDLE TAXI SCAMS

I have never had a problem with taxis in Rome, so I don't want to alarm you. I always ask the estimated price before getting into a cab, and I look to make sure the driver turns the meter on. If he says it's not working, I get out of the taxi.

Always carry cash in small denominations — 5 euro bills and 1 and 2 euro coins. You cannot rely on the driver being able to make the right change for you, and if he smells tourist on you there is a good chance that he suddenly might not have change. (Again I have heard of this but have never experienced it myself.) If I did feel like someone was trying to scam me I would just say "No problem, let's just call the police" or even better, the Guardia di Finanza (the tax police). No one wants to deal with that kind of attention!

PRIVATE DRIVER

You can hire a private driver to get you places, but that gets quite expensive. If I am going to see the Aqueducts or the Via Appia I normally have a driver stay and wait for me, because I either have others with me or I don't want to get stranded outside of town in the dark. It will seem silly to some but I don't want to be riding around on public transport outside of town at night. I know plenty of people who do though and get home just fine with more money in their pockets than I have left after paying my driver!

BUSES & TRAMS

Buses and trams are a very cost effective way to get around above ground. (I avoid them during rush hours because being packed inside with a full load of passengers raises the likelihood of being pickpocketed.) Don't forget to validate your ticket when you get onboard. If you are unable to walk up to the validation machine because the bus/tram is too full you can just pass your ticket forward and everyone will keep passing it until it gets to the person nearest the machine. They will validate it and everyone will pass it back to you.

VALIDATING TICKETS

When you buy a ticket for a train, bus or tram, generally that ticket is open for use across a broad stretch of time. When you want to use it, you must put it in the validating machine and validate it. That tells the ticket inspector (should there be one) that you are legitimately on board and not scamming the system. Without validation you could theoretically ride around all over the city on one ticket for days on end.

Some tickets will be valid for 90 minutes after validating (for example), others are simply a single use ticket.

Be aware that there is a zero tolerance policy on unvalidated tickets. An unvalidated ticket could earn you a serious fine. The officials won't care that you are a tourist and don't know the rules — plenty have tried that scam and learned the hard way.

If you are traveling by train, tram or bus, make sure you validate your ticket!

TRAINS

The Metro in Rome is quite small compared to the big cities in the US, so people who commute by subway in the US will find the Roman system very easy to use.

If you need help to navigate the train system, I suggest getting my first book, *Glam Italia! How To Travel Italy* on the kindle app on your smartphone and following my step-by-step guide for how to navigate the trains and the train stations. (Plus, if you're reading it on your phone you'll look like you know what you're doing and are just updating Facebook or texting with friends while using the ticket machines.)

Be wary inside the train stations. There are scammers there hoping to take advantage of you. Scam artists, who look like they are dressed in employee uniforms (but when you look closer you see they aren't) will come up to you and offer to help you. Sometimes they'll expect a cash tip, other times they'll do it to steal from you. If they know you don't know what you're doing, it's easy for them to distract or confuse you and get your money. I have shooed them away many times, but they are relentless.

Genuine Trenitalia and Italo employees are only ever dressed in full uniform, and each will only help you with their own trains — Italo employees won't help you to purchase a ticket from the machine for any train that is not an Italo train. The same goes for Trenitalia employees and their trains. Neither will come up to you and spontaneously offer to help.

MIND YOUR MONEY

My big piece of advice when using public transport is to be wearing a cross-body bag and keep your hand on it (I know, I've said it before). I heard stories in Barcelona about thieves waiting until the last second before the Metro doors closed and grabbing handbags and running away down the platform as the train pulled out. I've never seen it happen, but *wherever* I am traveling in the world I wear a cross-body bag and keep a firm grip on the bag itself. A little caution goes a long way. Men should wear a money belt under their clothes and keep their hand in the jacket pocket that holds their wallet.

Planning

When you are planning your days in Rome and figuring out your itinerary try not to pack your schedule too full. If you have read this book then you know there are tons of fascinating places to pop into close to the big sites on your itinerary, so you can add things spontaneously if you find that you have extra time on your hands.

The worst way to experience Rome is to race from one busy attraction to the next. You will end up frazzled and exhausted (and you might become one of those people who say they don't like Rome).

SHORT ON TIME?

Vatican tours normally take three hours, as do Colosseum and Forum tours. Count on the fact that you'll be waiting in line for a while to get in before the tour even begins. At the time of writing this book the Vatican is getting 25,000 visitors per day, so unless it's the most important thing on your list you may want to skip it in lieu of some of the other churches in this book. They won't disappoint!

If you don't have a lot of time in the city, I suggest you skip the tour of the Colosseum too. Walk around the outside instead. Maybe see Basilica San Clemente or the Case Romane, add in Palazzo Valentini and then walk through the Jewish Ghetto and over to the Trastevere.

If you are on a cruise and only have a couple of hours in Rome, I suggest you take the train to Trastevere station and from there you can catch a tram up to the Garibaldi Bridge or the Piazza Venezia and spend your time wandering in this small but fabulous area.

You will experience so much more of Rome, and while everyone else is waiting in line and getting hot and stressed out you will be eating gelato, sipping espresso, having a fabulous lunch and still have time for a glass of wine before heading back to your cruise ship.

Drinking Water in Rome

One of my pet peeves when traveling is seeing the mounds of single-use plastics left behind by tourists. Most of these are water bottles.

Here in the US it is quite normal to walk around with a drink, be it a bottle of water or a Big Gulp soda. Tap water is less than delicious, so it is part of American culture to buy bottles of water and throw the empties in the trash when we are done. For the most part we don't think anything of it, but in some other countries the overflow of single use plastics can create a huge problem. With that in mind I want to tell you about water in Rome.

Never buy bottled water from vendor trucks around major tourist sites. They will charge you whatever they want. I've seen them charging 3 euros for a small bottle of water, and even up to 10 euros. Summer days in Rome get really hot, so you know in advance that you will need bottled water. Stop at a minimart or supermarket and buy water there. You will pay anywhere from 20 cents to 80 cents for a bottle. When your bottle is empty, instead of throwing it in the trash, keep it and refill it everywhere you go. Rome has free water everywhere. It is fresh and cool, tastes wonderful and is completely safe.

Nasoni

As you walk around the Eternal City you will see little water fountains everywhere, the most famous of which are the *nasoni*, named for their nose-like spout with constantly running water. There are more than 2500 nasoni around Rome, and they've been satisfying the thirst of locals and tourists alike since 1874. The water runs through them continuously, which stops any bacteria building up.

If you don't have a water bottle but have a mean thirst, no problem. The top of the "nose" has a small hole, and by covering the spout with your finger water flows up out of this hole like a drinking fountain.

(If you successfully pull off the drinking fountain maneuver please take a photo and tag me on your Instagram! I've never done it myself because I expect I would end up running around Rome in a wet T-shirt — no one wins in that scenario — so I refill water bottles instead. Add an @Corinnatravels or an @HowToTravelItaly tag so that I can see it and clap for you!!)

Tap water

Regardless of whether you are staying in a hotel, an apartment or a bed and breakfast (wherever you are staying in Rome), the tap water is not only drinkable but also tastes really good. The same water that sources the nasoni also comes out of the tap at your accommodation. Water in Rome is clean, fresh and delicious.

Save the planet. Use the nasoni.

Shoes

One thing I am always asked is what shoes to pack for Italy.

Rome is a walking city — the way to really experience Rome and to see as much as you can, is to walk and walk and walk. With that in mind you need some good footwear. I emphatically tell my Glam Italia travelers no flip flops, no ballet flats and also (for the sake of all things glam) no big ugly chunky sneakers!

Flip flops are a disaster waiting to happen. My travelers often bring Tory Burch flip flop sandals, which although chic and expensive are still a bad idea. There are endless cobblestoned streets in Rome, which are incredibly beautiful, add endless atmosphere to every photo you take, but can be murder on your feet if you are wearing flip flops or ballet flats. Those shoe styles don't offer any support for your feet, and they raise the chances of you hurting yourself. By the end of day one, you'll be begging for mercy. Just don't do it!

One time in Venice I had a traveler determined to wear her Tory Burch flip flop sandals even though I had told her several times not to. It rained, the cobblestone streets got really slick, and her footwear slipped right out from under her, not only sending her airborne but causing her to land on her derriere with the most resounding crack you have ever heard. I was sure she was going to need a trip to the hospital but thankfully she didn't — the only thing damaged was her pride and her brand new Prada handbag purchased just days before.

When I travel to Italy I pack flip flops for beach days or in case I stay somewhere with a skanky looking shower tub. (That hasn't ever happened, and even if it did I would be forced to stay dirty because I'm that girl who is *phobic* about unclean showers!)

SO WHICH SHOES DO I PACK?

I bring two pairs of shoes. One is a chic, fashionable-looking pair of sneakers (like Supergas, Soffts, Allbirds or the Adidas slimline sneakers that everyone was wearing in Paris a couple of years ago). Your sneakers need to not only look good, but be broken in and give the soles of your feet tons of support. I add an insole (I call all insoles Dr Scholls, so I have no idea what brand I actually buy, I just make sure they are really cushiony). If your shoes don't have adequate support your feet will hurt, and before long your lower back will hurt, and then as your upper back tries to compensate, it too will hurt. You didn't travel all the way to Italy to be a bag of aches and pains!

The second pair of shoes I pack is a good pair of sandals. Again I buy sandals with really good support that you can walk in all day every day, and which will go with all your outfits. Every summer I see tons of women wearing Birkenstock Gizeh sandals (they're the ones that look like a version of a flip flop but have the full Birkenstock sole) and Mephistos. It took me a long time to get on board with that, as I always thought the word *Birkenstock* was synonymous with homemade deodorant and not shaving your legs. Turns out I couldn't have been more wrong! Once I got past my mental block I wore them myself for multiple summers in Italy and they were incredibly comfortable. My other favorite travel sandals are made by Born and by Sofft. My priorities are that they look good and support my feet and lower back.

I recommend also packing some BandAids and foot relief products (like foot lotion or blister pads). Yes, they do sell BandAids in Italy, but you will probably need them at a time when it's not convenient to go find a store (and the idea of putting your sore feet back into your shoes to go buy them will horrify you).

Clothes

I believe that the ultimate travel wardrobe should be made up of simple pieces that you can layer up and down, and mix and match to create multiple outfits. This is not to say I always achieve that, but it's my goal!

Winter-wear is pretty standard, but spring and summer in Rome require more thought for two reasons — Rome does get *very* hot (and that's coming from someone who lives in Phoenix) and Rome is home to one of the world's major religions, so it's respectful to dress modestly. However, I would probably die trying to wear jeans there in the summer. Not happening. So instead I wear breathable fabrics, like cottons and linens and modal, in dresses and skirts and pants that work even on the hottest days.

Don't wear leisurewear — even if you are a yoga instructor or a Golden Girl from Florida! You will seldom see Italian women wearing workout clothes on the street, even on their way to the gym. They think it looks tacky. And when in Rome....

VISITING CHURCHES

Rome is the home of the Catholic church and is not only full of churches (more than 900 of them) but also has a dress code in many other places that mustn't be violated. Regardless of where your religious persuasion or lack thereof lies, at some point you will want to step inside the churches — to see the incredible art and architecture, or just to sit somewhere cool out of the blazing sunshine. You might not even realize that it is a church you are entering — often tourists don't realize the Pantheon is a church.

All the churches in Rome are working churches, not museums, and as such there is a dress code: no bare thighs, shoulders must be covered. I watched some women get turned away at the Pantheon last summer because they had sleeveless dresses on. I always carry a scarf to throw over my shoulders if needed. A little forethought paired with respect for local customs goes a long way!

Final Thoughts

I really hope that this book has inspired you to seek out more places to see and things to do in Rome, beyond the main attractions.

The most exciting, most beautiful and most memorable parts of your vacation in Rome are not likely to be the places filled with crowds and long lines. You are more likely to find them within the pages of this book, or when you duck around a corner on your way to the next place on your itinerary and find yourself in a gorgeous little ivy-walled piazza, or if you were to stumble upon some incredible set of ruins with no one else around.

Try not to do too much each day and make sure you allow yourself time to just breathe it all in. If your hips and knees allow for it, do your best to walk this city – this is when you will discover your own little secret places and find your own magical travel stories.

The best way to use this book is to pick and choose a handful of places and things to add into your trip. Definitely don't try to do all 101!

I have included stories about the various places and people because for me this is what brings a city to life. You can tell me about an interesting church to go look at, and maybe I will go see it but then again maybe I won't. But if you tell me a *great story* about a church clear across town I will move heaven and earth to get to see it, because the story brought it to life! I hope that knowing about the lives of the people who created all of this art and architecture and history will inspire you or make you smile.

Do try to see at least one of the Caravaggios, even if you're not much of an art lover. Knowing the stories behind them can change the experience entirely and might turn you into a Caravaggio fan like me!

GET IN TOUCH

So many readers of my first book, *Glam Italia! How To Travel Italy*, have taken the time to reach out to me either on social media, the blog or by email, and have told me how the book impacted their trip. From planning it to adding in extra places to their itineraries to trying new foods. Sometimes they are in Italy when they message me, other times they are back home. I want you to know how much this means to me. My goal with these books is to help you create the most amazing trip ever, and when I hear from you it makes my day!

NEWSLETTER

If you are not already on the list, join my Private Members Newsletter. This is specifically designed to give additional valuable travel information for readers planning trips to Italy, and covers the entire country. You can find links to join the list on every blog post on the Corinna B's World blog.

PINTEREST

For quick reference to information on other places and things to do in Italy, follow my Pinterest boards @Corinnamakeup. The different areas of Italy each have their own board and each pin links back to a blog post, so you can get to the information very quickly.

FACEBOOK & INSTAGRAM

Find me on Facebook at Corinna Cooke Author and on Instagram @Corinnatravels and @HowToTravelItaly. Tag me in your Italy pictures or @ me in the comments so that I can see what you're up to. I love being able to watch you on your trips!

WRITE A REVIEW

Finally, as a constant traveler I have often relied on good travel guide books when heading to a new country or to an area I haven't been to before. Over the years I have learned to read reviews on travel books before I buy them, and this has helped me to find some great books with incredible information. Please take a couple of minutes to write a review of this book on Amazon. It will help more travelers to find it and to experience more of Rome.

Have a wonderful trip to Rome – maybe I will see you in the piazza.

Andiamo!

Corinna

About The Author

Corinna Cooke is an international Makeup Artist, Blogger and Magazine Beauty Director.

Her non-stop travels to Italy and subsequent blog posts lead to an accidental boutique, private tour-guiding business. For two months every year she takes small groups of women on glamour filled, a' la carte tours of Italy, where feeling fabulous happens at affordable, real person prices.

Corinna's bestselling first book *Glam Italia! How To Travel Italy* is the perfect companion to this guide. It offers advice on everything, from planning your trip to creating your dream vacation and also offers substantial help once you are in Italy. Learn everything you'll need to know, from how to use Italian trains, to how to order coffee, to what to do if you get sick while you're away, and much, much more!

Glam Italia! How To Travel Italy is available from Amazon worldwide as an eBook or paperback.

Originally from New Zealand, Corinna has lived all around the world, and now lives in Phoenix with her son, two cats and a rescue dog named Frankie.

Acknowledgments

Very special thanks to beautiful Jennifer for a lifetime of encouragement and inspiration and for always supporting all my crazy ideas, plans, ventures and adventures. You infused my life with wanderlust, always made me feel I could go anywhere, do anything, be anything I wanted, and have always been in my corner. Thank you for tirelessly proof reading my books, thank you for being the most incredible mother I could ever have wished for, and for being my best friend. I love you.

To Anna Golden, once again I thank you for being my editor – I couldn't go through this without you, nor would I want to! You are always so warm and patient and kind, and instead of hushing my voice you give power to it. I look forward to writing many more books with you!

To Daniella Hunt, my God the fun we've had! Thank you for teaching me Rome, for working with me all these years and for being such a great friend. I know that when we are both old and grey we will still spend our evenings having drinks in the piazza, and I will still be bugging you for more stories about Trajan and Hadrian and Diocletian! You are wonderful my friend.

Marta Halama, I adore working with you. You are so incredibly talented. We have many more books to work on together – these two were just the beginning!

Anthony Doerr, thank you for your exquisite use of language and for writing one of my favorite books, Four Seasons In Rome. Not only were you in my favorite city, but you were also in my neighborhood! I have read your book so many times, and know every street you walk along. There is magic in your words.

Andrew Graham Dixon do you even know how much your work impacts other people's lives? You gave me Caravaggio, for which I will be eternally grateful. Your passion for and excitement about his work are infectious! Because of you I have been to see each of his publically displayed works in Rome, my well-worn copy of *A Life Sacred and Profane* under my arm, and because of you I will find my way to see as many as I can around the world. Thank you from the bottom of my heart.

And finally Tommy. Taking you to Rome that first time so many years ago made me fall in love with the city all over again. Always stay a global citizen, travel the world as much as you can, never lose sight of your dreams, and always know I love you more than life itself.

XO

CPSIA information can be obtained
at www.ICGtesting.com
Printed in the USA
LVHW050957230120
644553LV00003B/56